D1070361

Targum Pseudo-Jonathan:
Deuteronomy

THE ARAMAIC BIBLE

• THE TARGUMS •

PROJECT DIRECTOR
Martin McNamara, M.S.C.

EDITORS
Kevin Cathcart • Michael Maher, M.S.C.
Martin McNamara, M.S.C.

EDITORIAL CONSULTANTS
Daniel J. Harrington, S.J. • Bernard Grossfeld

The Aramaic Bible

Volume 5B

Targum Pseudo-Jonathan: Deuteronomy

Translated, with Notes

BY

Ernest G. Clarke

with the collaboration of Mrs. Sue Magder

A Michael Glazier Book
THE LITURGICAL PRESS
Collegeville, Minnesota

BS
709.2
.B5
1987
vol.5B

About the Translator:

Ernest George Clarke, B.D., M.A., Ph.D. (1927–1997) was born in Varna, Ontario, Canada. He earned the B.A., B.D., and M.A. at the University of Toronto, continued his studies at the University of Chicago, and was awarded the D.Lit. from Leiden University in 1962. He was Professor of Old Testament at Queens Theological College, Kingston, Ontario, from 1956 to 1961, and from 1961 until his retirement in 1992 was Professor in the Department of Near Eastern Studies, University of Toronto. He was a Visiting Fellow of the Institute for Advanced Studies, Hebrew University of Jerusalem in 1985–1986. He was the author of *The Selected Questions of Isho'Bar Nun* (1962) and *Wisdom of Solomon* (Cambridge Bible Commentary, 1972), and in this series edited, besides the present volume, *Targum Pseudo-Jonathan of the Pentateuch: Text and Concordance* (1984), and *Targum Pseudo-Jonathan: Numbers, Translation and Notes* (1995).

Copyright © 1998 by The Order of St. Benedict, Inc., Collegeville, Minnesota. All rights reserved.

No part of this publication may be reproduced or transmitted in any form or by any means, electronic or mechanical, including photocopying, recording, or any information storage and retrieval system, without permission in writing from the publisher.

Library of Congress Cataloging-in-Publication Data

Bible. O.T. Deuteronomy English. Clarke. 1998.
Targum Pseudo-Jonathan : Deuteronomy / translated, with notes by
Ernest G. Clarke.
p. cm. — (The Aramaic Bible ; v. 5B)
"A Michael Glazier book."
Includes bibliographical references and index.
ISBN 0-8146-5863-6
1. Bible. O.T. Pentateuch. Aramaic. Targum Pseudo-Jonathan-
-Translations into English. I. Clarke, Ernest G. (Ernest George)
II. Title. III. Series: Bible. O.T. English. Aramaic Bible.
1987 ; v. 5B.
BS709.2 .B5 1998 Vol. 5b
[BS1273]
221.42 s—dc21
[222'.15042] 97-22398
CIP

Logo design by Florence Bern.
Printed in the United States of America.

JESUIT - KRAUSS - McCORMICK - LIBRARY
1100 EAST 55th STREET
CHICAGO, ILLINOIS 60615

TABLE OF CONTENTS

EDITORS' FOREWORD

While any translation of the Scriptures may in Hebrew be called a Targum, the word is used especially for a translation of a book of the Hebrew Bible into Aramaic. Before the Christian era Aramaic had in good part replaced Hebrew in Palestine as the vernacular of the Jews. It continued as their vernacular for centuries later and remained in part as the language of the schools after Aramaic itself had been replaced as the vernacular.

Rabbinic Judaism has transmitted Targums of all books of the Hebrew Canon, with the exception of Daniel and Ezra-Nehemiah, which are themselves partly in Aramaic. We also have a translation of the Samaritan Pentateuch into the dialect of Samaritan Aramaic. From the Qumran Library we have sections of a Targum of Job and fragments of a Targum of Leviticus, chapter 16, facts which indicate that the Bible was being translated in Aramaic in pre-Christian times.

Translations of books of the Hebrew Bible into Aramaic for liturgical purposes must have begun before the Christian era, even though none of the Targums transmitted to us by Rabbinic Judaism can be shown to be that old and though some of them are demonstrably compositions from later centuries.

In recent decades there has been increasing interest among scholars and a larger public in these Targums. A noticeable lacuna, however, has been the absence of a modern English translation of this body of writing. It is in marked contrast with most other bodies of Jewish literature for which there are good modern English translations, for instance the Apocrypha and Pseudepigrapha of the Old Testament, Josephus, Philo, the Mishnah, the Babylonian Talmud and Midrashic literature, and more recently the Tosefta and Palestinian Talmud.

It is hoped that this present series will provide some remedy for this state of affairs.

The aim of the series is to translate all the traditionally-known Targums, that is those transmitted by Rabbinic Judaism, into modern English idiom, while at the same time respecting the particular and peculiar nature of what these Aramaic translations were originally intended to be. A translator's task is never an easy one. It is rendered doubly difficult when the text to be rendered is itself a translation which is at times governed by an entire set of principles.

All the translations in this series have been specially commissioned. The translators have made use of what they reckon as the best printed editions of the Aramaic Targum in question or have themselves directly consulted the manuscripts.

The translation aims at giving a faithful rendering of the Aramaic. The introduction to each Targum contains the necessary background information on the particular work. In general, each Targum translation is accompanied by an apparatus and notes. The former is concerned mainly with such items as the variant readings in the Aramaic texts, the relation of the English translation to the original, etc. The notes give what explanations the translator thinks necessary or useful for this series.

Not all the Targums here translated are of the same kind. Targums were translated at different times, and most probably for varying purposes, and have more than one interpretative approach to the Hebrew Bible. This diversity between the Targums themselves is reflected in the translation and in the manner in which the accompanying explanatory material is presented. However, a basic unity of presentation has been maintained. Targumic deviations from the Hebrew text, whether by interpretation or paraphrase, are indicated by italics.

A point that needs to be stressed with regard to this translation of the Targums is that by reason of the state of current targumic research, to a certain extent it must be regarded as a provisional one. Despite the progress made, especially in recent decades, much work still remains to be done in the field of targumic study. Not all the Targums are as yet available in critical editions. And with regard to those that have been critically edited from known manuscripts, in the case of the Targums of some books the variants between the manuscripts themselves are such as to give rise to the question whether they have all descended from a single common original.

Details regarding these points will be found in the various introductions and critical notes.

It is recognized that a series such as this will have a broad readership. The Targums constitute a valuable source of information for students of Jewish literature, particularly those concerned with the history of interpretation, and also for students of the New Testament, especially for those interested in its relationship to its Jewish origins. The Targums also concern members of the general public who have an interest in the Jewish interpretation of the Scriptures or in the Jewish background to the New Testament. For them the Targums should be both interesting and enlightening.

By their translations, introductions, and critical notes the contributors to this series have rendered an immense service to the progress of targumic studies. It is hoped that the series, provisional though it may be, will bring significantly nearer the day when the definitive translation of the Targums can be made.

Kevin Cathcart Martin McNamara, M.S.C. Michael Maher, M.S.C.

ABBREVIATIONS

Ab.Zar.	Abodah Zarah
Ant.	Josephus, *Jewish Antiquities*
b.	Babylonian Talmud
B	First *Biblia Rabbinica.* Venice, Bomberg, 1517–18
BL	British Library
BM	British Museum (now British Library)
CG	Cairo Genizah
Cant. R.	Canticles Rabbah
Ctg (B, etc.)	Cairo Genizah (Pal.) Targum manuscript
Deut. R.	Deuteronomy Rabbah
Exod. R.	Exodus Rabbah
Frg. Tg(s).	Fragment Targum(s)
Gen. R.	Genesis Rabbah
Giṭṭ.	Giṭṭin
Hall.	Hallah
HT	Hebrew Text
j.	Jerusalem (Palestinian) Targum
Kel.	Kelim
L	Fragment Targum Leipzig Manuscript
LAB	Ps.-Philo, *Liber Antiquitatum Biblicarum*
LXX	Septuagint
Meg.	Megillah
Mek.	Mekilta de R. Ishmael
Meturg.	Elias Levita's *Meturgeman*
MSmg	Marginal reading of Ps.-J. manuscript

MT	Masoretic Text
NEB	New English Bible
Nf	Neofiti
Nfi	Neofiti interlinear gloss
Nfmg	Neofiti marginal gloss
NJB	New Jerusalem Bible
N	Nürnberg Fragment Targum Manuscript
NRSV	New Revised Standard Version
Num. R.	Numbers Rabbah
Onq.	Onqelos
OT	Old Testament
P	Paris BN Fragment Targum Manuscript
Pal. Tg.	Palestinian Targum
PRE	*Pirqe de Rabbi Eliezer*
PRK	*Pesiqta de Rab Kahana*
Ps.-J.	Targum Pseudo-Jonathan
REB	Revised English Bible
RSV	Revised Standard Version
Sam. Tg.	Samaritan Targum
Shabb.	Shabbath
Shebi.	Shebiith
Sifre Deut.	Sifre to Deuteronomy
Sifre Num.	Sifre to Numbers
Sukk.	Sukkoth
Tanḥ.	Tanḥuma
Tg.	Targum
V	Vatican Library Fragment Targum Manuscript
VM	Philo, *De Vita Mosis*
Vulg.	Vulgate

Journals and Series

AO	Acta Orientalia
BASOR	Bulletin of the American Schools of Oriental Research

BibThB	Biblical Theology Bulletin
BiblZeit	Biblische Zeitschrift
CCL	Corpus Christianorum, Series Latina
EJ	Encyclopaedia Judaica
HUCA	Hebrew Union College Annual
ITQ	The Irish Theological Quarterly
JAOS	Journal of the American Oriental Society
JBL	Journal of Biblical Literature
JJS	Journal of Jewish Studies
JNSL	Journal of Northwest Semitic Languages
JPS	Jewish Publication Society
JQR	Jewish Quarterly Review
JSJ	Journal for the Study of Judaism
JSOT	Journal for the Study of the Old Testament
JSS	Journal of Semitic Studies
JTS	Journal of Theological Studies
MGWJ	Monatschrift für Geschichte und Wissenschaft des Judentums
NTS	New Testament Studies
PIBA	Proceedings of the Irish Biblical Association
PL	J. P. Migne, *Patrologia Latina*
RB	Revue Biblique
RevHistRel	Revue d'Histoire des Religions
RSR	Recherches de science religieuse
SBL	Society of Biblical Literature
SNTU	Studien zur Umwelt des Neuen Testament
TDNT	Theological Dictionary of the New Testament
VT	Vetus Testamentum
VTSuppl	Supplement to Vetus Testamentum
ZAW	Zeitschrift für die Alttestamentliche Wissenschaft

INTRODUCTION

This volume on Ps.-J. of Deuteronomy represents the last volume of the Pentateuch in this series. It includes the translation and notes of Ps.-J. of Deuteronomy as well as an index for this volume. Many of the methods of translation unique to Ps.-J. noted in volumes 1B 2, 3, 4 are also to be found in Deuteronomy. However, the following variants are partially discussed or not discussed in the previous volumes.

1. Terms for sacrifices are not as common in the book of Deuteronomy as in Leviticus and Numbers. When they do occur they are as follows: for HT *šlmym, zbḥ šlmym* "peace sacrifice(s)" the translation in Deuteronomy is *nykst qwdšyn* "sacrifices of holy things" (Deut 12:6, 11, 27; 23:24; 27:7); HT "fire-offering" (*ʾiššeh*) is rendered in Deuteronomy by *qwrbnʾ* (Deut 18:1) but the more usual term is Aramaic *ʿlwt* (Deut 12:6); HT *terumah* is translated by *ʾpršw* "separated offering" in Ps.-J. (see Deut 12:6, 11, 17).

2. The Hebrew "field" (*śdh,* 17x) is translated by *ḥqlʾ* always in Onq. In Ps.-J. *ḥqlʾ* is the usual translation but in 20:19 and 22:27 *ʾnpy brʾ* and in 7:22 and 22:25 only *brʾ*. However, in Nf *ʾ(n)py brʾ* appears eight times (11:15; 14:22; 20:19; 21:1; 22:25, 27; 28:16, 38) and *ḥqlʾ* or an entirely different word in the other instances. Ps.-J. and Nf agree in 20:19 and 22:27. The third Aramaic word used in the Tgs (*tḥwm*) is not found in Deuteronomy of Ps.-J.[1]

3. In Deuteronomy the phrase "King Messiah" (*mlkʾ mšyḥʾ*) is found only in Ps.-J. (25:19; 30:4) whereas it is found in Ps.-J. eleven times in the other books of the Pentateuch and several times in Nf in the other books of the Pentateuch.[2] The phrase "Master of the World/Universe" (*mry ʿlmʾ*) is unique in the Tgs, in Ps.-J. of Deuteronomy (23:22; 28:12; 32:9, 51; 34:6). The phrase "Lord of all Ages" (*rbwn kl ʿlmyʾ*) is found in Ps.-J. in 32:4 only whereas there are two instances of the phrase in Nf (16:16; 32:4).

4. The word *gywr* in its verbal and nominal forms[3] occurs twenty times in Deuteronomy as "sojourner/alien" and three times as "proselyte." Deuteronomy 24:14 differs in the way various translators have treated the word but I consider the meaning in that verse to be "sojourner/alien" (see n. 28 on Chapter 24).[4]

5. As McNamara[5] has noted Nf always translates the HT *zkn* "elder" as *ḥkym* "wise man." Onq. usually translates the HT literally with the parallel Aramaic vocabulary, *sb* "elder";

[1]See McNamara, *The Aramaic Bible* 1A, 57 n. 9 and 4, 6–7 n. 16.

[2]S. A. Kaufman and M. Sokoloff, *A Key-Word-in-Context Concordance to Targum Neofiti. A Guide to the Complete Palestinian Aramaic Text of the Torah* (Baltimore: The Johns Hopkins University Press, 1993) 899–901.

[3]See Clarke (1984) 139–140.

[4]See McNamara, *The Aramaic Bible* 2, 6 n. 28; 4, 7 n. 24, and the Introduction in *The Aramaic Bible* 5A, 6 n. 16.

[5]*The Aramaic Bible* 2, 4 n. 12 and 4, 7 n. 18.

however, Ps.-J. agrees with Nf in most instances. There is one telling instance in Deut 21:3 (*ḥkymy sby*) when Ps.-J. seems to combine both *ḥkym* of Nf and *sb* of Onq.

6. Aramaic *šlyṭ,* as McNamara[6] has noted, is often preferred to the HT *mlk*. The phrase *rb wšlyṭ* is found in Nf of Exod 2:14 and 7:1. Kaufman and Sokoloff[7] indicate that the idiom is frequent in Nf of Genesis. As for Ps.-J. of Deuteronomy, the compound phrase is found only in 33:16.[8]

7. Regarding Aramaic *prq* "redeemed," McNamara[9] noted that Nf regularly adds this idea when reference is made to Israel's delivery from Egypt. As far as Ps.-J. is concerned the usual translation of the HT is literal although there are a few instances when "redeemed" is added (Deut 5:6; 6:12, 23; 7:8, 19; 8:14; 13:11; 20:1).

8. Aramaic *šbq* "forgive" is found 12x in Deuteronomy: 8x for HT *ʿzb,*[10] once for HT *nśy,* once for HT *rpy,* once for HT *slh,* and once for HT *nṭš* (Deut 32:15). Onq. consistently has *šbq*.[11] Nf uses *šbq* in all instances except three: Deut 1:9 HT *nśy* "bear" by *sbl;*[12] Deut 4:31 *rpy* and Deut 32:15 where Nf uses *nśy* but the Interlinear reading is *šbq*. McNamara[13] notes that Nf uses *šry wšbq* for the single HT word. Ps.-J. of Deuteronomy never uses the double expression whereas it is used in Ps.-J. of Exodus, Leviticus, and Numbers.

9. HT "flowing with milk and honey" *(zbt ḥlb wdbš):* in Ps.-J. the phrase appears 10x as in the HT but in four other instances (6:3; 11:9; 26:9, 15) we find *šmyntn kḥlb wḥlyyn kdbš* "rich as milk and sweet as honey." Onq. has *(ʿbdʾ ḥlb wdbš)* which is similar to the HT. Nf in the same variant passages (as well as 11:9 and 31:20) expands "pure as milk and sweet and tasty as honey" *(wnqyyn kḥlb wḥlyyn wṭʿymyn ldbš).* See McNamara[14] for the expression in Nf of Exodus and Deuteronomy.

10. Aramaic *mlʾk* "angel(s)" in Ps.-J. of Deuteronomy is added in 9:19; 10:14; 32:8; 34:5, 6 but in 33:2 "holy angels" *(mlʾkyn qdyšʾyn)* specifies the HT "holy ones" *(qdš).* There is, however, difficulty in the HT because *qdš* is singular. The note in BH Stuttgartensia is misleading. It should read as the MS of Ps.-J. reads: *rybw rybwwn mlʾkyn qdyšyn.*

11. Aramaic *dyn/dynyn/dynyʾ* is the translation for HT *mšpṭ/mšpṭym.* Unlike other books in the Pentateuch, as noted by McNamara[15] and Maher,[16] for Ps.-J. of Deuteronomy the usual translation for the HT is some form of *dyn* alone. However, in four (Deut 1:16; 32:5; 33:10, 21) of the some thirty-nine instances of *mšpṭ* in Ps.-J.[17] only these four passages agree with the usual translation form of Nf, using *sdr(y) dynyʾ.*

12. Hebrew itp *šḥh* is expressed in Ps.-J. of Deuteronomy by *sgd* and/or *plḥ*. McNamara[18] notes that Nf translates the HT with a number of different Aramaic words if it refers to God

[6]*The Aramaic Bible* 2, 6 n. 25.
[7]S. A. Kaufman and M. Sokoloff, *Concordance* 1295–1296.
[8]Clarke (1984) 573–574.
[9]*The Aramaic Bible* 2, 5–6 n. 23 and Introduction in *The Aramaic Bible* 5A, 6 n. 15.
[10]In Deut 12:19 Ps.-J. translates *ʿml* "defraud" for HT *ʿzb*.
[11]In Onq. (Deut 1:9) the translation is with the poël of *sbr* alone.
[12]See previous note.
[13]*The Aramaic Bible* 2, 5 n. 21.
[14]*The Aramaic Bible* 2, 5 n. 15 and Introduction, *The Aramaic Bible* 5A, 5 n. 12.
[15]*The Aramaic Bible* 2, 4 n. 9.
[16]*The Aramaic Bible* 3, 119 n. 26.
[17]Clarke (1984) 158–160 *dyn*.
[18]*The Aramaic Bible* 2, 5 n. 10 and Introduction, *The Aramaic Bible* 5A, 5 n. 13.

but that if it is the worship of idols only *sgd* is used. In Ps.-J. of Deuteronomy when the reference is to idol worship Deut 8:9; 11:16; 17:3 write *plḥ* plus *sgd* while Deut 4:19; 5:9; 30:17 express this with *sgd* plus *plḥ*. Deuteronomy 29:25 has *plḥ* only but Nf has the itp *šṭḥ*. On the other hand Deut 26:10 (Ps.-J.) translates *sgd* for the worship of God.

The vocabulary distributions discussed above suggest that although Ps.-J. often follows Onq. there are times when Ps.-J. follows Nf and still other instances when Ps.-J. goes its own way. The editor(s) of Ps.-J. represent a creative literary style that resulted in a targumic text with its own character and individuality independent from, for instance, both Onq. and Nf.

The examples above that delineate some of the editorial characteristics of Ps.-J. are not the totality nor do they fully reflect the parallel nature of the text of Ps.-J. to material in the other targums or Ps.-J.'s true independence. Ps.-J. is in many ways a unique targum (which may also be said for Onq. and Nf) and any attempt to identify its sources leaves a student just as far from a solution as ever. Sometimes it is possible to identify the same argumentation in other rabbinic sources as is found in specific passages in Ps.-J. However, the chronological line of development is often impossible to establish. Did Ps.-J. borrow directly from source "x" or did Ps.-J. and source "x" have a common source from which both borrowed?

The question of when, where, and by whom the targum was composed is unanswerable. The present text of Ps.-J. is the result of much editing and reediting, copying and recopying. The only certain fact we know is the sixteenth-century date of the present manuscript. The London British Museum manuscript (Add. 27031) is the only witness to Ps.-J. still extant. An *editio princeps* appeared in the Second Rabbinic Bible printed in Venice in 1591.[19] Hence an extreme position is that additions and changes could have been made to the MS of Ps.-J. up to the very time of copying the MS. On the other hand it is most unlikely that any significant changes were made so late in time. The present text of Ps.-J. is the result of many authors editing and revising what may have been the "original." The history of the MS is not as important as the contents of the MS. Authorship per se was not important to the ancients. The purpose of the targum was to update the meaning of Scripture and so the presentation of that meaning for the contemporary audience was paramount.

[19]R. Le Déaut, *Introduction à la Littérature Targumique* (Rome: Pontifical Biblical Institute, 1966) 101.

Targum Pseudo-Jonathan: Deuteronomy

Translation and Notes

CHAPTER 1[1]

1. These are the words *of reproof*[2] that Moses spoke with all of Israel. *He gathered*[3] *them before him when they were* on the other side of the Jordan. *He answered and said to them: "Was not the Law given to you* in the desert[4] *at Mount Sinai and explained to you on the plains of Moab?*[5] *How many miracles and wonders the Holy One blessed be he*[6] *performed for you from the time when you crossed by the shore of* the Reed Sea *where he made for you a way for every single tribe!*[7] *But you, you have deviated*[8] *from his Memra and you incited his anger*[9] at Paran *because of the spies' report;*[10] *and you have charged him with lying*[11] *and you have murmured about the manna*[12] *that he caused to come down white*[13] *from heaven for you. You have*

Notes, Chapter 1

[1]See A. Díez Macho, *MS Neophyti I, Deuteronomio* 5.575–629 for an extensive list of rabbinic parallels that É. Levine has prepared. The rabbinic references in the following notes highlight the rabbinic citations although not necessarily completely.

See the detailed discussion of Deut 1:1-8 by Maher (1994) 264–290.

[2]The phrase in the HT "These are the words that Moses spoke to the Israelites beyond the Jordan in the wilderness" is interpreted in the Tgs. and rabbinic literature, generally, as words of rebuke *(pytgmy ʾwkḥwtʾ)* for the way the Israelites behaved in the wilderness (only Frg. Tg.[P] does not mention "rebuke" specifically); see *Sifre Deut.* 23 and *PRK* 13:7. The Aramaic phrase *pytgmy ʾwkḥwtʾ* is found also in Deut 28:15 introducing the curses in vv. 15-68. When one compares the various texts of the Tgs. and the rabbinic literature there are additions and omissions. Ps.-J. offers some additions such as God's anger at Paran being due not only to complaints against the manna (Onq.) but also to the spies' report (also Frg. Tgs.[PV]). Ps.-J.'s reference to the sin of the golden calf is differently interpreted. Onq. considers the making of the golden calf as one of the causes for God's reproof. Nf says that "by reason of the calf which you made, the Lord decreed in his *Memra* to blot you out." However, a positive view is found in Ps.-J. where there is mention of the miracles performed for the Israelites as well as the help obtained by the merits of the Fathers, the Tent of Meeting, etc., to facilitate atonement for their sins, especially the sin of making the golden calf; see McNamara's extended note on the meaning of *dbr* and Grossfeld, *The Aramaic Bible* 9, 18 n. 2 for a discussion of the various rabbinic explanations for the rebuke.

[3]Aramaic *knp* used only here in Ps.-J. as a verb and in Num 33:25 in its nominal form *(kynwpyʾ)* in Ps.-J.; see Clarke (1984) 299. Only Ps.-J. specifically says that Moses "gathered" *(knp)* the people and *Sifre Deut.* gives three reasons for Moses doing so. The second reason (*Sifre Deut.* 24) is closest to Ps.-J.: "Moses gathered them *(knsm)* . . . and said to them 'I am about to rebuke you. If anyone has anything to say in rebuttal, let him come forth and speak.'"

[4]HT "in the wilderness": Ps.-J. *(mdbrʾ)* considers it the place where the Law was given at Mount Sinai.

[5]HT "the Arabah": Ps.-J. considers the plains of Moab as the place where the Law was explained; see Num 36:13 and the discussion in *b.Ḥag.* 6a-b.

[6]See Maher, *The Aramaic Bible* 1B, 89 n. 21 for the other occurrences of the phrase in Ps.-J. and the later discussion in Maher (1994) 270. Contrary to Maher the phrase is not found in the MS of Gen 25:21.

[7]See Exod 14:21 (Ps.-J.) for the same idea of twelve roads for the twelve tribes; see *PRE* 330 "the waters were made into twelve valleys, corresponding to the twelve tribes" and Maher, *The Aramaic Bible* 2, 201 n. 28 for other rabbinic references.

[8]Aramaic *sṭy* "deviate" but Nf and Frg. Tgs.(PV) *rgz* "anger."

[9]Aramaic *rgz* in Nf and Frg. Tgs.(PV) for the first verb (see n. 8 above) and *srb* "rebel/refuse" for the second verb; see Maher (1994) 272.

[10]See Num 13:31-33; 14:11-20 (Ps.-J.), Numbers 13 and also Nf and Frg. Tgs.(PV) for the association of Paran with the affair of the spies, but Num 21:5 (Onq.) associates Paran with the incident of the manna.

[11]HT the place name "Tophel" is here Aramaic *ṭpl* "charged falsely" which Cook (1986) 239 considers to be from a Hebraic idiom. The use of the Aramaic word maintains the word play. As Maher points out (1994, 275) the Pal. Tgs. do not present the same play on "Tophel" and "Laban."

[12]HT the place name "Laban" seems to be interpreted as the manna being white; see Exod 16:31 (HT) and Num 11:7 (Ps.-J.). Aramaic "murmured" *(rʿm)* is also found in Num 21:5-7 (Ps.-J.) whereas Nf has the vocabulary of Num 21:5.

[13]Aramaic *ḥywwr;* see Exod 16:31 (HT).

demanded meat at Haseroth;[14] *and it was fit for you to be destroyed from the midst of the world*[15] *but because it is remembered for you by the merits of your fathers,*[16] *the righteous ones, the Tent of Meeting, the ark of the covenant, and the holy vessels that you covered with pure gold, he has atoned for you concerning the sin of the golden calf.*[17] 2. (It is) *a march*[18] of eleven days from Horeb, *by the way of Mount Gabla*[19, 20] *to Reqem Gea.*[21] *But because you strayed*[22] *and incited anger*[23] *before the Lord, you have been delayed for forty years.*"[24] 3. And it was *at the end of*[25] forty years in the eleventh month, *that is the month of Shevat,*[26] on the first of the month, Moses spoke with the Israelites according to all that the Lord commanded him for them. 4. After he had defeated[27] Sihon, King of the Amorites, who lived in Heshbon, and Og, King of *Mathnan,*[28] who lived in Ashtaroth in Edrath, 5. on the other side of the Jordan in the land of Moab, Moses began to teach[29] *the words of*[30] this Law, saying: 6. the Lord our God spoke with us at Horeb, *but* it is not I myself[31] (who has spoken), saying: "(As for your sojourn here) it is enough for you and until now *it has been gratifying for you because you have received the Law, you have made the Tent and its accessories and you have appointed*

Notes, Chapter 1

[14]See Num 11:34-35 (Ps.-J.). This tradition is found in all the Tgs.

[15]Maher (1994, 276) rather than seeing the destruction as due to asking for meat sees this phrase as destruction "for all the sins that have been referred to." The phrase here is found in *Sifre Deut.* 26, "liable to extinction," because the Israelites worshiped idols: here Aramaic *šyṣy;* see Clarke (1984) 567–568 for the 122 uses of this verb in Ps.-J.

[16]I.e., Abraham, Isaac, and Jacob (as in Nf). The idea of the merits of the patriarchs being beneficial is found frequently in the Tgs.; see also Deut 9:19; 28:15; 33:15, 28, and Marmorstein (1968). In Deut 28:15 (Ps.-J.) the idea of the merits of the patriarchs is combined with the idea of God's covenant with the patriarchs. The patriarchs are called "the righteous ones" here as in Num 23:9 (Ps.-J. and Nf).

[17]HT: the place-name "Di-Zahab" is associated with the golden calf incident in the Tgs. and rabbinic literature. The gold of the holy vessels atones for the golden calf. In Nf the Tent of Meeting and the ark are also covered with fine gold but the sacred vessels are not mentioned; see *Sifre Deut.* 26 and Ginzberg, *Legends* 6.63.

[18]Although HT does not specifically use the word "journey" it is implied and so here, Onq., and Frg. Tgs.(PV) *mhlk* but Nf *ʾrḥ mhlk* "distance of a march" and Nfmg only *ʾrḥ.*

[19]HT "Mount Seir": see Maher, *The Aramaic Bible* 1B, 56 n. 19.

[20]MS and *editio princeps* incorrectly *ʿm* for *ʿd.*

[21]HT "Kadesh Barnea"; also v. 19; see note on Num 32:8 (Ps.-J.) and Clarke, *The Aramaic Bible* 4, 282 n. 8; here and Deut 2:14; 9:23 (Ps.-J.) and Davies (1972), who considers the place to be Petra.

[22]Aramaic *sṭy* as in v. 1 but Nf and Frg. Tgs. *ḥṭʾ;* see n. 8 above.

[23]Aramaic *rgz* with preceding note as in v. 1; see n. 9 above.

[24]*Sifre Deut.* 27–30 says that had Israel behaved meritoriously during the eleven-day journey they would have entered directly into the Promised Land but since they did not so act they were compelled to spend "forty years" in the wilderness. *Exod. R.* 20:13-16 gives several other reasons for the delay. Ps.-J. uses *ʾḥr* as also in Num 32:15 where Nf has *ṭlṭl.* Here Nf uses itp *ʿkb,* "delayed/detained."

[25]Also Nf, Nfmg, and Frg. Tg.(V).

[26]The month, Shevat, is identified only here in the Tgs.—a characteristic of Ps.-J.; see Num 1:1, 18; 9:11; 8:14 (Ps.-J.).

[27]HT *nkh* "defeated" (RSV): both here and Onq. *mḥʾ* but Nf *qṭl* "slay"; see Maher (1994) 280 for a study of the distribution of the verbs in the Tgs.

[28]HT "Bashan": Nf *bwtnyn* but Onq. and Ps.-J. *mtnn.* Ps.-J. represents the shift of *b>m* and *š>t;* see Num 21:33 (Ps.-J.) and McNamara's note on the verse of Nf in *The Aramaic Bible* 4, 123 n. 37 and Clarke's note, 250 n. 65.

[29]HT *bʾr* "explain" (RSV): also Onq. and Nf *prš,* but Ps.-J. uses *ʾlp* "to teach"; see Maher (1994) 282 for a fuller discussion of the distribution of the various vocabularies.

[30]HT "this Law": Onq. adds "teaching of" *(ʾlpn)* and Nf "the book of" and Nfmg "praise of" *(šbḥ)* or "praiseworthiness."

[31]*wlʾ ʾnʾ bʾnpy npšy* "not I, only (separately)" (Jastrow 99); *Sifre Deut.* 31 says "I am not speaking on my own—what I am saying to you comes from the mouth of his holiness." This idea is unique in Ps.-J. of all the Tgs.

leaders[32] *over you but from now it would be wrong for you to wait* at this mountain.[33] 7.[34] Turn and journey *to ʿArad and Hormah*[35] and ascend the mountain of the Amorites and toward all *the inhabitants of Ammon, Moab, and Gabla, in the plain of the forest,*[36] in the hill country, in the Shephelah, in the south and on the sea coast, *Ashkelon and Caesarea,*[37] the land of the Canaanites *as far as Callirrhoe*[38] and Lebanon, *the place of the mountain of the sanctuary*[39] as far as the Great River, the river Euphrates. 8. See[40] *that* I have delivered[41] *the inhabitants of* the land before you *and you shall have no need to take up arms.*[42] Enter and take possession of the land *and set up markers*[43] *there and divide it (the land)*: just as the Lord[44] promised your fathers, Abraham, Isaac, and Jacob to give to them and to their[45] children after them."[46] 9. And at that time I said *not to abandon you to one judge because*[47] I cannot carry you alone. 10. *The Memra of* the Lord your God has increased you and you have become today in quantity as (numerous as) the stars of the heavens. 11. May the Lord, the God of your fathers, add to you the like a thousand times *in virtue of this blessing*[48] *of mine,* and may he bless you *without number* just as he promised[49] you. 12. How will I be able to endure alone the burdens *of your skeptical ways*[50] *and the planning of evil against me as well as your words of dispute,*[51] *(you)*

Notes, Chapter 1

[32]Aramaic *rbnyn*.

[33]*Sifre Deut.* 31 interprets the mountain sojourn as "a reward" for you or "as being bad" for you. The Hebrew *rb* is understood as (1) "gain/reward," i.e., "gift of Torah, appointed leaders" and (2) "bad" *(rʿ)* for you: your stay here has been wrong for you. Ps.-J. adds to the *Sifre Deut.* interpretation by saying that a further delay at the mountain would not be beneficial. Nf translates the HT literally.

[34]The Tgs. and *Sifre Deut.* 32 identify the various references in the HT: "the plain" is "Arabah"; "the south" is "Negeb." HT *pnw;* Onq. and Ps.-J. itp *pny* but Nf pa *kwn;* see Maher (1994) 284–286 for a discussion of the vocabulary distribution in the Tgs.

[35]See Num 21:1-3 where the two places are noted, as also *Sifre Deut.* 32.

[36]See *Sifre Deut.* 32 for the same identification; see also Maher (1994) 286 for other comments.

[37]See *Sifre Deut.* 32 "and by the sea—Gaza, Ashkelon, and Caesarea."

[38]Aramaic *qlrhy:* see Gen 10:19 (Ps.-J. and Nf) for the same place-name (HT "Lasha"); Deut 2:32 (Nfmg) for HT "Jahaz"; *Gen R.* 37:6 recognized the place as having warm springs; see note in Maher, *The Aramaic Bible* 1B, 48 n. 36.

[39]HT "Lebanon," also Onq.: here and Nfmg "Lebanon" is understood as the site of the Temple; see *Sifre Deut.* 32 and also Deut 3:25; 11:24 (Ps.-J.). *Pesher Habakkuk* (12, 3-4 on Hab 2:17) already made a similar identification; see Vermes (1961) 26–39.

[40]Plural here and v. 21; see Drazin (1982) 61 n. 10 for comment on the singular vs. the plural; *Sifre Deut.* 33 says not "an estimate" or "a vague rumor" but "that which you can see with your own eyes."

[41]HT "set" *(ntn):* Aramaic here *msr* as Nf and Nfi but Onq. and Nfmg *yḥb*. Maher (1994) 288 notes that the HT idiom *ntn byd* or *ntn lpny* is usually translated in the Tgs. by *msr* but that *ntn* is translated by Aramaic *yḥb*.

[42]*Sifre Deut.* 33 says "you will need no weapons—just take a compass and divide it up."

[43]MS *dypty*ʾ*;* Jastrow 297 *dywptyn* "compasses"; Gk *diabētes* "carpenter's level"; see Maher (1994) 289 for other interpretations of the word; *editio princeps dpty*ʾ*;* see *Sifre Deut.* 33 "went to work to improve it."

[44]MS and *editio princeps* but omitted in later editions.

[45]MS "your."

[46]MS "after you."

[47]See *Yalqut* I, 802.

[48]Lit. "this my blessing"; "mine" refers to Moses and his additional blessings.

[49]Lit. "spoke."

[50]Aramaic *ʾpwqy* from *ʾpykyrws* (Jastrow 104) "epicure"; *Sifre Deut.* 36 "we learned that they are *ʾApikorsim* (skeptics)," defined in *Sifre Deut.* 396: "an *apikoros* is 'one who scoffed at the sages' i.e., 'making free, irreverence, contempt of the Law and its teachers'" (Jastrow 107); Onq. and Nf *ṭrḥ* "troubles/problems"; see also Le Déaut V, 20 n. 19 and Sysling (1991) 133–134.

[51]HT *rybkm* "bickering"; MS *dynnykwn* and *editio princeps dynnkwn* but better Onq. *dynkwn* and Nf *dynykwn* which Le Déaut V, 20 n. 20 suggests should be read as "the words of your judges"; see *Sifre Deut.* 36 which suggests that they were "litigious" ("delighting in trials" *Sifre Deut.* 396 n. 5).

who bring out one sela in order to extract two. 13. *Appoint* for yourselves wise men, intelligent *in their thoughts*[52] *and instructions* according to your tribes and I shall appoint them chiefs[53] over you. 14. So you answered me and said: "The thing that you have proposed[54] to do[55] is right." 15. Then I took the chiefs of your tribes *and spoke to them at length,* men wise and educated, *but I could not find men intelligent in their thoughts,*[56] and I appointed them chiefs over you, leaders[57] of thousands, leaders of hundreds, leaders of fifty—*twelve thousand*—leaders of tens—*six myriads*—and commanders[58] for your tribes. 16. At that time I appointed your judges *with the regulations concerning the judicial procedures, saying*: "Listen to your brothers (complaints): *that one shall not speak all his words that he has spoken while the other is forced to cut short his words; and when you have heard their words it shall not be possible for you not to judge*[59] *them.* You shall bring judgment in truth *and full settlement* between a man and his brother and *the one who stores up*[60] *(against him) grievances.*[61] 17. You shall not show partiality[62] in judgment. You shall listen to *the words of*[63] the lesser (person) as well as *the words of*[63] the great (person); and have no fear before a *rich* man *or a ruler* because the judgment is from *the Lord who sees every secret.* The matter that is difficult for you, you shall bring to me and I shall hear it." 18. And I have prescribed for you, at this time, all *the ten ways*[64] in which you should act *in civil cases*[65] *and capital cases.*[66] 19. Then we decamped from Horeb and traveled that entire great and fearful desert where you saw *serpents*[67] *like logs*[68] *and scorpions like archers, lying putrid*[69] *before you,* by the way of the hill country of the Amorites, just as the Lord our God commanded, and we came to *Reqem*

Notes, Chapter 1

[52]Aramaic *mrʿywnhwn;* Onq. *mdʿn* and Nf *ḥkmyn;* see also v. 15 and Exod 18:21 (Ps.-J.) "trustworthy men *(gwbryn dqšwṭ)* who hate to accept money through dishonesty" and Maher, *The Aramaic Bible* 2, 213 n. 25 and *Mekilta* to Exod 18:21 (II, 183) "men of truth . . . when sitting in judgment hate to accept money."

[53]HT and here *ryšyn* "heads" (also v. 15) but Nf "lords" (also v. 15).

[54]Lit. "you have spoken."

[55]MS *lmymr* but Ginsburger reads *lm>ʿbd* as also Onq., but Nf *špr* "good."

[56]Aramaic *mrʿywnyhwn,* see v. 13. In Exod 18:21 Jethro speaks of men with four qualities: "able men," "men who fear God," "trustworthy men," and "men who hate dishonest gain" but here Moses speaks only of "men wise and educated"; *Sifre Deut.* 38 speaks of these as "one of the seven qualities which Jethro mentioned to Moses."

[57]Aramaic *rbnyn.*

[58]Aramaic *srkyn.*

[59]According to *Sifre Deut.* 39 because "you are, nevertheless, servants in the service of the community."

[60]HT *gērô* "the alien that is with him" (RSV) is interpreted in Onq. and Nf literally as "the stranger" but in Ps.-J. the HT is understood as from *ʾgr* "to accumulate/heap up"; see *b.Sanh.* 7b.

[61]See *Sifre Deut.* 40 "the one who piles up *(ʾgr)* charges"; see preceding note.

[62]HT *nkr pnym* "be partial": here and Onq. *ʾštmwdʿ* "be recognized/be partial" (Jastrow 131) but Nf *nsb ʾpyn. ʾŠtmwdʿ* is the translation of the Hebrew phrase in Deut 16:19 (Onq.), 33:9 (Ps.-J.), and 21:17 (Nfmg); otherwise the Hebrew is rendered in the Tgs. by *nsb.*

[63]HT "hear the small and the great alike": Tgs. add "words," which is implied. *Sifre Deut.* 41 notes that nothing should be decided until the words of each are heard.

[64]HT "all the things" as also Onq. and Nf: *Sifre Deut.* 42 "this refers to ten points of difference between civil cases and capital cases" according to *m.Sanh.* 4:1.

[65]Aramaic *mmwnʾ.*

[66]Aramaic *npšṭʾ;* see also *Sifre Deut.* 42.

[67]See Deut 8:15 (Ps.-J.).

[68]Aramaic *kšwr* "beam" (Sokoloff 270); see also *Sifre Deut.* 42 "serpents as large as beams and scorpions as bows stretched out. . . ."

[69]Aramaic *sryyn* "putrid" (Jastrow 1026); *Sifre Deut.* 42 *srwhyn* conveys the same sense.

Gea.[70] 20. And I said to you: "You have come to the hill country of the Amorites that the Lord our God has given to us. 21. See *that* the Lord *your* God has given *you* the land. Go up and possess it just as the Lord *your* God spoke *to you.* Do not fear and do not be dismayed."[71] 22. Then you, all of you, approached me *in confusion,* and said: "We will send men before us in order that *they may note,* for us, *the faults*[72] *of* the land, and they will bring back to us a report about the route by which we should go up and about the cities where we shall enter." 23. And the report was good in my eyes and I took twelve *proven*[73] men from among you, one man to a tribe. 24. Then they turned and ascended to the hill country and came to the River of the Grape *and they noted its faults.* 25. And they took in their hands some of the fruit of the land and they removed (it) for us and they brought back to us a report and *Caleb and Joshua*[74] said: "The land that the Lord our God has given us is good." 26. But you did not choose to go up; *you believed the report of the ten wicked ones* and rebelled against *the Memra of* the Lord your God. 27. And you spoke rebelliously[75] in your tents, *taking your sons and your daughters to your bosoms, saying: "Woe to you, you afflicted ones, tomorrow you will be slain.*[76] It is *because* the Lord hated us that he has brought us out of the land of Egypt to give us into the hands of the Amorites in order for them to destroy us. 28. Where shall we go up? Our brothers have made our hearts faint, saying: 'The people are greater and mightier than we; the cities are large and fortified (with walls)[77] *almost to the heavens*[78] and we have seen there even the sons *of Ephron, the giant*!'" 29. And I said to you: "Do not be dismayed[79] and do not fear them! 30. It is *the Memra of*[80] the Lord, your God, who goes before you; it is he who will fight[81] for you according to all that he did for you in Egypt in your sight,[82] 31. and also in the desert where you saw *the burning serpents full of deadly poison* and the Lord your God carried you *by the clouds of Glory*[83] *of his Shekinah,* just as a man carries his son the entire way that you went

Notes, Chapter 1

[70]See n. 21 on this place-name in v. 2 above.

[71]Aramaic itp of *tbr* "to be dismayed" (Sokoloff 575) here and Onq., but Nf *bhl* "to be frightened" (Sokoloff 86); the same vocabulary distribution is found in v. 29 and 2:25 for Onq. and Nf but Ps.-J. uses in 2:25 *rtt* "to tremble/shake" (Jastrow 1504); see also Deut 20:3 and 33:29 (Ps.-J.) for *rtt;* see Clarke (1984) 555 for all occurrences in Ps.-J.; 1QapGen 21:32; 22:9 *tbr* to imply "defeat."

[72]HT *hpr* "explore": here *trgn* "to espy the fault" (Jastrow 1696) which Levy (II, 407) understands from *twr* "to explore" and *rgn* "to slander," but Cook (1986) 247 and Dalman (398) consider the form as an itp of *rgn.* See Clarke (1984) 545 for the three instances of the verb in Ps.-J. Onq. and Nf *ʾll* "spy out." The same distribution is in v. 24. See also v. 27 below *(rgyntw).*

[73]Aramaic *gwbryn bryryn; bryr* "clear/pure/certain" (Jastrow 194) from *brr* itp "to be selected" (Jastrow 197). In Deut 29:12 (Ps.-J.) "a chosen nation." In *Sifre Deut.* 44 the word *brwryn* is explained as "the best and finest among you."

[74]See Num 13:30 and 14:30 (Ps.-J.).

[75]The meaning of the HT is unclear but here and Nf *rgn* "to quarrel/create discontent" whereas Onq. *rʿm* "to murmur"; see n. 72 above.

[76]Aramaic *tbr* as in v. 21; see *Sifre Deut.* 45 "O afflicted ones . . . O suffering ones, tomorrow some of you will be slain."

[77]Aramaic *krykn* here and Onq. from *krk* "to wrap around" (Sokoloff 269) but Nf *tlyln* "fortified"; see Deut 9:1 where the vocabulary distribution among the Tgs. is the same.

[78]HT "in the heavens"; see the same formula in Deut 4:11; 9:1 (Ps.-J.) and see also Drazin (1982) 66 n. 27 on this phrase.

[79]Aramaic itp *tbr* "to be broken" (Sokoloff 575 "be dismayed") as in Onq. but Nf *bhl.* See n. 71 above.

[80]Onq. as here but Nf "Glory of the *Shekinah.*"

[81]Onq. as here *(gyḥ)* while Nf *ʿbd nṣḥny qrbykwn* which is the usual idiom "to do battle."

[82]HT "to your eyes"; Nf "your eyes have seen."

[83]Frequently in Ps.-J.; see Maher, *The Aramaic Bible* 1B, 22 n. 11.

until the time when you came to this place. 32. But in this matter you were not believing in *the Memra of*[84] the Lord your God, 33. who went before you on the way to prepare[85] a place of encampment in order for you to camp *with the pillar of* fire at night to light for you the way in which you should go and *the pillar of* cloud during the day." 34. And the voice of your words was heard *before*[86] the Lord and he was angry and swore, saying: 35. "Not a single man among these men of this evil generation shall see the good land that I swore to give to your fathers, 36. except for Caleb bar Jephunneh; he shall see it and to him shall I give the land *of Hebron* in which he walked and to his sons because he has acted perfectly according to the Fear[87] of the Lord." 37. Even against me was there anger *before* the Lord because of you, saying: "Even you shall not enter there. 38. It is Joshua bar Nun *who serves in your house of instruction*[88] who shall enter there. Make him strong because he will make Israel possess it. 39. But your children about whom you said that they will be for spoil,[89] and your children who are unable to distinguish, this day, between good and evil, they are the ones who shall enter there and to them shall I give it and they shall possess it. 40. But as for you, turn yourselves about and return to the desert by the way of the Reed Sea." 41. And you answered and said to me: "We have sinned before the Lord. We shall go up and battle according to all that the Lord our God has commanded us." Each one of you has put on his war equipment *and begun* to ascend to the hill country. 42. Then the Lord said to me: "Say to them: Do not go up and do not do battle, *for my Shekinah*[90] does not *go* among you, lest you be broken by your enemies." 43. And I spoke to you but you did not heed and you rebelled against *the Memra of*[91] the Lord *and were wicked;* then you went up to the hill country. 44. So the Amorites who live in that hill country came out against you and chased you, just as wasps[92] *sting*[93] *and flee,* and destroyed you[94] *at Gabla* as far as Hormah. 45. Then you returned and cried before the Lord; but the Lord did not accept your *prayers*[95] and did not listen *to your words.*[96] 46. So you lived in *Reqem* as many days as the days that you dwelt (in other places)."

Notes, Chapter 1

[84]Also Onq., but Nf "the Name of the *Memra* of."

[85]HT "to seek out *(twr)* (a place to camp)"; the Tgs. *tqn* "to prepare"; see Num 10:33 and John 14:2-4; see McNamara (1983) 239–241 on this verse.

[86]Also Onq.

[87]Here and Onq., but Nf "the *Memra* of the Lord"; see Sysling (1991) 191 n. 21.

[88]Aramaic *byt ʾwlpn,* only in Ps.-J.; see Sysling (1991) 9 n. 88.

[89]Here Aramaic *ʿdy,* but Onq. and Nf *bzz* "to despoil" (Sokoloff 89).

[90]Here and Onq., but Nf "the Glory of my *Shekinah.*"

[91]Here and Onq., but Nf "the mouth of the decree of the *Memra* of."

[92]Here Aramaic *ʾwrʿyytʾ* "wasps," but Onq. *dbyrtʾ* "bees" and Nf "wasps of bees."

[93]HT "do": the MS of Ps.-J. has a double translation: *ḥrr* and *ḥwš*. The MS has *ḥnn* but read with Ginsburger *ḥdd* "to sting" (Jastrow 425) and *ḥwš* "to flee," whereas Onq. and Nf translate with one verb: (1) Onq. *ntz* "to fly away" (Jastrow 943) is made clear in *b.Sotah* 48b, "R. Joshua b. Levi said: 'It is the honey which comes from the hills. How is it known? As R. Shesheth translated "as the bees do" (Deut 1:44): When the bees spring forth and fly in the heights of the world . . .'" and (2) Nf *rdp* "pursue."

[94]HT *nkh* "beat down" (RSV): here *mḥy* "wipe out/destroy" but Onq. *ṭrd* "beat into a retreat," Nf *ktt* "crush" and Frg. Tg.(V) *qṭl;* see also Grossfeld, *The Aramaic Bible* 9, 21 n. 24.

[95]HT "hearken to your voice" in Ps.-J. refers to prayer as also in Onq., but Nf "the voice of your weeping"; see Maher, *The Aramaic Bible* 1B, 104 n. 7 for other instances in Ps.-J.

[96]HT "give ear *(ʾzn)* to you": the Tgs. "listen (ap of *ṣwt,* Sokoloff 462) to your words."

CHAPTER 2

1. Then we turned and set out for the desert by way of the Reed Sea, just as the Lord spoke to me, and we circled Mount *Gabla*[1] for many days. 2. And the Lord said to me, saying: 3. "It is enough for you that you have circled this mountain; turn to the north 4. and give a command to the people, saying: You will be passing through the territory of your brothers, the sons of Esau who live in Gabla.[2] They shall fear you, be very careful: 5. do not attack them because I shall not give you any of their land even as much as to set a foot for I have given Mount *Gabla* as an inheritance to Esau, *because of the honor that he did to his father.*[3] 6. You shall buy natural *grain* from them with silver, that you may eat, and even water shall you buy from them with silver, that you may drink. 7. *Be careful not to trouble them,* for the Lord *your* God blessed you in all the works of your hands, *furnishing all your needs*[4] on your travels in this great desert. During these forty years (with) *the Memra of* the Lord your God supporting[5] you, you lacked nothing." 8. So we crossed *opposite* our brothers, the sons of Esau who lived in *Gabla,* from Elath and from *the city of Tarnegola*[6] and we turned and crossed by way of the Moab desert. 9. Then the Lord said to me: "Do not annoy the Moabites and do not battle against them[7] for I shall not give you as an inheritance any of their land for I have given *Lehayyat*[8] as an inheritance to Lot's sons. 10. The *Fearsome Ones*[9] lived there from early times, a great and numerous people and strong[10] as giants.[11] 11. *The giants who lived in the Plain of the Giants*[12] were considered, even they, *as giants who were destroyed in the flood*[13] and the Moabites called them *Fearsome Ones.*[14] 12. And at *Gabla* the *Nobles*[15] lived from early times; but the

Notes, Chapter 2

[1]HT "Mount Seir," also Onq., but Nf reads as here.

[2]MS reads *bḥqlʾ* "in the country," which a scribe partially erased.

[3]See Gen 38:8, 12 (Ps.-J.); Jacob feared that Esau, having received merit by serving his father, might prevail over his brother; see Maher, *The Aramaic Bible* 1b, 113 n. 8; see also *Deut. R.* 2, 3 (18) and *b.Meg.* 16a–17b.

[4]HT "he knew all your ways": here and Onq. substitute "needs" for "ways" but Nf "your ways were revealed before God."

[5]HT "The Lord your God has been with you": Tgs. Onq. and here add (1) Memra and (2) "help" (*sʿd* "aid/support") instead of HT "with you," but Nf has only "at your aid" *(sʿd);* see McNamara's note on this verse in *The Aramaic Bible* 5A, 27 n. 6.

[6]HT "Ezion-Geber," also Onq., but Nf as here.

[7]The Tgs. add *sdr qrb* to clarify the meaning; see the same process in vv. 19 and 24.

[8]HT "Ar": the Tgs. translate as here; see v. 18 below and Num 21:15 (Ps.-J.), Clarke, *The Aramaic Bible* 4, 248 n. 33, and Grossfeld, *The Aramaic Bible* 8, 127 n. 9, and McNamara's note on this verse in *The Aramaic Bible* 5A, 27 n. 8.

[9]HT "Emim": the Tgs. *ʾymtnyʾ;* see Gen 14:5 (Ps.-J. and Nf); Deut 2:10 is the source for the etymology of Gen 14:5 in the Tgs.; see Maher, *The Aramaic Bible* 1B, 56 n. 18.

[10]Aramaic *ḥsyn* but Onq. and Nf *tqp;* see Deut 9:2 where the vocabulary distribution is the same.

[11]MS *gynbryʾ;* Onq. *gybbryʾ* "giants," but Nf reads *gwbryh* "men." Clearly Ps.-J. and Onq. with *yodh* suggest "giants" whereas Nf with *waw* suggests "men." The fact that a scribe has marked the *waw* in Nf with a dot to produce *gbryh* suggests an attempt to read (incompletely) with Onq. and Ps.-J.; Nfmg has *gwbryh;* see also vv. 11, 20.

[12]That is, "the plains of the Rephaim" are called by the Moabites "Emim" (HT Deut 2:11). The idea of "giants" comes from the tradition reflected in the Tgs. of Josh 12:4; 13:12; 15:8; 1 Chr 11:15; 14:9; 20:4, 6 where "Rephaim" are called "giants." Also LXX translated "Rephaim" with *gigantēs.*

[13]See Gen 3:11 (Ps.-J.); Gen 14:13 (Ps.-J.); Maher, *The Aramaic Bible* 1B, 57 n. 26; and *Gen. R.* 42, 8 and *Deut. R.* 1, 25.

[14]See n. 9 above.

[15]HT "Horites" as Onq. and Nfmg: Ps.-J. *gnwsyyʾ* and Nf *ḥwwrnyyh* (as in Gen 36:20, 21 [Nf]); LXX *gennaios;* see also Maher, *The Aramaic Bible* 1B, 122 n. 7.

sons of Esau drove (them) out and destroyed (them) from before them and lived in their place, just as Israel did to the land of its inheritance[16] that the Lord gave them. 13. So now rise and cross over the River *Tarvayya*."[17] We crossed the River *Tarvayya*. 14. And the period of days in which we traveled from *Reqem Gea*[18] until we crossed the River *Tarvayya* were thirty-eight years until the entire generation of men of war were wiped out from *the midst of* the camp just as the Lord promised them. 15. But *a plague from before* the Lord *was hurled* against them to destroy them from the midst of the camp until they ceased to exist. 16. Now when all the men of war had been eliminated[19] from the midst of *the camp,*[20] 17. then the Lord spoke with me saying: 18. "You are going to cross on this day the border of the Moabites[21] (to) *Lehayyat.*[22] 19. When you shall approach the Ammonites, you shall not surround them nor attack them by engaging them in battle for I shall not give you any of the land of the Ammonites as an inheritance for I have given it as an inheritance to the sons of Lot, *because of the merit of Abraham.*" 20. It was also considered a land of *giants;* in earlier times *giants*[23] lived there and the Ammonites called them *Zimthanay,*[24] 21. a great and strong people like the giants. *The Memra of* the Lord destroyed them from before them and drove them out and they lived in their place 22.[25] until the time of this day.[26] 23. *And the remainder of the surviving Canaanites* who were camped in *the cities of Rephiah*[27] as far as Gaza, *the Cappadocians*[28] who came out from *Cappadocia* destroyed them and dwelt in their place. 24. Rise, journey and cross over the tributaries[29] of the Arnon; see *that* I have delivered into your[30] hands Sihon, King of Heshbon, and the Amorite, along with his land. Begin *to drive him out*[31] and make war against him. 25. On this day I am beginning to put terror and fear of you on the faces of all the nations who are under the whole heaven; those who shall hear the report of your *merit: how the sun and the*

Notes, Chapter 2

[16]HT "their possession": here and Onq. *yrt* but Nf *ytb,* "settlement."

[17]HT "the brook Zered": also Onq. and Nf but here *trwwyy'* (Jastrow 550); see Num 21:12 (Ps.-J.) and Clarke, *The Aramaic Bible* 4, 248 n. 24 for another explanation of "Zered": "the wadi producing reeds, sedge, and violets."

[18]HT "Kadesh Barnea": see n. on Deut 1:2 and Davies (1972).

[19]HT "had perished and were dead": here *psq* "separate out" to die; Onq. af of *šlm* "ceased to die" (Grossfeld) and Nf *swp* "perished/came to an end" (and died).

[20]HT "the people," also Onq. and Nf but here *mšryt'.*

[21]*Editio princeps* and Onq. "Moab" but Nf as here.

[22]HT "Ar"; see n. 8 above.

[23]HT "Rephaim": see n. 12 above.

[24]HT "Zamummim" but here and Nf *zmmtnyyh* (Sokoloff 179); but Onq. "Heshbani" from *ḥšb* "think" suggesting possibly "inhabitants of Heshbon."

[25]The first part of v. 22 is omitted in the MS due to homoioteleuton on *b'tryhwn* "in their place."

[26]MS *'d zmn ywm' hdyn* as Nf but *editio princeps 'd ywm' hdyn* "until this day" as also Onq.

[27]HT "Chatzerim," obviously a contemporary geographical location here.

[28]HT "the people of Caphtor": all the Tgs. "Cappadocians"; see Gen 10:14 (Ps.-J.) and Maher, *The Aramaic Bible* 1B, 48 n. 31, and Wainwright (1956).

[29]The plural *nḥly* may be an error since Onq. and Nf have singular here but Ps.-J. has instances of both plural (Deut 3:8, 16; 4:48) and singular (Deut 2:36). In the plural it may refer to the various tributaries that flow into the Arnon; see n. 40 below.

[30]HT "your" singular as Onq., but here and Nf plural.

[31]HT "take possession": here and Onq. use *trk* "expel/drive out" but Nf translates literally with *yrt* "possess"; see Grossfeld, *The Aramaic Bible* 9, 23 n. 12.

moon stood[32] *because of you, and have ceased speaking a song during a day and a half, and they remained in their dwellings until you arranged war against Sihon;* so they will tremble and shake[33] from before you. 26. Then I sent messengers *from Nehardea*[34] *which is close to the* desert Kedemoth to Sihon, King of the Amorites,[35] (with) words of peace, saying: 27. "Let me cross through your land! I shall go by the road *that is the main*[36] *road,* I shall not stray *to cause you damage* to the right or to the left. 28. You shall sell me natural grain for money, that I may eat, and you shall give me water for money, that I may drink, only would I pass through. 29. (It is there) that the sons of Esau, who live in *Gabla,* and the Moabites, who live in *Lehayyat,* did to me until the moment when I would cross the Jordan to (enter) the land that the Lord our God has given to us." 30. But Sihon, King of Heshbon, did not choose to let us cross through the midst of *his territory* for the Lord your God hardened *the inclination of* his spirit and hardened his heart in order to deliver him into your hand as at this day. 31. Then the Lord said to me: "*See, in the prolongation of the sun and the moon,* I have begun to deliver him into your power, Sihon and his land. Begin to drive him out in order to possess his land." 32. So Sihon came out toward us, he and all his people *to battle* at Jahaz. 33. And the Lord our God delivered him before us. We destroyed him and his sons along with all his people. 34. At that time we captured all the cities and destroyed[37] all the cities, men,[38] women, and children. We did not leave (any) survivor. 35. Only the cattle we plundered for ourselves, and we stripped the cities that we captured. 36. From Aroër which is on the banks of the tributary of the Arnon river, and the city that was built in the middle of the valley,[39] to Gilead, there was not a city *too powerful*[40] for us: all of them the Lord our God delivered before us. 37. However, we did not approach the land of the Ammonites, every region of the tributary of the Jabbok and the cities of the hill country, according to everything that the Lord our God had commanded.

Notes, Chapter 2

[32]The connection with the story of Joshua is because the Hebrew verb *ʾḥl* "to begin" is translated with *šry* in Deut 2:25 and Josh 3:7; see Ginzberg, *Legends* 3.340; 6.46 (see Le Déaut V, 35 n. 29 and his criticism).

[33]HT "tremble and be in anguish": here *zwʿ* and *rtt,* but Onq. *zwʿ* and *šbr* "tremble" and "be broken" and Nf *rgz* and *bḥl* "tremble" and "be frightened." *Rtt* appears in Ps.-J. in seven instances (Clarke 1984, 555).

[34]Here is the only mention in the Tgs. of this place-name; it should not be identified with the famous Jewish Academy in Babylonia.

[35]HT "Heshbon" as Onq. and Nf: see v. 24.

[36]Aramaic *kbyšʾ* "grade/make a path" (Jastrow 610); Onq. *ʾwrḥʾ ʾyzyl* "main road" (Grossfeld) and Nf *bʾḥrʾ ʾhlk* "by the road I will walk." In Num 20:19 Grossfeld translates *ʾwrḥ kbyšʾ* in Onq. as "main road." In Ps.-J. Num 20:19 the vocabulary differs *(ʾsrṭyʾ dmlkʾ).* Grossfeld translates "main" for both *kbyšʾ* and *ʾyzyl* which comes from *ʾzl* "to go."

[37]HT *ḥrm* "utterly destroyed": here and Onq. *gmr* but Nf *šyṣy.*

[38]HT *mtm* "utterly" (RSV) but the meaning is unclear: here and Onq. translate "men" and Deut 3:6; 4:27 (HT) but Nf "fortified towns."

[39]Aramaic *nḥlʾ:* see n. 28 above.

[40]HT "too high": here and Onq. *tqp* but Nf itp *šyzb* "to be saved."

CHAPTER 3

1. So we turned and went up by way of *Mathnan.*[1] Og, King of *Mathnan* came out to meet us, he and all his people, *to battle* at Edreath. 2. Then the Lord said to me: "Have no fear of him for I have given him and all his people and his country into your power. You will do to him just as you did to Sihon, King of the Amorites, who lived in Heshbon." 3. And the Lord our God delivered into our power even Og, King of *Mathnan,* along with all his people. We battled him until no survivor was left. 4. At that time we captured all his cities. There was not a city that we did not take from them, sixty cities, all the territory *of the province*[2] *of Targona,*[3] the Kingdom of Og, in *Mathnan.* 5. All these were fortified[4] cities, *surrounded by high* walls, *closed by* doors and bolts, besides very many unwalled cities. 6. And we destroyed[5] their *cities* just as we did to Sihon, King of Heshbon, thus we destroyed all the cities, men,[6] women, and children. 7. But all the cattle and spoils of the cities we plundered for ourselves. 8. We took at that time from *the control of* the two kings of the Amorites the land that was on the other side of Jordan, from the tributaries[7] of the Arnon to the Mountain of Hermon:[8] 9.[9] the Sidonians had called Hermon *the mountain that produced tasteless fruit*[10] and the Amorites called it *the Snow Mountain*[11] *for snow never ceased from it, neither in the summer nor in the winter,* 10. all the cities of the plain and all Gilead and all *Mathnan* to *Seleucia*[12] and Edreath, the cities of the Kingdom of Og in *Mathnan.* 11. For only Og, King of *Mathnan,* remained of *the giants,*[13] *the rest of whom had been destroyed in the flood.*[14] Behold his couch was an iron couch. *It was placed in the house of archives,*[15] at Rabath of the Ammonites. Its length was nine cubits and

Notes, Chapter 3

[1]HT "Bashan": here and Onq. "Mathnan" but Nf "Butnin." The same vocabulary distribution is found in vv. 3, 4, 10, 13; Num 21:13. "Mathnan" represents the consonantal shift of *b>m* and *š>t*.

[2]HT *ḥbl* "region": here *tḥwm plk* seems to be a conflation of Onq. *plk* "district" and Nf *tḥwm* "territory."

[3]HT "Argob": Onq. and Nf *trkwnʾ/h* but Nfmg *ʾtrgwnʾ;* see Deut 3:13 (Ps.-J.); Luke 3:1 ("Trachonitis"); and see Grossfeld, *The Aramaic Bible* 9, 25 n. 2 for possible geographical location in northeast Transjordania, known as Bashan in the OT; the place is also mentioned in 1 Kings 4:13; see Schürer (1973) 1.337.

[4]See note on 2:24.

[5]Aramaic *gmr* as in Onq., but Nf *šyṣy;* see 2:34 for the same vocabulary distribution.

[6]See n. 38 on the Aramaic word *(gwbryyʾ)* in Deut 2:34.

[7]Aramaic *nḥly* "wadies" or "tributaries"; see note on 2:24 and Maher, *The Aramaic Bible* 1B, 160 n.47 suggests the translation "wadi(es)."

[8]HT "Hermon," also here and Onq., but Nf *twr tlgh* "Mount of Snow."

[9]The *editio princeps* offers a different text from that found in the Frg. Tgs. The order of verses (3:9, 11 before 3:2 in Frg. Tgs.) suggests the secondary nature of these recensions; see Klein (1975) 129–135; see also the following notes.

[10]HT "Sirion": here and Nf *msry pyrwy* (as if derived from the af of *sry* "to make unsavory," Jastrow 1026); see also 4:48 (Frg. Tgs. and Nfmg); Onq. "called Hermon, Sirion."

[11]HT "Senir" as also Nf, but Onq. as here. The Frg. Tg.(V) has "a land that increases the fruits of the tree for Hermon." See Klein (1975) 129–135 for a discussion of the order of the various Frg. Tg. recensions; see Grossfeld, *The Aramaic Bible* 9, 25 n. 3 for rabbinic notes.

[12]HT "Salecah" (RSV): see McNamara on this verse in *The Aramaic Bible* 5A, 32 n. 9.

[13]HT "Rephaim," also v. 13: see nn. 11 and 12 for 2:10-11.

[14]See the note on 2:11; Maher, *The Aramaic Bible* 1B, 57 n. 26 for rabbinic sources.

[15]Aramaic *byt ʾrkywn;* Nfmg and Frg. Tg.(P) read *ʾprkwn* "eparchy." Le Déaut V, 41 n. 12 says that the phrase "the archives of the Jews" is mentioned in papyri and inscriptions.

its width was four cubits, by his own cubit.[16] 12. And we took possession of that land at that time. From Aroër, which was on[17] the bank of the river, and half the hill country of Gilead along with its cities, I gave to *the tribe of* Reuben and to *the tribe of* Gad. 13. But the rest of Gilead and all of *Mathnan,* Og's kingdom, I gave to the tribe of Manasseh, the entire territory of *the province of Targona,* all of *Mathnan* which was called the land of *the giants.* 14. *And*[18] Jair, son of Manasseh, took the entire *territory of the province of Targona* to the frontier of Korzi[19] and Epikoros[20] and called them by his name, "the towns of Jair," until this day. 15. And to Makir I gave Gilead. 16. And to *the tribe of* Reuben and to *the tribe of* Gad I gave from Gilead as far as the tributaries[21] of the Arnon, the middle of the river being its border, and as far as the Jabbok *whose* river makes the border of the Ammonites, 17. with the plain and the Jordan, and the territory from *Gennesaret*[22] as far as the sea of the plain *and the city of Tiberias*[23] *which lies close to the* Salt Sea, below *where the waters empty*[24] from the heights[25] to the east. 18. At that time I commanded *you, the tribe of Reuben and the tribe of Gad and half the tribe of Manasseh* saying: "the Lord your God gave you that land to possess; all who are equipped for war shall cross over armed before your brothers, the Israelites. 19. Only your wives and your children and your cattle, (I[26] know that you have much cattle), shall remain in *your* cities that I have given you, 20. until the time when the Lord allows your brothers to rest like you and they will possess, even they, the land that the Lord your God has given you.[27] Then you will return, each man to his inheritance that I have given to you." 21. To Joshua I commanded, at that time, saying: "Your eyes have seen everything that the Lord your God has done to these two kings: so shall the Lord do to all the kingdoms through which you shall cross. 22. Do not fear them for *the Memra of*[28] the Lord your God is fighting for you." 23. At that time *I sought compassion from before* the Lord, saying: 24. "*In prayer, in compassion from before you,* Lord God! It is you who began to show your servant your greatness and the power of your strong hand. Because you are God *and there is no one other than you whose Shekinah dwells*[29] in the heaven *above,* and there is no dominion on earth that can do as you do or as

Notes, Chapter 3

[16]HT "a common cubit" (RSV); Onq. *bʾmt mlk* "royal cubit" and Nf *ʾmtyh dmlkʾ*. Ps.-J., which uses *grmyh,* may be translating the HT literally or may understand the cubit of a giant, that is, King Og.

[17]MS *wʿd* instead of *wʿl* as in Onq. and Nf.

[18]"And" not in HT but is in the Hebrew lemma found in the MS.

[19]Aramaic of the MS *qwrzy* seems an error; Onq. and Nf *gšwrʾh* "Geshorah" (as in HT and Tg. Josh 12:5; 13:11, 13); Frg. Tg.(V) *qryyt ʾpyqwrs* "City of Epikaros." Jastrow 104 suggests reading the MS as in Frg. Tg.(V).

[20]HT "Macathites": MS *ʾntyqyrws;* Onq. and Frg. Tg.(V) *ʾpykwrws;* Nf has a censorial erasure that might suggest the reading "Epicureans" as original; see as well Tg. Josh 12:5; 13:11, 13; 2 Sam 23:34; 2 Kings 25:23.

[21]Aramaic *nḥly;* see note on 2:24.

[22]HT "Kinnereth": *gnsyr* in Tgs. from the Greek *gennesaret;* see Num 34:11 (Nf). First mentioned in 1 Macc 11:67.

[23]See Alexander (1975) 222.

[24]Aramaic *špkwt;* see Lev 1:16 (Nf) and Jastrow (1616).

[25]HT "Pisgah": here, Onq. and Nf *rmtʾ* "Ramtah"; see Num 21:20; 23:14; Deut 3:17, 27; 4:49; 34:1, and Grossfeld, *The Aramaic Bible* 8, 127 n. 15.

[26]The text reads "we" as Onq., but Nf reads *ydʿ ʾnh.*

[27]Onq. and Nf add "beyond the Jordan."

[28]Onq. as here but Nf does not add "*Memra.*"

[29]See Exod 15:11 (Ps.-J. and Nf) for the inspiration for this paraphrase; see McNamara, *The Aramaic Bible* 2, 66 n. 11, and Maher, *The Aramaic Bible* 2, 204 n. 22.

your power (does). 25. So I would cross and see the good land that is on the other side of the Jordan, that good hill country *on which is built the city of Jerusalem and the hill country of* Lebanon[30] *on which, in the future, your Shekinah will rest.*" 26. But the Lord was angered against me because of you and did not heed *my prayers.*[31] And the Lord said to me: "It is enough for you! Do not continue to speak about this matter before me! 27. Go up to the top of the height[32] and lift up your eyes to the west, to the north, to the south, and to the east and see with your eyes;[33] for you shall not cross over this Jordan. 28. Then command Joshua and encourage him and strengthen him for it is he who will cross over before this people and he will give them possession of the land that you see." 29. And we dwelt in the valley, *crying because of our sins that joined*[34] *us to the worshipers of the idols* Peor.

CHAPTER 4

1. And now, Israel, hear the statutes and judgments that I am teaching you to do in order that you shall live and enter and take possession of the land that the Lord, the God of your fathers, is giving to you. 2. *You are not permitted* to add to the matters that I am commanding you nor shall you diminish anything of that *which concerns* keeping the commandments of the Lord your God that I am prescribing for you. 3. With your eyes you have seen what *the Memra of*[1] the Lord has done to[2] the *worshipers of the idols of* Peor,[3] for every man *who strayed after the idols* of Peor the Lord your God destroyed from among you. 4. But you who adhere to *the Fear of*[4] the Lord your God are alive, all of you, today. 5. See that I taught you the statutes and judgments just as the Lord my God commanded me to do, so (you should act) in the midst of the land that you are entering to possess. 6. You shall keep and do the Law, for it is your knowledge and your intelligence in the sight of the (other) peoples who will hear about all these

Notes, Chapter 3 (Cont.)

[30]That is, the "temple" as in Onq. *(byt mqdš᾽)* and Nf *(twr byt mwqdšh)* and Nfmg 2 "this goodly Mount Zion and the sanctuary"; see Deut 1:7 (Ps.-J.) and Grossfeld, *The Aramaic Bible* 9, 27 n. 10 for the rabbinic evidence for the interpretation of Lebanon as the Temple; see Vermes (1961) 26–39 for a full discussion of the various interpretations of "Lebanon" in the Tgs.

[31]HT "to me": Onq. "he did not listen to me"; Nf "hear the voice of my prayer."

[32]See n. 25 above.

[33]Aramaic *ʿynk;* here and Onq. singular, but plural in Nf.

[34]HT "we remained in the valley opposite Beth-peor"; here the Aramaic *᾽zdwwgnn:* the verb *zwg* in itp suggests sexual union as in Deut 5:30 (Ps.-J.); Nf and Frg. Tg.(V) *dbq.*

Notes, Chapter 4

[1]HT and Onq. "the Lord," but here and Nf "*Memra*" is agent of the action.

[2]HT "at Baal-Peor," but here the preposition *beth* "to/with" plus "the worshipers of the idols of."

[3]HT only "at Baal-Peor."

[4]HT "the Lord": see also vv. 20, 29, 30; Onq. translates consistently as here, "Fear of"; Nf v. 4 translates "the Law of the Lord" but Nfmg "the Name of the *Memra* of the Lord." In v. 20 Ps.-J. and Nf translate "the *Memra* of the Lord" and in vv. 29, 30 Ps.-J. translates, as here, "The Fear of the Lord," but Nf has only "the Lord"; see Sysling (1991) 191 n. 21 for other passages. Grossfeld, *The Aramaic Bible* 9, 29 n. 1 observes on the basis of *b.Ketub.* 3b that "Fear" was introduced to prevent human intimacy with God Himself.

statutes and will say: "Surely a people knowledgeable and wise is this great people!" 7. For what people is (so) great as to have a god[5] close to them as *the Name of the Memra of* the Lord our God? *It is the way of the nations to carry their gods*[6] *on their shoulders; they appear close to them but they are far away because they do not hear with their ears. But the Memra of the Lord sits on his throne high and lifted up, and he hears our prayer* every time when we pray before him and he fulfills[7] our petitions. 8. And which is the great people that has statutes and judgments as just as all this Law that today I laid before you? 9. Only take heed[8] *for yourselves* and watch[8] yourselves exceedingly, lest you forget the things that you saw with *your* eyes *at Sinai* and lest they turn from your heart all the days of your lives. You shall teach them to your sons and the sons of *your* sons. 10. *And you shall make yourselves pure in your study (of the Law),* as the day when you stood before the Lord your God at Horeb at the time when the Lord said to me: "Gather *before*[9] me the people that I may make them hear my words in order that they learn[10] to fear *before*[9] me, all the days that they will live on the land and that they will teach their children." 11. So you drew near and stood on *the slopes of* the mountain while the mountain was burning with fire and *its flame was reaching up* to the heavens, in darkness and dense cloud. 12. Then the Lord spoke with you *at the mountain* from the midst of the fire. You were hearing the sound *of (my) Dibbur*[11] but an image you did not see, only a voice *speaking*. 13. And he taught you his covenant that he commanded you to do, the ten Memras, and he wrote them on two tablets *of sapphire*.[12] 14. And the Lord commanded me at that time to teach you the statutes and judgments so that you may do them in the land to which you are crossing over to possess. 15. So take heed to yourselves for you did not see any image on the day when the Lord spoke to you (at Horeb)[13] from the midst of the fire; 16. be careful that you not act corruptly and make for yourselves a likeness or image *of any idol,* a male or female image, 17. an image of any animal that is in the land, an image of any winged bird that flies in the air of the firmament of the heavens, 18. an image of any reptile that is on the land, an image of any fish that is in the waters under the land. 19. And lest when you lift[14] your eyes toward the heavens and you see the sun and the moon and the *principal*[15] stars, the entire galaxy of the heavens, you will stray[16] and bow down to them and worship them. *It is through them* that the Lord

Notes, Chapter 4

[5]HT "God" *(ʾlhym)*: Tgs. singular *ʾlh* (Ps.-J. *ʾlqʾ*) to avoid suggestion of polytheism. *B.Sanh.* 38b considers the reference to God but *y.Ber.* 9.11 interprets this as an idol; see also 4:35, 39; 5:7; 32:39. Onq. adds "to accept its prayers in time of tribulation"; see Grossfeld, *The Aramaic Bible* 9, 29 n. 3.

[6]Lit. *dḥlthwn* "their Fears."

[7]HT "whenever we call upon him" as Onq., but Nf "answer" *(ʿny)* and Ps.-J. "fulfill" *(ʿbd)* complete the idea of the HT phrase.

[8]HT "take heed/keep," both times *šmr,* but Tgs. write itp of *šmr* first and then *nṭr* for the second occurrence.

[9]HT writes *ly* and *ʾty,* but Onq. and Ps.-J. translate with *qdm* in both instances; Nf uses *qdm* only in the second instance.

[10]HT *lmd* "learn": the Tgs. *ʾlp* meaning "to teach themselves."

[11]Aramaic *dbwrʾ,* which often serves as a metonym for God; however in Onq. "the sound of words" *(ql ptgmyn),* Nf "my words" *(dbryy),* and Nfmg "words" *(dbyryn);* see Exod 33:11 (Ps.-J.) and Num 7:89 (Nf).

[12]HT "stones" as Onq. and Nf: "sapphire" here and Deut 34:12 (Ps.-J.), but Deut 5:22; 9:9, 10, 11; 10:1, 3 (Ps.-J.) "marble" *(mrmyryn);* see Clarke (1984) 371 and *Cant. R.* 5.14 (246).

[13]HT, Onq., and Nf, but MS omits.

[14]HT "lift *(nsʾ)* your eyes": here *tly* as Nf but Onq. *zqp*. Ps.-J. always has *zqp* for HT *nsʾ,* following Onq., except here.

[15]Aramaic *ryš,* but Nf "the course *(sdr)* of the stars."

[16]Aramaic *ṭʿy* "to err/go astray" in all Tgs.

your God has allotted[17] *the knowledge of*[18] all the peoples that are (found) beneath the entire heavens. 20. But you, *the Memra of* the Lord has taken (you) *for his portion*[19] and has brought you out with an iron *yoke,*[20] from Egypt, in order to be for him a people, a possession as (you are) today. 21. Now there was anger against me *from before* the Lord concerning *your words that you murmured about the waters;* and he swore that I would not cross the Jordan and that I would not enter the (good)[21] land that the Lord your God will give you (as an inheritance).[22] 22. Because I will die in this land, I will not cross over the Jordan but you will cross over and will possess this good land. 23. Take heed to yourselves, lest you forget the covenant of the Lord your God that he made with you and you make for yourselves *a likeness,* an image of anything that the Lord your God commanded *you not to make*. 24. Because the Lord your God, *his Memra*[23] is a *consuming* fire, *that fire is* a jealous God *and he takes revenge in jealousy*.[24] 25. When you give birth to sons and to sons of sons, and you grow old in the land and you corrupt your deeds and you make *for yourselves a likeness,* an image of anything, then you will do what is evil *before*[25] the Lord your God, to provoke him to anger. 26. I call to witness against you, this day, *everlasting*[26] *witnesses,* heaven and earth, because you will surely be destroyed quickly from upon the land to which you are crossing over the Jordan to possess; you will not lengthen days on it because you will surely be destroyed. 27. Then the Lord will scatter you among the nations and you will remain as a small nation among the nations to which the Lord shall lead you into exile. 28. And there *you will be constrained* to serve *the worshipers of* idols, the works of human hands, *of* wood and stone that neither see, nor hear, nor eat, nor breathe. 29. Then from these you will seek *to return to the Fear of* the Lord your God, and you will find *mercy* if you seek from *before* him, with all your heart and with all your soul. 30. When you will be in distress and all these things befall you, at the end of days, then you will return to *the Fear of* the Lord your God and will heed *his Memra*.[27] 31. For the Lord your God is a God of mercy; he will not abandon you nor will he destroy you nor will he forget the covenant of your fathers that he covenanted with them. 32. If you would ask now about *the generations* that are *from the beginning of days,* who were before you from the day when the Lord created Man on the earth, and from one extreme to the other of the heavens: whether such a great thing as this has ever been or *whether the like of this* has ever been heard? 33. Has it *been possible* that a nation has heard the voice of *the Memra of* the Lord,[28] *the eternal God,*

Notes, Chapter 4

[17]HT "allotted" *(ḥlq):* here and Nf *plg* "allotted," but Onq. "designated" *(zmn).*

[18]That is, the Lord has given knowledge to the Gentiles through the heavenly hosts, but to Israel directly (v. 20). LXX ". . . in order to give the light to all the people."

[19]Aramaic *lḥwlqyh,* which is a play on HT *lqḥ* "taken" by metathesis.

[20]HT, Onq., and Nf *kwr* "furnace," but here *nyr.*

[21]HT and Onq., but omitted in MS as also in Nf where it is added in red ink in the margin by an annotator.

[22]Aramaic *ʾhsnʾ* "inheritance"; found in HT, Onq., and Nf, but omitted in MS.

[23]Also Onq.

[24]See Exod 20:5; 34:14 (Ps.-J. and Nf) for the same idea.

[25]HT "in the sight of" becomes in the Tgs. "before"; see also 6:18; 8:18; 12:25, 28; 13:19; 17:2; 21:9; 31:29.

[26]Aramaic *qyymyn;* see Deut 32:1 (Ps.-J. and Nf).

[27]HT "his voice," Onq. as here, but Nf "the voice of the *Memra* of the Lord."

[28]HT "the voice of a god": the Tgs. all interpret as a reference to God. Onq. as here but Nf "the voice of the living God" *(ʾlh ḥyyh).*

who spoke from the midst of the fire, as you heard, and remained alive? 34. Or whether *the miracle*[29] *the Lord did, revealing himself, in order to separate*[30] *to himself* a nation by lot[31] from the midst of another nation, by miracles, by signs, by wonders, *by the victorious battles,* with a raised arm, and by many visions, like all that the Lord your God did for you in Egypt, and that your eyes have seen? 35. Is it to you[32] *that these wonders* have been shown in order for you to know that it is the Lord who is God;[33] there shall be no other except for him. 36. From the heavens *on high*[34] he made you hear the voice *of his Memra* to rebuke *you by his teaching;*[35] on the earth he showed you his great fire and his words you heard from the midst of the fire. 37. And because he loved your fathers, *Abraham and Isaac,* therefore he chose *the sons (of Jacob)* who came[36] after him and brought you out from Egypt, with his good will and great power, 38. by driving out before you the many and stronger nations than you by bringing you into and giving you their land as an inheritance, as is (the case) today.[37] 39. So you will know this day and reflect[38] that the Lord is God,[39] *whose Shekinah*[40] *dwells* in the heavens above and rules over the earth below; there is no other *apart from him.* 40. Then you should keep his statutes and his commandments that I am prescribing for you today that he may do good to you and to your children after you and so that you may prolong (your) days[41] on the earth that the Lord your God gives to you for all time." 41. Behold, therefore, Moses separated three cities on the other side of the Jordan toward the east, 42. to where a murderer could flee who had slain his friend unintentionally and he did not hate him formerly, so he will flee to one of these cities and survive. 43. It is *Kewatherin*[42] in the desert, in the land of the plain, for *the tribe of* Reuben, and Ramtha in Gilead, for *the tribe of* Gad, and Dabra[43] in *Mathnan*[44] for *the tribe of* Manasseh. 44. And this is the instruction of the Law that Moses set before the Israelites. 45. These are the testimonies and statutes and judgments that Moses decreed for the Israelites at the time of their departure from Egypt. 46. *And Moses instructed*[45] *them,* beyond the Jordan,

Notes, Chapter 4

[29]Aramaic *nysʾ,* a play on the HT pi of *nsh* "to attempt" (RSV); Onq. *(nsyn)* and Nf *(nysyyh)* are plural.

[30]HT "take" *(lqḥ)*: here *pšr,* Onq. "redeem" *(prq),* Nf "choose" *(bḥr),* Nfmg "seek" *(bsr),* and Frg. Tg.(V) "select" *(brr).*

[31]See Deut 32:8-9 (Ps.-J.).

[32]HT and Onq. singular, but plural in MS and Nf.

[33]Aramaic *ʾlh* (singular); see note on vv. 7, 39.

[34]Aramaic *mrwmʾ* is a phrase not entirely exclusive to Ps.-J. but frequently so, as Maher notes, *The Aramaic Bible* 1B, 51 n. 19; see Deut 28:15; 34:5 (Ps.-J.) and a variant in 33:26 (Ps.-J.).

[35]HT "discipline": Onq. "instruct" *lʾlpwtwt,* and Nf "chastise" *lmrdy,* but Ps.-J. combines the two traditions (*ksn* "rebuke" and *ʾlp*) found in the other Tgs.

[36]MS supplies *dpqwn* (*npq* "to go out/come") whereas Onq. and Nf have only "after him" without specifying "the sons" as the sons of Jacob.

[37]MS reads *kzmn ywmʾ hdyn* whereas Onq. reads *kywmʾ hdyn* "as it is this day" which may reflect Ps.-J.'s reading; Nf reads *bywmʾ hdyn* "at this day."

[38]Aramaic *twb lyb;* also in other Tgs.

[39]Ps.-J. *ʾlqym* as in HT *(ʾlhym)* and Onq., but Nf *ʾlh* (singular) as Ps.-J. in v. 35.

[40]Onq. as here, but Nf "Glory of his *Shekinah.*"

[41]MS reads *ywmʾ dyn* instead of *ywmyn* as in Onq. and Nf.

[42]HT "Bezer" as also Onq. and Nf: Jastrow (627) considers this reading in Ps.-J. uncertain. Rieder (1974) 261 without any corroborative evidence suggests reading *bwtyryn* "cluster of grapes" which could be taken from *bsr* "to cut grapes" (Jastrow 185) or *boser* "grapes" (Jastrow 147).

[43]HT "Golan": Nf as here, but Onq. as HT.

[44]HT "Bashan": see n. 28 on Deut 1:4.

[45]Aramaic *tnnwn* from *tnʾ* "to repeat"; not in Onq. or Nf.

in the valley (opposite Beth Peor),[46] in the land of Sihon, King of the Amorites, who lived in Heshbon, whom Moses and the Israelites had smitten in their exodus from Egypt. 47. And they took possession of his land and the land of Og, King of *Mathnan*: the two kings of the Amorites who were on the other side of the Jordan, toward the east; 48. from Aroër which is on the border of the tributaries[47] of Arnon to the Mountain of Sion,[48] *that is the Mountain of Snow,* 49. with all the plain on the other side of the Jordan to the east as far as the sea which is the plain beneath the slopes of the heights.[49]

CHAPTER 5

1. Then Moses called all Israel and said to them: "Hear, Israel, the statutes and the judgments I speak *before* you this day. You shall learn them and do them carefully." 2. The Lord our God has made a covenant with us at Horeb: 3. not with our fathers did the Lord make this covenant but with us, we, all of us, living *and enduring* here today. 4. *Directly,*[1] the Lord spoke with you on the mountain, from the midst of the fire. 5. I, at that time, was standing between *the Memra of* the Lord and you to transmit to you the Word of the Lord for you were afraid before *the sound*[2] *of the Memra of the Lord that you heard from the midst of* the fire but you did not go up on the mountain when he said: 6. "*My people, Israelites,*[3] I am the the Lord your God who has delivered and brought you out *redeemed*[4] from the land of the Egyptians, from the house where slaves were enslaved.[5] 7. *My people, Israelites,* you shall not have any other god except me. 8. You shall not make for yourselves a likeness or any image that is in the heavens above or that is on the earth below or that is in the water below the earth. 9. You shall not bow down to them nor shall you worship *before* them for I, the Lord your God am a jealous and *avenging* God, *taking revenge in jealousy, remembering the* sins of their *wicked* fathers on

Notes, Chapter 4 (Cont.)

[46]MS omits but found in Onq.; Nf reads "near the idols of Peor."

[47]Aramaic *nḥly* "wadies" or "tributaries"; see n. 29 on Deut 2:24; Maher, *The Aramaic Bible* 1B, 160 n. 47.

[48]HT "Sirion" (that is, "Mount Hermon") (RSV): Frg. Tg.(V) "whose fruit is tasteless" *(msry pyrwy hw')*; see n. 10 on Deut 3:9.

[49]HT "Pisgah"; see n. 25 on Deut 3:17 for other instances.

Notes, Chapter 5

[1]HT "face to face": here *mmll qbl mmll* and basically the same expression in Onq. "Literally" (Grossfeld) and Nf "speech against speech" (McNamara). Le Déaut V, 61 "de vive voix"; Etheridge (685) "word for word"; see Gen 32:31; Exod 33:11; Num 12:8 (Ps.-J. and Nf) and Deut 34:10 (Ps.-J.) for a similar idiom.

[2]HT "because of the fire," also Onq. and Nf "before *(mn qdm)* the flames of fire." Here following the *editio princeps mn qdm ql mymr'* but MS *mn ql pwnyn* (Jastrow 1143 *pwn* "change/alternate") which Le Déaut V, 61 translates as "le bruit de l'écho de la Parole."

[3]A liturgical phrase in Ps.-J.; see the same phrase in the following verses of the chapter.

[4]Aramaic *pryqyn* added often in Ps.-J. but not as frequently as in Nf; see Clarke (1984) 390–392 for other instances in Ps.-J.

[5]HT "house of bondage" (RSV); Nf literal but Ps.-J. and CG expand similarly *(š'bwd 'bdy')*.

the rebellious sons[6] to the third and to the fourth generation of those hating me *when the children were consumed with sin*[7] *after their fathers,*[8] 10. but keeping kindness *and goodness* for thousands *of generations of those loving me, the righteous,* and for those keeping *my statutes and* my Law. 11.[9] *My people, Israelites, no one of you* do swear in vain, by the Name of *the Memra of* the Lord your God, for the Lord, *on the great judgment day,*[10] will not acquit anyone who swears in vain, by his Name. 12. *My people, Israelites,* keep the Sabbath day to sanctify it just as the Lord your God commanded[11] you. 13. (During) six days shall you work and do all your work; 14. but on the seventh day, rest and *be quiet before* the Lord your God; you shall not do any work, you, your sons, your daughters, your menservants, your maidservants, your oxen, your asses, all your animals, your strangers who are in your cities[12] in order that your menservants and your maidservants shall be quiet like you. 15. And you shall remember that you were slaves in the land of Egypt and the Lord your God *redeemed* and brought you out from there with a strong hand and upraised arm; therefore the Lord your God commanded you to keep the Sabbath day. 16.[13] *My people, Israelites, every man be careful with the* honor of *his* father *and the* honor of *his* mother just as the Lord your God commanded you in order that you lengthen your days and in order that he do good to you in the land that the Lord your God is giving you. 17. *My people, Israelites,* do not be murderers, *neither companions nor partners with murderers, nor shall there be seen in the congregation of Israel (those who have a part) with murderers; lest your sons who arise after you also*[14] *learn to be with murderers; for it is because of murderers that the sword emerges upon the world.*[15] 18. *My people, Israelites,* do not be adulterers, *neither companions nor partners with adulterers, nor shall there be seen in the congregation of Israel (those who have a part) with adulterers, lest your sons who arise after you also*[16] *learn to be with adulterers; for it is because of the sins of adulterers that death emerges upon the world.* 19. *My people, Israelites,* do not be thieves, *neither companions nor*

Notes, Chapter 5

[6]Aramaic *mrwdyn* both here and in Nf; see Exod 20:5 (Ps.-J. and Nf); Lev 26:39 (Ps.-J.); Ginzberg, *Legends* 3.48.

[7]MS incorrectly reads *lmyḥmy* "by seeing"; read with Onq. *lmḥṭyʾ* "sinning" (Aramaic *ḥṭʾ*) and the sense of Nf.

[8]Also Onq.; Nf "before me"; see Tg. Jer 32:18; LAB 11,6. The idea of punishing children for the sins of their parents is contradicted in Deut 24:16 (Ps.-J. and Nf) as in Jer 31:29 and Ezek 18:20 (HT).

[9]For vv. 11-21 see Exod 20:7-17 (Ps.-J. and Nf).

[10]The phrase also in Nf; in addition to this passage see Ps.-J. on Gen 3:19; 4:7; 9:6; 39:10; 49:22; Exod 15:12; 20:7; 34:7; Num 14:18; 15:31; 31:50; see Sysling (1991) 69 and Maher, *The Aramaic Bible* 1B, 29 n. 41 for other comments.

[11]This phrase which is not found in the parallel passage in Exodus refers to the Sinai event and so is found in all the Tgs.

[12]HT "gates" in Tgs. "cities" as in Gen 22:17 (Tgs.); see Grossfeld, *The Aramaic Bible* 6, 87 n. 13 for fuller comments.

[13]Verses 16-33 are paralleled in the text of Ps.-J. in Exod 20:12-26. See Maher, *The Aramaic Bible* 2, 217–220 and McNamara's comments in the same volume (pp. 83–90). An article on the question of an original Palestinian Targum of Exodus 20 is found in Kaufman and Maori (1991), which has some relevance for the material in Deuteronomy 5. For our purposes here a comparison of the texts of Exodus and Deuteronomy results in the observation that in Deut 5:16-21 the texts of Ps.-J. in Exodus and Deuteronomy are similar. In Deut 5:22-30 the text of Ps.-J. in Exodus deviates greatly from Deuteronomy. The text of Deut 5:31-33 is not found in Exodus. The text of Ps.-J. Deut 5:16-33 is paralleled in Nf. Differences will be indicated in the following notes. There is no witness to these vv. in Frg. Tgs.(PV) but Deut 5:22-29 is found in the Cairo Geniza MS T-S B 8.1r–1v (= MS D plates 44–45; see Klein [1986] 1, 334–337).

[14]MS *lhwn,* an error for *lhwd* as in Nf; see Exod 20:13 (Ps.-J. and Nf).

[15]See Exod 20:13 (Ps.-J.) for the same idiom *(ḥrbʾ npyq ʿl ʿlmʾ).*

[16]Correctly here *lhwd;* see n. 14 above.

partners with thieves, nor be seen in the congregation of Israel with thieves; for[17] *it is because of their sins that famine emerges upon the world.* 20. *My people, Israelites,* do not carry yourselves as false witnesses, *neither companions nor partners of those who act as false witnesses; nor shall there be seen in the congregation of Israel with those who act as false witnesses; for it is because of the sins of false witnesses*[18] *that clouds come forth but rain does not fall and that drought emerges upon the world.* 21. *My people, Israelites,* do not be coveteous *neither companions nor partners with people who covet; nor shall there be seen in the congregation of Israel with coveteous ones lest your children who arise after you (also)*[19] *are to be with covetous ones. Neither shall anyone of you desire his companion's* wife, *nor anyone of you desire his companion's* house, *nor* his field, *nor* his manservant, *nor* his maidservant, *nor* his ox, *nor* his ass, *nor* anything that his companion has; *for it is because of the sins of coveting that the Kingdom attacks men's possessions to take them and that banishment emerges upon the world."*[20] 22. These words the Lord spoke with (all)[21] your assembly on the mountain from the midst of the fire, from the clouds *and from the mist,* a great voice without interruption.[22] And *the sound being spoken*[23] was written on two *marble*[24] tablets and he gave them to me. 23. However, it shall be when you have heard *the sound being spoken*[25] from the midst of darkness while the mountain was lit by fire, you should approach me, all the chiefs of your tribes and your *wise men.*[26] 24. And you said: "Behold *the Memra of* the Lord our God has shown us the *Shekinah* of his Glory and the greatness *of his praise* and the sound of *his Memra* we have heard from the midst of the fire. Today we have seen that the Lord has spoken with a man *who has the holy spirit in him* and is (still) alive. 25. So now why should we die? For the great fire may consume us. If we continue still to hear the voice of *the Memra of* the Lord our God, then we shall die. 26. For what *man of* flesh heard the sound of *the Memra of* the living God speaking from the midst of the fire, like us, and has lived? 27. Draw near and hear everything that the Lord our God shall say; then you, you shall speak with us everything that the Lord our God spoke to you; we shall hear[27] (it) and do (it). 28. And the sound of your words when you were

Notes, Chapter 5

[17]Ps.-J. omits the phrase "lest your sons arise up after you and learn also to be people who steal" which is found in Nf as well as Exod 20:15 (Ps.-J. and Nf); Nfmg "they also learn to be thieves."

[18]Nf reads here "for by the sins of false witnesses wild beasts attack the sons of men" but the idea of the clouds not giving rain is found in v. 21 in Nf: "clouds go up, and rain does not carry down, and scarcity comes upon the world. . . ." There is no parallel to this midrash in any of the other Tgs.

[19]MS omits, but read *lhwd* as in Nf; see nn. 14, 16 above in vv. 17, 18.

[20]Nf reads here "the kingdoms attack the sons of men and covet their property and take them"; for the text of Nf at this point see n. 17 above; vv. 19-21 are omitted in Ginsburger. Also Onq. has a very different text from Ps.-J. and Nf in these verses. There are no parallels in the other Tgs. for this midrash found in Ps.-J.

[21]MS omits, but found in Nf.

[22]HT "and he added no more" (RSV) *(wlʾ ysp)* from *swp,* not *ysp:* see *Mekilta* on Exod 20:1 (II, 228) "God spoke the Ten Commandments with one utterance—something impossible for creatures of flesh and blood."

[23]HT and here *qwl* but here also the Aramaic *dbyrʾ;* Le Déaut V, 69 translates "Dibbur" ("ce qui disait le Dibbur") but the form suggests a passive participle.

[24]See Deut 4:13; 34:12 (Ps.-J.) "sapphire," but here and 9:9, 10, 11; 10:1, 3 "marble"; Onq. and Nf only "two tablets of stone" *(tryn lwḥy ʾbnyʾ).*

[25]See n. 23 above.

[26]HT "elders" as Onq., but Nf as here.

[27]Aramaic here *qbl,* as also Onq., but Nf *šmʿ.*

speaking with me *was heard before* the Lord and the Lord said to me: "All[28] this people's words that they spoke with you *have been heard;* everything that they speak is good. 29. *Would that the inclination of* their heart *be perfect* in this their *ambition* to fear *before* me and to keep all my commandments all the days so that it will be good for them and for their children forever. 30. Go, say to them: *he has permitted you to join with your wives*[29] *(again) since you have been separated now for three days.*[30] 31. But you, *remain apart from your wife*[31] *because in the Sanhedrin that is above, you should stand at my side*[32] and I shall speak with you the[33] commandments and the statutes and judgments you will teach[34] them that they will observe (them) in the land that I shall give them to possess." 32. *And now* do carefully just as the Lord your God commanded you, do not stray to the right *nor* to the left. 33. In every way that the Lord your God has commanded you, you shall walk in order that you will live and he will do good to you and you will prolong (your) days in the land that you will possess.

CHAPTER 6

1. Now this is *the instruction of* the commandments, statutes, and judgments that the Lord your God commanded (me) to teach you to do in the land into which you are crossing over to possess, 2. in order that you will fear before[1] the Lord your God to keep, all the days of your life, all the statutes and commandments that I am commanding you: you, your son, and your son's son, in order to lengthen your days. 3. So, Israel, you will heed and do carefully in order that it shall be good for you and you will increase accordingly, just as the Lord, the God of your fathers, said to you; in a land *whose fruits are rich as* milk *and sweet as*[2] honey. 4.[3] And it was, *when the time was reached for our father Jacob to be gathered from the midst of the world, he was afraid lest there be a defect*[4] *among his sons. He called them*[5] *and asked them:*

Notes, Chapter 5 (Cont.)

[28]MS *kl* but *editio princeps ql* as Onq. "the tone of your words" (Grossfeld) and Nf "the voice of your words" (McNamara).

[29]HT "tents" as Onq. and Nf, but Ps.-J. interprets midrashically, understanding "tents" as the wife who is found in the tent; see Lev 14:8 (Ps.-J.); see Maher, *The Aramaic Bible* 3, 158 n. 10 for rabbinic citations.

[30]Nf has only "return in peace to your tents"; see *b.Šabb.* 87a.

[31]*b.Šabb.* 87a.

[32]Nf omits this midrash that is found in Ps.-J.; *PRE* 359 "he did not approach his wife."

[33]HT "all" as Onq. and Nf but omitted here.

[34]Here and Onq. plural *(tlpwn)* but Nf singular *(tlyp).*

Notes, Chapter 6

[1]HT *ʾt:* Onq. and Ps.-J. replace the sign of the accusative with *qdm;* Nf inserts *Memra.*

[2]See the Introduction (# 8) and McNamara's note on this verse in *The Aramaic Bible* 5A, 49 n. 3.

[3]HT contains the *Shema;* the Tgs. reflect the ideas of Genesis 49, i.e., Jacob's final blessing and his fear that his sons contain some defect (v. 2); see McNamara's note on this verse in *The Aramaic Bible* 5A, 49 n. 4. For the midrash interpretation found here and at Gen 49:2 see *Sifre Deut.* 55–59.

[4]See *Sifre Deut.* 6:4 (55–59) ". . . perchance such unworthy ones will issue from me as they did issue from my forefathers," i.e., Ishmael from Abraham and Esau from Isaac; Tosephta Targum (T-S AS 71, 4v, 217r = MS Z); Gen 49:2; Klein (1986) 1.164; *Deut. R.* 64.

[5]See Gen 35:22 (Ps.-J.) and Gen 49:2 (Ps.-J. and Nf).

is there any guile in your[6] *hearts? All of them replied as one and said to him*: "Hear, Israel, *our father,* the Lord our God, the Lord is one." *Jacob answered and said: "Blessed be his glorious Name for ever and ever."*[7] 5. *Moses, the prophet, said*[8] *to the people, the Israelites: follow the true worship of your fathers* and love the Lord *your* God[9] *following your hearts' inclination even if he take your lives along with all your wealth.*[10] 6. And these words that I am commanding you today are *written* on *the tablet of* your heart. 7. And you shall teach them to your son(s)[11] and you shall be meditating on them in your dwelling, *in your houses at the time of your occupation with your wedding (plans)*[12] and when *you* are walking in *your* way and in the evenings *close to your bedtime* and in the morning[13] *close to your* arising. 8. And you shall tie them as written signs on your left hand[14] and they shall be as phylacteries[15] *on your forehead*[16] between your eyes. 9. You shall write them o*n your doorposts*[17] and *you shall attach them to the upper third, fixed* on the doorpost of your house, and on your door *to the right when you enter.*[18] 10. And it shall be when the Lord your God brings you into the land he promised to your fathers, to Abraham, Isaac, and Jacob, to give you many and good cities that you did not weary yourselves to build, 11. and houses filled with everything good that you were not occupied with filling and wells dug that you did not work to dig, vineyards and olive groves that you did not prepare for planting, (when) you shall eat and be satisfied, 12. beware lest you forget *the Fear of*[19] the Lord *your God who redeemed* and brought you out *redeemed* from the land of Egypt, from the house where slaves are enslaved. 13. You shall be afraid *before* the Lord your God[20] and *before* him shall you worship and in the Name of *his Memra* shall you

Notes, Chapter 6

[6]MS "their."

[7]The phrase is an addition in Ps.-J. here and in Deut 11:26; 28:12; 29:9; 32:4, 14. In Nf it is only an addition in Deut 32:3, 4, 14. Gordon (1994) 74–82 discusses such an addition in the Tgs. Possibly this phrase is inserted to get the attention of the people much as is the phrase "my people, children of Israel."

[8]Nfmg *ʿd lʿlmyn* "for eternity"; see Cortès (1976) 343–365.

[9]Nf "the teaching of the law of"; see Deut 11:1 (Ps.-J.), also *Sifre Deut.* (59–62) "with both your inclinations, the inclination to good and the inclination to do evil" (59).

[10]HT "with all your might" *(mʾd): b.Ber.* 54a explains that "with all your might" means "with all your money." The Tgs. use different words to express the same idea: Onq. *nks(h);* here and Nf *mmwn;* see McNamara on this verse in *The Aramaic Bible* 5A, 50 n. 6.

[11]MS singular as Onq. but Nf plural.

[12]See Deut 11:19 (Ps.-J.); *b.Ber.* 11a–16a, and McNamara's note on this verse in *The Aramaic Bible* 5A, 50 n. 8.

[13]MS incorrectly "evening" *(rmšʾ)* but Ginsburger corrected to *sprʾ*.

[14]HT and Onq. and here "hand" but Nf "arms" *(ʾdrʿ)*. Only Ps.-J. adds "left"; see Deut 11:18.

[15]Aramaic *tpylyn;* see Exod 13:16; Deut 11:18; 22:5; 28:10 (Ps.-J.); see Clarke (1984) 606 for all the instances of this word.

[16]HT "as frontlets" (RSV); *mwqrʾ* "forehead" (Jastrow 748 "brain") only in Ps.-J. here, Deut 11:18, and Deut 28:28, but 28:35 "knees."

[17]Aramaic *mzwzyyn;* see Deut 11:20; 20:5; see Le Déaut V, 75 n. 15, who considers the words as referring to both container and contents; see Deut 11:20 "scrolls." See McNamara's note on this verse in *The Aramaic Bible* 5A, 50 n. 12.

[18]See *Sifre Deut.* 69 "on the right side as one enters."

[19]HT "the Lord": Onq. as here *(dḥltʾ)* but Nf "teaching of the Law of the Lord," as also in Deut 8:11, 14, 19; but Ps.-J. translates similarly, as here, in Deut 8:11, 14, 19.

[20]HT "the Lord": Onq. as here but Nf "the Glory of the *Shekinah* of the Lord your God"; see McNamara on this verse in *The Aramaic Bible* 5A, 51 n. 14.

swear, *in truth.* 14. You shall not go after *the idols of the nations, among the divinities of*[21] the nations around you, 15. for God is jealous and the Lord your God takes *revenge,* his *Shekinah*[22] rests among you; lest the anger of the Lord your God be strong against you and he destroy you[23] quickly from upon the face of the earth. 16. *My people, Israelites, be careful* not to test the Lord your God as you tested him *by the ten tests.*[24] 17. You shall surely keep the commandments of the Lord your God and his testimonies and his statutes that he prescribed for you. 18. And you shall do what is right and proper[25] *before*[26] the Lord in order that he do good to you and you shall enter and possess the good land that the Lord promised to your fathers, 19. by driving[27] out all your enemies from before you, as the Lord spoke. 20. When your son shall ask you tomorrow, saying: "What are the testimonies and statutes and judgments that the Lord our God commanded you?" 21. You shall say to your sons: "We were enslaved to Pharaoh in Egypt and *the Memra of* the Lord brought us out from Egypt with a strong hand. 22. And *the Memra of* the Lord *let loose* signs and many wonders and *evil plagues* against Egypt, against Pharaoh and against all *the men of* his house *while we saw (all this)* with our (own) eyes. 23. But us he brought out *redeemed* in order to bring us out to give us the land that he promised to our fathers. 24. The Lord commanded us to do all these statutes, to fear *before* the Lord our God all the days, to maintain[28] us, as is the case today. 25. And merit[29] shall be kept for us *in the world to come* if we do carefully all the statutes, all this commandment,[30] before the Lord our God as he commanded us.

Notes, Chapter 6

[21]HT "other gods, of the gods": Onq. and here *(tʿwwt ʿmmyyʾ)* and Nf *tʿwwn ʾḥrnyyn.* Ps.-J. interprets HT "other" as "of the nations," which clarifies Nf's "other idols" which could suggest that God is an idol. In the parallel in the HT "of the gods" Ps.-J. has an error in the MS: *mnḥlt* is an error for *mdḥlt.* ("Fears" = "divinities") which is a metonym for "deities."

[22]Onq. as here, but Nf "the Glory of whose *Shekinah*"; see McNamara's note on God's jealousy in *The Aramaic Bible* 5A, 51 n. 16.

[23]MS incorrectly "them."

[24]See Num 14:22 (Ps.-J.) and Clarke, *The Aramaic Bible* 4, 228 nn. 23, 24, and Ginzberg, *Legends* 3.350; 6.121; see *b.Arak.* 15a for the list.

[25]HT "what is right and good": here *tqyn* and *kšr;* Onq. reverses the order. Nf *špr* and *tqn;* see note on Deut 12:8 (Ps.-J.) below.

[26]HT "in the sight of."

[27]HT has a rare word "thrusting out" (RSV): see also Deut 9:4 (Ps.-J.) and Josh 23:5; Onq. pael *tbr* "to shatter"; here *dḥy* "push away" (Jastrow 291) and Nf *dḥp* "thwart" and Nfmg *šyṣy* "destroy."

[28]Aramaic *lqyymwtnʾ;* Onq. *yytb lnʾ* "that we may fare well" and Nf *lmyytbh ln* "do good to us."

[29]HT "be righteous" *(sdqh):* Onq. *zkwt* and Nf *zkw* interpret "merit" as now but Ps.-J. speaks of "merit in the world to come."

[30]HT "this commandment" as Onq. *yt tpqydtʾ hdʾ* and Nf *yt kl mṣwwth hdh;* Ps-J. *yt kl qyymyyʾ yt kl tqpydtʾ* agrees with Nfmg *qyymyh hʾylyn* and conflates. See Cook (1986) 46 on conflation.

CHAPTER 7

1. When the Lord your God will have brought you to the land where you will enter to possess it and he will have removed many peoples from before you: the Hittites, the Girgashites, the Amorites, the Canaanites, the Perazzites, the Hivites, and the Jebusites, the seven nations, greater and stronger than you, 2. (When) the Lord your God will have handed them over before you and you will have smote them you will completely destroy[1] them *by the Lord's curse.*[2] You shall not make a covenant with them nor love them. 3. You shall not marry with them; your daughters you shall not give to their sons and their daughters. You shall not take for your sons, *for anyone who marries with them, it is as if he married with their idols.* 4. For *their daughters* shall lead your sons astray from my *service*[3] and they shall serve *the idols of the nations,*[4] so the Lord's anger will be strong against you and he shall destroy you quickly. 5. However thus you shall do to them:[5] their (heathen) altars[6] shall you tear down, their statues shall you break, the trees that they worship[7] shall you cut down, and the images of their idols shall you burn with fire. 6. For you are a holy people *before*[8] the Lord your God; and the Lord your God has chosen you in order to be his favored[9] nation from all the nations that are on the face of the earth. 7. This is not because you are more *exalted*[10] than all the (other) nations that the Lord desired you and chose you but rather because you are *humbler in spirit and kinder than*[11] all the nations. 8. But it is because the Lord loves you and because he keeps the covenant he promised to your fathers, he has brought you out *redeemed* with a strong hand and redeemed you from the house where slaves are enslaved,[12] from the hand of Pharaoh, King of Egypt. 9. So you shall know that the Lord your God is a *judge, strong* and faithful, who keeps the covenant and *benevolence, to a thousand generations, to his friends,* the righteous,[13] and to those who keep his commandments;[14] 10. who pays, *in this world,* to those who hate him, *the reward of their good works* in order to destroy them *in the world to come*[15] and who does

Notes, Chapter 7

[1]HT *ḥrm* "utterly destroy": here *gmr,* also Onq., but Nf *qṭl*; see v. 16.

[2]Aramaic *šmtʾ* "curse/ban," used only in Ps.-J. in this context; see Gen 42:37; Num 21:24; Deut 7:2, 26 (2x); 13:18 (Ps.-J.). See Clarke (1984) 582; Maher, *The Aramaic Bible* 1B, 141 n. 27, and Cook (1986) 259; Cook notes that this meaning of *šmt* "occurs otherwise in the Babylonian Talmud and Mandaean."

[3]HT "me": here *pwlḥny;* Onq. *dḥlty;* Nf "my *Memra.*" Grossfeld, *The Aramaic Bible* 8, 109 n. 24 notes the use of "Fear" *(dḥltʾ)* or "Worship" *(pwlḥnʾ)* to express metonym for God.

[4]Onq. as here, but Díez Macho (1978) suggests reading the Aramaic text as *tʿwwn ʾḥrnyyn* for a confused text in Nf.

[5]MS *lkwn.*

[6]Aramaic *ʾgwrʾ* "heathen altar" (Jastrow 12); here as Onq., but Nf *mdbḥ.*

[7]Aramaic *ʾylny sygdyhwn;* Onq. and Nf "you shall cut down *(qss)* their Asherah"; see *b.Abod. Zar.* 48a.

[8]HT "to": Tgs. "before."

[9]HT *sglh* "a people of unique value": Tgs. *ḥbyb* "beloved."

[10]See *b.Hul.* 89a.

[11]HT and Onq. "fewest," but Nf "smallest" *(qlylyn).*

[12]See the same expression in Deut 5:6; 8:14 (Ps.-J.).

[13]Aramaic *sdyqyyʾ;* see Exod 20:6 (Ps.-J. and Nf); Deut 5:10 (Ps.-J. and Nf); see McNamara's note on this verse in *The Aramaic Bible* 5A, 54 n. 6.

[14]See Gen 3:24 (Ps.-J.) and Maher, *The Aramaic Bible* 1B, 31 n. 60.

[15]See Gen 3:24 and Maher, *The Aramaic Bible* 1B, 30 n. 58 for a list of other targumic passages dealing with rewards and punishment; Gordon (1977) 113–130 and Marmorstein (1968) 39.

not delay (the retribution) of those who hate him *but while they are living pays them, in this world, their recompense.*[16] 11. So you shall keep the commandments and the statutes and the judgments that I am commanding you[17] to do.[18] 12. And it shall be because[19] you shall heed these judgments and you do them carefully, then the Lord *your* God shall keep the covenants and the kindness he swore to your fathers. 13. Then he will love you and bless you and make you numerous; and he will bless *the children* of your loins and the fruit of your land, your grain, your wine, your oil, your herds of oxen and your flocks of sheep. 14. You will be more blessed than all the nations; there will be no barren *men* or barren *women* among you nor will your animals *be barren from wool and milk and young*. 15. And the Lord will remove from you all sickness and all afflictions that you knew that the Lord *let loose upon evil* Egypt; he shall not inflict them on you but let them loose against all your enemies. 16. And you will destroy[20] all the nations whom the Lord your God shall give you; your eye shall not pity them nor shall you worship their *idols* for they shall be a stumbling block for you. 17. *Lest* you say in your heart: "These nations are greater than I; how will I be able to drive them out?" 18. Do not be afraid of them; remember *the mighty acts* that the Lord did to Pharaoh and to all the Egypt*ians*, 19. the many miracles that you saw with your eyes, the signs, the wonders, and *the mightiness* of the strong hand and *the victories of* the raised arm when the Lord your God brought you out *redeemed*. It is so that the Lord your God shall do to all the nations before whom you have fear. 20. Only the Lord your God will let loose *a plague of stinging* hornets against them[21] until those who remain and those who hide themselves are destroyed before you. 21. Do not be broken (in spirit) before them for *the Shekinah of*[22] the Lord your God is among you, the great and fearful God. 22. So the Lord your God will remove slowly these nations *before* you; you will not be able to destroy them quickly lest the wild beasts increase against you *when they come to eat their bodies*. 23. But the Lord your God will deliver them before you and confound them with a great confusion until they are destroyed. 24. And he will deliver their[23] kings into your hand*s* and you shall destroy *the memory of* their names under *the whole* heaven: no man will endure *before* you until you have destroyed them. 25. You shall burn with fire the images of their *idols,* you shall not covet the silver nor the gold upon them or take it for yourselves lest you stumble because of them; because it is an abomination[24] before the Lord your God. 26. Nor shall you bring into your houses the abominations[25] of *idols*

Notes, Chapter 7

[16]See Nfmg "(and repays) the reward of the light precepts that are in their hands in this world in order to blot them out in the world to come"; also the same idea in Frg. Tgs.(PV); *Gen. R.* 8.1 (257) and Drazin (1982) 115 n. 14 for a rabbinic explanation.

[17]MS "them."

[18]HT, Onq., and Nf add "this day."

[19]HT "because" *(ʿqb):* Tgs. *h(w)lp d(y),* which is a common preposition in Ps.-J.: see Clarke (1984) 227–228.

[20]HT "destroy": here and Onq. *gmr* but Nf pa *kly* "you shall consume all the possessions of the nations" *(nksy ʾmyyh);* Nfmg "the booty of your enemies" *(bzt bʿly dbbykwn).*

[21]*Editio princeps* incorrectly "you" *(kwn* for *hwn).*

[22]Nf "the Glory of whose *Shekinah* is leading."

[23]MS incorrectly "your."

[24]HT "abomination" *(twʿbh);* Tgs. *mrḥq;* see also Deut 17:1; 18:12; 22:5; 23:19[MT]; 25:16, 19 (Ps.-J.) and Clarke (1984) 549, *rḥq*.

[25]Aramaic *mrḥq;* see previous note.

and their (cult) utensils[26] so that you will not be cursed[27] like them; you shall utterly *abominate them as an unclean abomination* and you shall surely loathe *them* because they are cursed.[27]

CHAPTER 8

1. You shall do carefully every commandment I am prescribing for you today, in order that you live, multiply, enter and possess the land that the Lord promised to your fathers. 2. Now you should remember the entire journey on which the Lord your God led[1] you in order to afflict you and in order to test you to know[2] whether you will keep his commandments or not. 3. And he humiliated you and caused you to hunger, then he fed you the manna that you did not know nor did your fathers know, in order to make you know that not by bread alone does man live but by everything that *is created*[3] *by the Memra of* the Lord does man live. 4. Your clothing was not worn out upon your *bodies,* and your *feet* did not *walk barefoot*[4] these forty years. 5. Understand, then, with *the thoughts of your* heart that just as a man trains[5] his son, the Lord your God trains[6] you. 6. So you shall keep the commandments of the Lord your God, by going in the ways that are proper *before* him and by fearing him. 7. For the Lord your God is bringing you into the land *renowned for its fruit,* a land whose rivers *of clear*[7] water are flowing *from wells of sweet* springs and *(from) deep (pools) that do not dry up,* emanating from valleys and mountains; 8. a land *that produces* wheat and barley, *and grows* vines *from which sweet and dry wine come forth, and produces* figs and pomegranates, a land *whose* olives *make oil and whose (date) palms make* honey;[8] 9. a land where you will not eat bread in want,[9] where

Notes, Chapter 7 (Cont.)

[26]See *b.Šabb.* 82b.

[27]See note on "curse" *(šmt)* in v. 2.

Notes, Chapter 8

[1]HT "these forty years in the wilderness": also Onq. and Nf, but MS and *editio princeps* omit.

[2]HT "what was in your heart": also Onq. and Nf (Nf inserts "the thoughts of") but MS and *editio princeps* omit.

[3]HT "everything that proceeds out of the mouth of the Lord": here *ʾtbry ʿl mymrʾ dyyy;* Onq. *ʾpqwt mymr mn qdm ywy,* and Nf *dnpq mn pm gzyrt mmryh dyyy* "everything that comes from the mouth of the decree of the Memra of"; Nfmg omits *mn pm.*

[4]HT "feet did not swell" *(bsq):* Tgs. *yḥp* "barefoot" (Jastrow 575); see Clarke (1984) 263, who notes Deut 8:4 as the only instance in Ps.-J.

[5]HT "disciplines" (RSV): Onq. "to teach" *(ʾlp);* Nf "chastise" *(rdy)* and Nfmg "chastise" *(prgl),* "whip" (Sokoloff 575). The MS has *sqr,* found only here in Ps.-J. (Clarke, 1984, 415). Jastrow (1019) and Dalman (299) correct to *sqd* "to goad/train."

[6]See the previous note for the same vocabulary distribution.

[7]Aramaic *ṣll;* see Gen 1:21; Exod 7:24 (Ps.-J.).

[8]See Lev 2:12 (Ps.-J.) which links dates with making honey, but see Maher, *The Aramaic Bible* 3, 126 n. 14 for another view of whether it is honey or not and also Lev 12:11 for the prohibition of honey as an offering. Nf reads "whose dates are as sweet as honey" whereas Nfmg is as Ps.-J. "whose dates make honey."

[9]HT "without scarcity": here *ḥwsrnʾ;* Onq. and Nf "scarcity" *(mskn).*

nothing will be lacking; a land *whose wise men*[10] *enact decrees clear as iron and whose disciples ask questions bright as* brass. 10. *So you shall be careful at the time when you* are eating and are sated, *to be thankful* and bless *before* the Lord your God for all *the fruits* of the renowned[11] land that he has given you. 11. Watch yourselves lest you forget *the Fear of*[12] the Lord your God so as not to keep his commandments and judgments and his statutes that I am prescribing for you today, 12. when you have eaten and been satisfied and built *beautiful*[13] houses and dwelt (in them), 13. and your oxen and sheep multiplied, and your silver and gold increased for you and everything of yours increased, 14. then your heart would be lifted and you would forget *the Fear of* the Lord your God who brought you *redeemed* out of the land of Egypt, from the house where slaves are enslaved;[14] 15. he who led you *with love* through the great and fearful desert, *a place full of* poisonous serpents and *stinging* scorpions, a parched land,[15] *a place* without water, who brought forth water for you from the flinty rock; 16. he who fed you the manna in the desert which your fathers did not know *in order to afflict*[16] *you* and in order to test you to do good to you at your end (of time). 17. *Be careful that* you not say in your heart: it is *our* own strength and our strong arm *that has obtained for us* these properties. 18. So you shall remember the Lord your God for he is the one who has given you *the advice*[17] to obtain the properties in order to keep, as is the case today, the covenant he promised to your fathers. 19. However, if you should ever forget *the Fear of* the Lord your God and go after *the idols of the nations*[18] and worship them and bow down to them, I testify against you, today, that you shall surely perish. 20. For like the nations the Lord *is removing* before you, so shall you perish just because you did not heed[19] *the Memra of* the Lord your God.[20]

Notes, Chapter 8

[10]HT "stones" as Onq. and Nf, but here "wise men"; see *b.Ta'an.* 4a.

[11]Aramaic *mšbḥ'*, but Onq. and Nf *ṭbt'*.

[12]HT "Lord our God": here and Onq. "Fear," but Nf "the teaching of the Law of the Lord": see vv. 14, 19. This distribution distribution of the idiom is common in the Tgs.

[13]HT "goodly" as Nf, but here and Onq. "beautiful" *(špr).*

[14]Aramaic *byt š'bwd 'bdy':* found frequently in Ps.-J. and Nf; see Exod 13:3, 14 (Ps.-J.); Deut 5:6; 6:12; 13:6, 11 (Ps.-J.).

[15]HT "thirsty ground": here (MS) and Onq. *ṣhw(w)n'*, which Jastrow (1272) lists under *ṣhwn* "parched" (also a number of Onq. MSS), but the *editio princeps* reads *skwwn'*, which Jastrow (1281) considers a corruption for *ṣhwn.*

[16]Here pa *sgp;* Onq. *'ny* and Nf *s'r.*

[17]HT "Power": Onq. "advice" *('ys'); here mylk',* but Nf as HT.

[18]HT "other gods": here and Onq. add "nations" to "idols" *(t'wwt 'mmy')* but Nf only "idols"; see Clarke (1984) for the twelve instances of the phrase in Ps.-J.

[19]Aramaic *qbl* here and Onq., but Nf *šm'* "hear."

[20]HT "voice of the Lord your God": Onq. and here add "the *Memra* of" and Nf "the voice of the *Memra* of."

CHAPTER 9

1. Hear, Israel, you are crossing over the Jordan today, to enter to dispossess the nations many and stronger than you, many cities fortified (with walls)[1] toward the heavens,[2] 2. a nation *strong and haughty as the giants* about whom you know and have heard: "Who will be able to stand before the children *of Ephron the giant*?"[3] 3. And you shall know today that the Lord your God *whose glorious Shekinah*[4] goes before you and whose *Memra* is a consuming fire,[5] will destroy them *and he will drive them out before you* and you will drive them out and destroy them quickly just as the Lord *your God*[6] spoke to you. 4. When the Lord your God pushes them out before you do not say in your hearts, saying: "By my (own) merit the Lord has brought me in to possess this land" when it is because of the sins of these peoples the Lord is driving them out before you. 5. It is neither because of your merits nor because of the uprightness of your heart that you are possessing their land; but because of the sins[7] of these peoples is the Lord your God driving them out before you and in order to fulfill the word that the Lord swore to your fathers, to Abraham, Isaac, and Jacob. 6. And you must know that it was not because of your merit that the Lord your God has given you that *renowned*[8] land to possess, for you are a stiff-necked people. 7. Remember, do not forget, how you provoked anger *before*[9] the Lord your God in the desert; from the day when you came out from the land of Egypt until your coming to this place you have been rebelling before the Lord. 8. And at Horeb you provoked anger *before* the Lord and the anger before the Lord was against you to destroy you. 9. When I ascended the mountain to take the *marble*[10] tablets of the covenant that the Lord made with you, I was on the mountain forty days and forty nights; I did not eat bread[11] nor did I drink water. 10. The Lord gave me the two *marble*[10] tablets inscribed by the Lord's finger and on which *were written according to* all the words that the Lord spoke with you on the mountain, from the midst of the fire,[12] on the day of *the gathering of*[13] the assembly. 11. However, at the end of forty days and forty nights the Lord gave me the two *marble* tablets, the tablets of the covenant. 12. So the Lord said to me: "Arise, go down for the people *who are*

Notes, Chapter 9

[1]Aramaic *krykn* "fortified": see Num 13:28; 32:36; Deut 1:28; 2:8; 32:11, 13 (Ps.-J.); Nf "tell" *(tlyln)* in the same passages.

[2]See n. 78 on this phrase in Deut 1:28 (Ps.-J.).

[3]HT "Anak": Onq. "the giant"; Nf "Anak, the giant"; *editio princeps* "the giant"; Deut 1:28 (Ps.-J.) as here. This is another example of how Ps.-J. clarifies the HT.

[4]NF "the Glory of whose *Shekinah*."

[5]Aramaic *ʾyšʾ ʾklʾ* here and Onq., but Nf "it is the *Shekinah* as a consuming fire."

[6]Also Nfmg

[7]HT "wickedness": Tgs. *ḥwb;* see Grossfeld, *The Aramaic Bible* 9, 41 n. 5.

[8]Aramaic *šbḥ;* Onq. and Nf "good *(ṭb)* land"; see Deut 8:10 (Ps.-J.).

[9]Onq. as here; Nf "provoked the *Memra* . . . to anger."

[10]See n. 23 on Deut 5:22 (Ps.-J.) "marble" and n. 12 on Deut 4:13 (Ps.-J.) "sapphire."

[11]HT "bread" as here and Onq. *(lḥm),* but Nf *mzwn* "food"; see v. 18 below.

[12]HT "fire" as here and Onq., but Nf "flames *(lḥby)* of fire."

[13]HT "the assembly" as Onq. *(qḥl),* but Nf as here *(knyšt qḥlʾ).*

called by your name, whom I brought out from Egypt, have corrupted[14] their ways."[15] 13. Then the Lord said to me, saying: "*The stupid acts*[16] *of this people are revealed before me*: it is indeed a stiff-necked people. 14. Desist *from your prayer to me;*[17] I shall destroy them and erase their name from beneath the heavens and make you into a stronger and more numerous nation than they (are). 15. So I turned and descended from the mountain while the mountain was burning with fire and the two tablets of the covenant were in my two hands. 16. And I looked and behold you have acted stupidly *before* the Lord your God: you made for yourselves a calf, a molten *image*. You strayed quickly from the way the Lord prescribed for you. 17. So I took hold of the two tablets and threw them from my two hands and broke them, *while you saw, when the tablets were breaking, the letters were flying off.*[18] 18. *Then I sought for mercy from*[19] before the Lord as previously; forty days and forty nights I ate no bread[20] nor drank water, because of all your sins in which you sinned, doing what was evil before the Lord, causing anger before him. 19. *At that very time five angels were sent forth from before the Lord, destroyers*[21] *to destroy Israel: Anger, Wrath, Ire, Destruction, and Rage.*[22] *When Moses, the lord*[23] *of Israel, heard he went and recalled the great and glorious Name; then Abraham, Isaac, and Jacob rose up from their graves and stood in prayer before the Lord; and immediately three of them were restrained and two remained, Anger and Wrath. Moses sought mercy and even the two of them were restrained. He dug a pit in the land of Moab and hid them (there) with the oath of the great and fearful Name. For so it is written:* "Because I was afraid before the anger and wrath that the Lord had expressed against you to destroy you. But the Lord heeded my prayer,[24] even at this time. 20. And against Aaron there was extreme anger before the Lord to the point of destroying him; but I prayed even for Aaron at that time. 21. I took *your stupid act*[25] of making the calf,[26] and burned it with fire and I ground it *thoroughly with a pestle* until it became crushed like dust and I threw the dust into the river that descended from the mountain. 22. *At the Brazier and the Testing and at the Graves of Lust* you were causing anger *before* the Lord. 23. And at the time when the Lord sent you from *Reqem Gea,*[27] saying: "ascend and possess

Notes, Chapter 9

[14]Aramaic pa *ḥbl* (Sokoloff 185 no. 3); see also Deut 4:16, 25; 31:29; 32:5 (Ps.-J.), but Onq. and Nf add an explanation of how the people have corrupted their ways "by straying *(prʿ)* from the path"; see next note.

[15]Onq. and Nf follow the HT and add: ". . . that I ordered them (to take); they made for themselves a molten image."

[16]Aramaic *srḥ* "stupid acts"; Onq. and Nf *qšy* "stiffnecked"; see Clarke (1984) 416.

[17]HT "let me alone" *(ḥrp);* Onq. and here ap of *nwḥ* and add "your prayer to me"; Nf "Refrain *(mnʿ)* yourself before me from begging mercy for them"; see Exod 32:10 (Ps.-J.) and see Grossfeld, *The Aramaic Bible* 7, 89 n. 6 for rabbinic evidence.

[18]See Exod 32:19 (Ps.-J.); see Maher, *The Aramaic Bible* 2, 253 n. 39 for rabbinic citations and Ginzberg, *Legends* 6.54.

[19]HT "I prostrated before the Lord" as Onq., but Nf "I prostrated myself in prayer and begged mercy before the Lord"; see n. 17 above.

[20]See n. 11 above.

[21]See *Deut. R.* 9:1 (78) and *Exod. R.* 32:13 (512).

[22]See Num 17:11 (Ps.-J.) where only "Ire/Rage" is mentioned, and Clarke, *The Aramaic Bible* 4, 237 n. 9; Ginzberg, *Legends* 3.124.

[23]Aramaic *rb;* see Clarke (1984) 540.

[24]Here and Onq. *qbl ṣlwt,* but Nf *šmʿ ql ṣlwt;* see Deut 10:10 (Ps.-J.).

[25]HT and Onq. "your sin" *(ḥwb)* but here *srḥ;* see n. 16 above on v. 13.

[26]HT, here and Onq. "calf," but Nf "idols."

[27]HT "Kadesh Barnea"; see Gen 14:7 (Ps.-J.) and Maher, *The Aramaic Bible* 1B, 56 n. 22; Num 32:8 (Tgs.) and Clarke, *The Aramaic Bible* 4, 282 n. 8 and Davies (1972) 160–163.

the land that I am giving to you," then you rebelled against *the Memra of*[28] the Lord your God and did not trust him or heed *his Memra.*[29] 24. You have been rebellious before the Lord from the day when I knew you. 25. And I prostrated myself *in prayer*[30] before the Lord, for forty days and forty nights, when *I lay prostrate in prayer* because the Lord has spoken of destroying you. 26. And I prayed *before* the Lord *and I said: "I beseech you, by the mercy before you,* Lord God, do not destroy your people and your inheritance that you redeemed by your strength, whom you brought out from Egypt by the power of your strong arm. 27. *Ah!* Remember your servants Abraham, Isaac, and Jacob, but do not consider[31] the hard-heartedness of this people, nor their wickedness nor their *stupid acts,*[32] 28. lest *the inhabitants*[33] of the land from which you brought them out say: "it is because the power[34] from before the Lord *became insufficient* to bring them into the land about which he had spoken to them and because you hated them so he brought them out to slay them in the desert, 29. now they are your people and your inheritance whom you brought out with your great power and with your upraised arm.'"

CHAPTER 10

1. At that time the Lord said to me: Hew *for yourself* two *marble*[1] tablets according to *the form of* the first ones and ascend *before* me on the mountain; and make for yourself a wooden ark.[2] 2. So I will write on the tablets the words that were on the first tablets which you broke[3] *with your entire strength,* and you will place them in the ark. 3. So I made an ark of acacia wood and I hewed two *marble* tablets according to the first *form,* then ascended the mountain with the two tablets in my hand. 4. He wrote on the tablets as the first writing, the ten words[4] that the Lord spoke with you on the mountain from the midst of the fire on the day *when the congregation was gathered;* then the Lord gave them to me. 5. So I turned and descended from the mountain and I placed the tablets in the ark that I had made. They were *kept* there as the

Notes, Chapter 9 (Cont.)

[28]Onq. as here, but Nf "decree of the *Memra* of."

[29]HT "his voice": all Tgs. as here.

[30]Onq. as HT ("so I lay prostrate before . . .") but Nf as here, adding "in prayer."

[31]HT *pnh* "pay attention to": Onq. as HT, but Ps.-J. and Nf itp *skl.* See Maher's discussion (1994, 284–285) on HT *pnh.*

[32]HT, Onq., and Nfmg *ḥṭʾ* "sin," but here and Nf *srḥ;* see n. 16 above on v. 13, and n. 25 on v. 21.

[33]See McNamara's note on this phrase in *The Aramaic Bible* 5A, 63 n. 36.

[34]Aramaic *ḥylʾ;* Onq. and here, but Nf *ykwlʾ* "ability."

Notes, Chapter 10

[1]HT "stones" as Onq. and Nf, but see notes on Deut 4:13 and 5:22 (Ps.-J.).

[2]Onq. and here as HT, but Nf "ark of the covenant" (*ʾrwn dqym);* see McNamara's note on this phrase in *The Aramaic Bible* 5A, 64 n. 2.

[3]See Exod 31:18 (Ps.-J.): the stones weighed "forty seahs"; Nfmg "which I broke" (either to excuse Moses or an error); see Ginzberg, *Legends* 3.129; 6.54. God approves of Moses' action (*b.Šabb.* 87a).

[4]*dbyryʾ* here and Nf, but Onq. *ptgmyn.*

Lord had prescribed for me. 6. So the Israelites decamped from *the villages of* the Wells[5] of the Sons of Yaakan to Moserah. *It is there that Amalek fought with them,*[6] *when he was King in Arad, because he had heard that Aaron had died, and that the clouds of Glory*[7] *had ascended. And as Israel was reluctant for that war they sought to return to Egypt, and returned six stages. The Levites pursued them and slew eight of their clans and they turned back. Even among the Levites four clans were slain. They said one to the other: "What caused us this slaying except that we were lax in the mourning of Aaron the pious one?" So all the Israelites established there a mourning just as if*[8] Aaron had died there and was buried there. After that Eleazar his son officiated[9] in his place. 7. From there they decamped to Gudgod and from Gudgod to Yotbath, a land *of running streams*[10] of water. 8. At that time the Lord set apart the tribe of Levi, *because they were jealous for his Name to slay for his Glory,*[11] to carry the ark of the covenant of the Lord, to stand before the Lord to minister to him, and to bless in his Name[12] until this very day. 9. Because of this *the tribe of* Levi had no share or inheritance with their brothers: *the gifts*[13] *that* the Lord *gave him*[14] were his inheritance just as the Lord your God spoke of it to him. 10. Now I remained on the mountain, *seeking and praying* as on the first day, for forty days and forty nights, and the Lord[15] heeded[16] *my prayers,*[17] also at that time, and the Lord did not desire to corrupt you. 11. So the Lord said to me: "Arise, go, *reconnoiter*[18] before the people so they may enter and possess the land that I promised their fathers to give to them." 12. So now, Israel, what does the Lord your God seek from you except to fear *before* the Lord your God, to walk in all the ways *that are right before him,*[19] and to love him and to worship *before* the Lord your God with all your heart, and with all your soul, 13. to keep the commandments[20] that I am prescribing for you today in order that it may go well with you. 14. Behold the heavens and the heavens above the heavens are the Lord your God's *and the band of angels through whom is the service maintained before him,*[21] the earth and all that is in it. 15. But it is only your fathers the Lord desired in order to love you and he will delight

Notes, Chapter 10

[5]HT "sons," but Onq., here, and Nfmg *byrʾ* "wells" (Sokoloff 101 *byr* no. 2); Nf as HT.

[6]See Num 21:1 (Ps.-J. and Nf); see Clarke, *The Aramaic Bible* 4, 246 nn. 1–8 and Ginzberg, *Legends* 3.330–334 for the following paraphrase.

[7]See Maher, *The Aramaic Bible* 1B, 22 n. 11 for a discussion of the same idiom.

[8]Aramaic *kʾylw*.

[9]Nf adds "as high priest."

[10]Here and Onq. *ngdyʾ nḥlyn,* but Nf *byt nḥylyn* "torrents of water."

[11]See Exod 32:26-29 (Ps.-J.) where the Levites are urged to do so on behalf of the Lord; Maher, *The Aramaic Bible* 2, 254.

[12]Onq. and here as HT, but Nf "the holy Name of his *Memra*."

[13]Aramaic *mtnn*.

[14]HT, Onq., and Nfmg "the Lord is his inheritance"; some Onq. MSS agree with Ps.-J.; Nf combines both ideas: "the Lord's offerings *(qrbn)* are his inheritance."

[15]Nf "the voice of the Memra."

[16]Aramaic *qbl* here and Onq., but Nf "heard *(šmʿ)* the voice of my prayers"; see Deut 9:19 (Ps.-J.). This represents the usual vocabulary distribution for this word in the Tgs.

[17]HT "me": Tgs. specify as here.

[18]HT "on your journey" (RSV) *(nsʿ)* and Onq. and Nf *nṭl* suggesting "journey," but here *twr*.

[19]Also found in Nf.

[20]HT adds "and statutes of the Lord"; also Onq. and Nf.

[21]Onq. as here.

in their *children* after them as you yourselves, more than all the nations *that are upon the face of the earth* as is (the case) today. 16. So *put aside* the obduracy[22] from your heart and do not stiffen your neck any longer. 17. Because the Lord your God is the God *of judges, and Master of Kings,*[23] the great God, strong and fearful, *before whom* is no respect of persons or even the taking of a bribe, 18. making judgments for the orphans and the widow and loving the stranger, giving him food and clothing. 19. So you shall love the stranger[24] for you were *temporary sojourners*[25] in the land of Egypt. 20. Before the Lord your God you shall fear and him shall you worship[26] and you shall stay close to his Fear[27] and shall take an oath in his Name. 21. He is your praise and he is your God who did for you these great and mighty deeds that you have seen with your eyes. 22. As seventy souls did your fathers descend into Egypt, and now the Lord your God has *made* you as many as the stars of the heavens.

CHAPTER 11

1. So you shall love the Lord[1] your God and keep the observance *of his Memra,*[2] his statutes, his judgments, and his commandments always. 2. Therefore you know today that not with your children who know not and saw not *the teaching of the Law*[3] of the Lord your God, his greatness, and his strong hand and his upraised[4] arm; 3. his signs and his actions that he did in the midst of Egypt to Pharaoh King of Egypt and to all *the inhabitants of* the land;[5] 4. and what he did to the Egyptian army, to their horses and to their chariots when he caused the waters of the Reed Sea to engulf them, when they chased after you[6] and the Lord destroyed them *once*

Notes, Chapter 10 (Cont.)

[22]HT "circumcise the foreskin of your heart": Nf also "circumcise" but here and Onq. *ʿdy* "put aside"; for "foreskin" here and Onq. substitute *ṭpš* ("obduracy") and Nfmg *qšyy'* ("hardness"); see Deut 30:6 (Ps.-J.) for the same vocabulary; see *b.Hag.* 12b.

[23]HT "God of gods and Lord of lords" is translated in the Tgs. to avoid any linkage of God with other gods and so Ps.-J. translates *dyyn'*, which is a difficult word and should be read as Onq. *'lh dynyn* "God of judges" (see *Mekilta* on Exod 21:6 [III, 14]). The HT reads "bring him unto God" and *Mekilta* says "to the court . . ."; Nf "For the Lord your God is the God above all gods and the Lord above all lords, the great, mighty, and terrible (God) who is not an accepter of persons in judgment and does not accept a bribe of money." The idea that God is subject to any pressure such as bribes is unacceptable.

[24]Aramaic *gyywr'*.

[25]Here and Onq. *dyyryn,* but Nf *gywryn.*

[26]HT "serve": here and Onq. *plḥ,* but Nf *ṣly* ("pray").

[27]HT "cleave *(dbq)* to him": here and Onq. "stay close (itp *qrb*) to his Fear *(dḥlt')*" but Nf "cleave *(dbq)* to the teaching of his Law"; see n. 18 on Deut 6:12 above for the same vocabulary distribution.

Notes, Chapter 11

[1]Nf adds "the teaching of the Law of" as in vv. 2, 13, 22; see also n. 8 on 6:5.

[2]Here and Onq., but Nf "his charges" *(mṭrtyh)* from *nṭr.*

[3]See n. 1.

[4]Onq. and here *mrmm',* but Nf *mnṭlth* "uplifted"; see also 4:34; 5:15; 7:19; 26:18 for the same distribution in the Tgs.

[5]HT "his land" as Onq., but here *'rʿ'* and Nf "the lands" *('rʿy'),* which Golomb (90) considers a "misspelling" for the singular; see McNamara on this word, which he suggests correcting to "his lands" in *The Aramaic Bible* 5A, 67 n. 4.

[6]MS incorrectly "them," as also some MSS of Onq.

and for all.[7] 5. And what he did for you in the desert before your arrival at this place, 6. also what he did to Dathan and Abiram, sons of Eliab son of Reuben, when the earth opened its mouth and swallowed them and *the men of*[8] their house[9] and all their *creatures*[10] who *were with* them in the midst of all Israel. 7. For you saw with your eyes all the great work of the Lord that he performed. 8. Therefore you shall keep all the commandments that I am prescribing for you today so that you will be strengthened and enter and possess the land you are crossing over to possess, 9. and in order to multiply your days on the land that the Lord promised to your fathers to give to them as well as to *their children,*[11] a land *whose fruit is rich as* milk and *sweet as* honey. 10. For the land you are entering to possess is not like the land of Egypt from which you came out, in which you sowed your seed and irrigated it *yourself*[12] as a *kitchen* garden. 11. But the land into which you are crossing over to possess is a land of mountains and valleys that are watered by the rain *that descends* from the heavens, 12. a land the Lord your God sought *by his Memra in order to do good continuously;*[13] the eyes[14] of the Lord your God have observed it from the beginning of the year to the end of the year. 13. So it shall be if you will surely heed my commandments that I am prescribing for you today, loving the Lord[15] your God and worshiping *(before)* him with all your heart and with all your soul, 14. then I shall give to your land the rain in its time, the early (rains) *in Marheshwan*[16] and the late[17] (rains) *in Nisan,* and you will gather your grain, your wine, and your oil. 15. I shall put the grass in your field for your animals; and you will eat and be satisfied. 16. Beware lest the inclination of your heart wanders and you go astray and worship *the idols of the nations*[18] and bow down to them. 17. Then the anger of the Lord will be great against you; and he will close *the clouds of* the heavens and they will not *let down* rain and the earth will not give the harvest and you will perish quickly from upon the excellent land that the Lord is giving you. 18. Put these words of mine on your heart and on your person and tie them, when they are written *on phylacteries,*[19] as a sign on your *upper left arm* and they will be *as phylacteries on your forehead* between your eyes. 19. You shall teach them to your children by reflecting[20] on them, in your houses, *even with your weddings,*[21] and when you are walking on the way and *in the evening*

Notes, Chapter 11

[7]Lit. "until the time of this day."

[8]Aramaic *ʾynwš,* also Onq. and Nf. It was a necessary addition in the Tgs. because no house *per se* existed in the desert; see McNamara's note on the phrase in *The Aramaic Bible* 5A, 67 n. 5.

[9]Onq. and Nf add "as well as their tents."

[10]HT "every living thing" *(hyqwm):* here *byryytʾ;* Onq. *yqwmʾ* and Nf *qʾmyh* "living things"; Nfmg "(and every) creature *(bryytʾ)* that was in the counsel of Korah in the midst of the Israelites"; see Gen 7:4, 23 (Nf) which agrees with Ps.-J.

[11]HT "seed" is regularly translated in the Tgs. as "sons" except in Nfmg *lzrʿyyt bnyn* "descendants of their children."

[12]Aramaic *bgrmk* is read incorrectly in Onq. and Nf as *brglk* "with your feet" as in HT.

[13]See *Sifre Deut.* 80–81 where a discussion is found of God's continuous beneficence to the people.

[14]See McNamara on this phrase in *The Aramaic Bible* 5A, 68 n. 11.

[15]Nf "the teaching of the Law"; see n. 1 above.

[16]See *Sifre Deut.* 86 "the former rain falls in Marheshwan."

[17]See *Sifre Deut.* 86 "the latter rain falls in Nisan" and Lev 26:4 and Deut 28:12 (Ps.-J.).

[18]HT "other gods": Onq. as here *tʿwwt ʿmmyʾ* but Nf "other idols"; see also Gen 35:2, 4; Exod 22:19; 23:13; Deut 6:14; 7:4; 8:19; 11:28; 12:2; 13:1, 7, 14; 17:3; 18:20; 29:25 (Ps.-J.) for a similar expansion.

[19]Aramaic *tpylyn;* see n. 14 on Deut 6:8.

[20]Aramaic *lmgrsʾ;* Onq. *mll* and Nf *ḥzy;* Jastrow (270) considers *grs* as a technical term in the study of Torah.

[21]See Deut 6:7 (Ps.-J.).

close to your bedtime and *in the morning close to* your rising. 20. And you shall write them *on scrolls on the mezuzoth and you shall attach them to the upper third,*[22] *fixed* on the doorposts of your houses and on your doors, 21. in order that your days will be multiplied on the earth that the Lord promised to your fathers to give them, as the number of days that the heavens exist over the earth. 22. For[23] if you observe carefully all that commandment that I am prescribing for you to do, to love the Lord your God,[24] to walk in all the ways *that he established before him,*[25] and *in order that* you bring yourself near to *his Fear.*[26] 23. Then *the Memra of* the Lord will drive out all these nations from before you and you will dispossess nations greater and stronger than you. 24. Every place where the toes of your feet shall walk shall be yours: your territory will run from the desert and *the mountains of* Lebanon *(those are the mountains of the Temple)*[27] from the *great*[28] river, the river Euphrates, as far as the *Ocean*[29] Sea, *these are the waters of creation, on the west side*. 25. No man will endure before you, the Lord your God will place your fear and your dread on all the inhabitants of the land through which you will walk just as he has spoken to you. 26. *Moses, the prophet, said:* "See! I am *arranging*[30] before you, today, a blessing and *its opposite:*[31] 27. the blessing, if you will heed the commandments of the Lord your God that I am prescribing for you today, 28. and *its opposite,* if you will not heed the commandments of the Lord your God and you go astray from the way that I am prescribing for you today *to wander after the idols of the nations* whom you did not know." 29. And it shall be, when the Lord your God brings you to the land into which you are entering to possess, then you will put *six tribes* on Mount Gerizim and *six tribes* on Mount Ebal: *those who are giving the blessing shall turn their faces toward Mount Gerizim and those who are giving the curse shall turn their faces toward Mount Ebal.*[32] 30. Have they not been situated nearer to the Jordan in the direction of the setting of the sun, in the land of the Canaanite who dwells on the plain opposite Gilgal *on the side of the Vision of Mamre?*[33] 31. For you are crossing over the Jordan to possess the land that the Lord your God is giving you and you shall possess it and dwell in it. 32. So you shall do carefully all the statutes and judgments that I have placed before you today.

Notes, Chapter 11

[22]See Deut 6:9 (Ps.-J.); *b.Menhoth* 33b and Tg. *Song of Songs* 8:3.

[23]MS *ʾry; editio princeps ʾrwm;* there are only six instances of *ʾry* in Ps.-J. (Gen 2:17; 19:2; 20:7; 26:16; 32:26; and here), otherwise *ʾrwm* is usual; see Clarke (1984) 75 and Maher, *The Aramaic Bible* 1B, 24 n. 35.

[24]NF "the teaching of the Law of"; see n. 1 above and the note on v. 13 and 6:5.

[25]HT "in all his ways."

[26]HT "him": Onq. as here *(dḥltyh)* but Nf "the teaching of his Law"; Nfmg "name of his *Memra*"; see Deut 11:1.

[27]See n. 39 on Deut 1:7 (Ps.-J.).

[28]HT "river": Nf as here, but Ps.-J. explicates the meaning in the parallel "the river Euphrates."

[29]HT "western sea," also Onq. and Nfmg; Nf "last" *(ʾḥrnyyh)* but here *ʾwqynws;* see n. 17 on Num 34:6 (Ps.-J.) in Clarke, *The Aramaic Bible* 4, 288 n. 17, "western border . . . the Great Sea, the Ocean. . . ."

[30]HT "set" *(ntn):* Onq. *yhb* but here and Nf *sdr*.

[31]I.e., "curses" as Onq. and Nf *(lwṭ);* see also Deut 11:26-29; 27:12-14; 30:1-10.

[32]See *Sifre Deut.* 112–113 "to teach us that the blessing is on Mount Gerizim and the curse on Mount Ebal."

[33]HT "oak *(ʾlwn)* of Moreh"; Onq. "plains of Moreh" *(myšry mwrh);* Nf "plains of Vision" *(myšry ḥzwh).* The Tgs. regularly translate HT *ʾlwn* as *myšr*. Ps.-J. seems to be a combination of the other two Tgs. In Gen 12:6 (Ps.-J.) we note "plain that had been pointed out" *(myyry);* see Maher, *The Aramaic Bible* 1B, 52 n. 7. Jastrow (772) considers *myyry* from a root *ʾry* "to point out," but Levy (2.33) derives it from *ʾmr* as a reference to Deut 11:29-30 and the blessings and curse; see Maher, *The Aramaic Bible* 1B, 55 n. 13; Aberbach and Grossfeld (1982) 79 explain the translation in Onq. as "plains" to avoid the suggestion of worshiping trees.

CHAPTER 12

1. These are the statutes and judgments that you shall do carefully in the land that the Lord, the God of your fathers, has given to you to possess all the days that you live on the earth. 2. You shall surely destroy all the places where the nations whom you are dispossessing worshiped and *their idols,*[1] on the high mountains and on the heights and beneath every tree *whose appearance is beautiful.*[2] 3. Then you shall tear down their pagan altars[3] and break their statues and you shall burn with fire their abominations and you shall cut down the images of *their idols* and destroy[4] their name from that place. 4. *You are not permitted to erase*[5] *the writing of the Name of* the Lord your God. 5. But you shall seek the land[6] where *the Memra of* the Lord your God has chosen, among all your tribes, *to cause his Shekinah*[7] to dwell, and there as a site[8] for his *Shekinah* you shall go.[9] 6. So you shall bring there your burnt offerings and your *sacrifices of holy things*[10] and your tithes and the levy[11] of your hands and your vows and your freewill offerings and the firstborn of your oxen and your lambs; 7. and it is there that you shall eat before the Lord your God and you[12] shall rejoice in all *the acquisitions of* your hands[13] with which the Lord your God blessed you. 8. *You are not permitted to* do as we have done till today, a man doing everything that is fit[14] in his eyes; 9. because you have not been brought yet *to the temple*[15] *that is* the house of rest nor to the inheritance *of the land* that the Lord your God is giving to you. 10. So when you shall have crossed the Jordan and shall live in the land that the Lord your God is giving you to inherit and you shall have caused youselves to rest there from all your enemies round about, then *you shall build the temple*[16] and after *that* you shall live in safety. 11. And it is to the place in which *the Memra of* the Lord[17] has chosen *to*

Notes, Chapter 12

[1]HT "gods": Aramaic *tʿwwt;* see vv. 3, 30, 31.

[2]HT "green": Onq. "leafy *(ʿbwp)* tree," here *špyr* and Nf "praiseworthy" *(šbḥ).*

[3]Aramaic *ʾgwryhwn* (for a pagan altar), also Onq., but Nf *mdbḥ. Sifre Deut.* 116 says the word *(ʾgwrʾ)* signifies an altar "hewn specifically for idol worship."

[4]Aramaic *šyṣy* here; Onq. *ʿbd* and Nf *swp* "exterminate."

[5]Aramaic *mḥq* here; Onq. and Nf *ʿbd.* Ps.-J. is citing Rabbi Ishmael in *Sifre Deut.* 117: "if one erases even one letter . . ." and *b.Šabb.* 102a that one may not blot out "even one letter from" the name of God in any writing.

[6]HT "place" *(ʾtr)* as Onq., but here and Nf *ʾrʿʾ,* which may be an error for *ʾtrʾ* that would be a literal translation of the HT as in vv. 11, 14.

[7]Nf "glory of his *Shekinah.*"

[8]Lit. "the place *(byt)* of his *Shekinah* you shall seek"; here *byt* implies "temple"; see *Sifre Deut.* 116 "if a house was built originally for idol worship."

[9]Here and Onq. *ʾtʾ* "to come/go," but Nf "you shall enter with fear" *(thwwn ʿlyn bdḥlh).*

[10]HT *zbḥykm* "your sacrifices": the Tgs. *n(y)kst qwdšyn* as also in vv. 11 and 27 below, 23:24, and 27:7; see Clarke (1984) 385 *nks* and McNamara's note on this verse in *The Aramaic Bible* 5A, 71 n. 7.

[11]HT "offering" *(trwmh):* in the Tgs. *ʾpršh* from *prš,* translated by Grossfeld "personal contribution" (*The Aramaic Bible* 9, 46) and McNamara "separated offering"; "a portion set aside as a priestly offering" (Sokoloff 71).

[12]HT, Onq., and Nf add "both you and all the men of your house."

[13]HT "in all that you undertake" (RSV) *(bkl mšlḥ ydkm),* Tgs. *ʾwšṭwt ydkwn.*

[14]HT *yšr:* here and Onq. *kšr,* but Nf *špr wtqn* "good and right"; see the same vocabulary distribution in vv. 25, 28; 13:19; 21:9, but in Deut 6:18 Ps.-J. and Onq. use both *kšr* and *tqn;* see n. 23 on Deut 6:18 (Ps.-J.)

[15]Aramaic *mwqdšʾ* here and Onq., but Nf omits. As in v. 5 above, *byt* implies the Temple in Jerusalem.

[16]See *Sifre Deut.* 121, "Three commandments were given . . . when they entered the land . . . to build the chosen house"; see also *b.Sanh.* 20b.

[17]HT, Onq., and Nf add "your God."

cause his Shekinah[18] *to dwell* that you shall bring there *all your sacrifices of holy things*[19] *and firstlings and tithes*[20] that I am prescribing for you; *it is there that you shall offer* your burnt offerings and *your sacrifices of holy things; there shall you eat* your tithes and the levy of your hands and the best of your vows that you vowed before[21] the Lord.[22] 12. You shall rejoice before the Lord your God, you, your sons and your daughters, your male servants and female servants, and also the Levite who is found in your cities[23] since he has no portion or inheritance with you. 13. Take heed not to offer your burnt offerings wherever you see (fit);[24] 14. but it is at the place that the Lord[25] has chosen, *the inheritance of* one[26] of your tribes, that you shall offer your burnt offerings and it is there that you shall do everything that I am prescribing for you. 15. Nevertheless, whenever you desire, you may slaughter and eat meat, in all your cities, according to the blessing that the Lord your God has granted you; *those who are unclean so as not to be able*[27] *to touch holy things*[28] *and those who are clean to touch holy things alike may eat it,*[29] *as (if it were) the meat* [30]*of the gazelle or the deer.* 16. Only *about the blood, take heed* not to eat it; you shall pour it upon the earth as water. 17. *You are not permitted*[31] to eat *in your* cities[32] the tithes of your grain, your wine, and your oil, the firstlings of your oxen and your lambs, or any of your votive offerings that you vowed, or your freewill offerings,[33] or the levy[34] of your hands. 18. But it is only before the Lord your God that you may eat it at the place that the Lord your God will choose, you, your sons and your daughters, your male servants and your female servants, as well as the Levites who are *in your cities.*[35] You shall rejoice before the Lord your God in all that your hands will have acquired. 19. Take heed lest *you defraud the* Levite, all the days *that you dwell* on your land. 20. When the Lord your God expands your borders, as he has spoken to you, and you reply "I shall eat meat" for your soul desires to eat meat, with all the desire of your soul you may eat meat. 21. If the place in which

Notes, Chapter 12

[18]HT, Onq. as here, but Nf adds "the glory of his *Shekinah.*"

[19]Aramaic here *qwrbnyy'*, but see n. 10 on v. 6 above.

[20]See *Sifre Deut.* 122 "applies to the firstborn and to tithes, sin-offerings, and guilt-offerings."

[21]HT and Nf "to," but here and Onq. *qdm.*

[22]Nf "the name of."

[23]HT "gates": all Tgs. as here; see also vv. 15, 17, 18, 21.

[24]HT "see" as here and Nfmg *(ḥmy)* and Onq. *(ḥzy),* but Nf *škḥ* "find" and Nfmg "(in every) place that you shall see."

[25]Rieder (1974) 272 incorrectly says that the MS reads *dyyy,* implying a text such as "*Memra* of."

[26]See *Sifre Deut.* 123 "but the site of the Chosen House came from only one tribe" and "R. Judah says 'The money is to come from all your tribes, but the chosen house from one'" (Neusner 1987, 203).

[27]HT "the unclean" *(ṭm'):* Onq. as HT; here the *mn* of *mn lmqrb* is awkward. I have translated as a negative *mn.* Nf seems to imply the same in *dmrḥq mn* "the one who is unclean for holy things" (Sokoloff 329).

[28]See *Sifre Deut.* 124 "proves that both of them (clean and unclean) may eat from the same dish."

[29]See n. 38 on v. 22 below.

[30]Added in Tgs. to clarify.

[31]See *Sifre Deut.* 125: although one is able to eat "within one's gates" one is not permitted. "It is not a question of ability but being forbidden to do so" (ibid., 425 n. 1).

[32]See n. 23 above on v. 12.

[33]Aramaic here *nsb'* whereas Onq. and Nf *ndb'.* In Ps.-J. *ndb'* is found only twice (Exod 35:29; 36:3); otherwise Ps.-J. uses *nsb'* for "freewill offering"; see Clarke (1984) 375, 388.

[34]See n. 11 on v. 6 above.

[35]See n. 23 on v. 12 above.

the Lord your God has chosen *to cause his Shekinah*[36] *to dwell* is far from you, you shall slaughter[37] some of your oxen and some of your sheep that the Lord your God has given you, as I prescribed for you, so you shall eat in your cities as much as your soul desires. 22. Only you shall eat as he who eats the meat[38] of the gazelle and the deer: *he who is unclean to touch holy things and he who is clean to touch holy things,* alike shall they eat it. 23. Only be resolute over *your inclinations* in order not to eat blood: for it is by the blood that the soul *exists;* do not eat blood with flesh *because it is by it that the soul exists.*[39] 24. Do not eat it; pour it on the earth as water. 25. Do not eat it in order for it to be good for you, for you as well as your sons after you, for you shall do what is proper[40] before the Lord. 26. Only animals that will be your tithes[41] as well as your holy vows you shall take and carry to the place that the Lord has chosen. 27. So you shall offer up[42] your burnt offerings *according to the rules*: flesh and blood on the altar of the Lord your God; but the blood of the rest of *your sacrifice of the holy thing*[43] shall you pour on the altar of the Lord your God, and the flesh *shall be fit* to eat. 28. Observe and heed all the words that I am prescribing for you in order that it be good for you, as well as for your sons after you forever, for you shall do what is proper[44] before the Lord your God. 29. When the Lord your God shall have destroyed the nations where you are entering to expel them before you, so that you shall have dispossessed them and you shall have been established in their land, 30. take heed lest you become ensnared after *their idols,* after they have been destroyed before you, or lest you seek *their idols,* saying: "*As did* these nations worship *their idols* so even we[45] shall also do so." 31. Do not do worship like this to the Lord your God; for everything that is abominable and hateful to the Lord they have done to their idols, even tying[46] their sons and their daughters and burning them with fire for *their idols.*

Notes, Chapter 12

[36]HT "name": here and Onq. "*Shekinah*" but Nf "the Glory of his *Shekinah*."

[37]See the same argument in Lev 17:5. Here it reflects a debate between R. Ishmael who said that in the wilderness it was forbidden to slaughter and eat at will, and R. Akiba who said that in the wilderness one could do so because ritual slaughter was not a law until the people settled in the land of Israel; see *Sifre Deut.* 128, 426 n. 3, and *b.Ḥul.* 16b, 17a.

[38]See n. 30 above.

[39]See Lev 17:11, 14 (Ps.-J.).

[40]HT "what is right" *(yšr):* here and Onq. *kšr* but Nf *špr wtqn;* see n. 14 on v. 8 above.

[41]Only Ps.-J. adds "tithes" contrary to the *halakah.*

[42]Here and Onq. *ʿbd,* but Nf *qrb.*

[43]HT "sacrifices": here and Onq. singular *(nkst qwdš)* but Nf plural.

[44]Aramaic *kšr;* see n. 14 on v. 8 above.

[45]HT, Onq., and Nf "I," but Nfmg as here.

[46]See *Sifre Deut.* 135, "This informs me only concerning their sons and their daughters."

CHAPTER 13

1. Every thing[1] that I am prescribing for you, you shall do carefully; you shall not add to them nor shall you reduce them. 2. When there shall arise among you *a false*[2] prophet or *a master of* impious dreams[3] and he give you a sign or a wonder, 3. and the sign or wonder come to pass, about which he had spoken with you, saying: "Walk after *the idols of the nations*[4] that you did not know, and let us worship before them," 4. do not heed[5] the words of that *false*[6] prophet or of that dreamer of dreams, for the Lord your God is testing you to know whether you are loving[7] the Lord your God with all your heart and with all your soul. 5. It is *the worship of*[8] the Lord your God you shall follow and it is him you shall fear; and you shall keep his commandments, you shall heed *his Memra, you shall pray before him* and you shall draw near *to his Fear.*[9] 6. But that *false* prophet or that dreamer of impious dreams shall be slain *by the sword*[10] for speaking revolt against the Lord your God, who brought you out from the Land of Egypt and who redeemed you from the house where slaves are enslaved, to lead you astray from the way in which the Lord your God prescribed for you to follow. So denounce the doers[11] of evil from among you. 7. If your brother, son of your (own) mother, *therefore*[12] *the son of your father,*[13] or your son, or your daughter, or the woman *who sleeps* on your bosom,[14] or your friend who is as dear to you as your (own) person, seeks to seduce you in secret, by evil counsel, saying: "Let us go and worship *the idols of the nations* that neither you nor your fathers have known," 8. among *the idols of the seven*[15] nations that surround you, who are near to you, *or (those) of the rest of the nations* who are distant from you from one extremity of the earth to the other, 9. do not desire him;[16] do not heed him and do not let your eyes have pity

Notes, Chapter 13

[1]Aramaic *ptgmʾ* in all the Tgs.

[2]*šqr* "to lie" or "to break the covenant"; here translated as "false"; see, for example, Deut 13:4, 6; 18:20, 22; 33:11 (Ps.-J.), and Clarke (1984) 588.

[3]In *Sifre Deut.* 136 the addition "dreamer of" suggests that the prophecy need not be identical to that of Moses.

[4]Aramaic *tʿwwt ʿmmyʾ;* Onq. as here, but Nf "other gods." This is the usual translation in Ps.-J. for HT "other gods"; see vv. 7, 8, 14.

[5]Onq. as here *qbl,* but Nf *šmʿ* "hear."

[6]See n. 2 above.

[7]See McNamara's note on this verse in *The Aramaic Bible* 5A, 75 n. 2.

[8]Here and Onq. *pwlḥnʾ,* but Nf "*Memra* of."

[9]HT "to him": here and Onq. "to his Fear"; Nf "to the teaching of his Law," and Nfmg "to the Name of his *Memra.*"

[10]See Deut 18:20 (Ps.-J.), *Sifre Deut.* 138 suggests death by "stoning," but *m.Sanh.* 11.1 as here.

[11]HT "evil," but Tgs. make concrete the abstract: "doers of evil." Onq. and here singular but Nf plural; see Deut 17:7, 12; 19:21; 21:21, etc. for the same interpretation of the HT; see also *Sifre Deut.* 138, "remove evildoers from Israel."

[12]Aramaic *kl dkn* is a technical expression (Jastrow 638), an idiom found seven times in Ps.-J.: Lev 10:19; Num 22:30; Deut 13:7; 14:21; 23:1, 19; 31:27.

[13]*Sifre Deut.* 138 "one betrothed to you."

[14]HT "bosom": Onq. "wife of your covenant" (Grossfeld); here *dmk ʿwb* as Deut 28:54, 56; see Clarke (1984) 166, 431, and Frg. Tg.(V) "who sleeps with you." Maher, *The Aramaic Bible* 1B, 62 n. 7 notes the same idea but with different vocabulary *(škb ʿytp).*

[15]HT "some of the gods of the peoples"; see Deut 20:17 (Ps.-J.) for a list of the nations.

[16]MS "them" is incorrect; see HT, Onq., and Nf.

on him, nor love him nor conceal him in a hiding place. 10. But you shall surely slay him. It is your hands that shall *stretch forth* against him first to slay him, then finally[17] the hands of all the people. 11. You shall stone him so he dies, because he sought to lead you astray *from the Fear of*[18] the Lord your God who brought you out, *redeemed,* from the land of Egypt, from the house where slaves are enslaved. 12. So all of Israel shall hear and fear and shall not continue to do a comparable evil deed among you. 13. If you hear that in one of your cities that the Lord your God has given you to live there, saying: 14. "Some *impious*[19] men have strayed *from the teachings of the sages* among you and are causing the inhabitants of your cities to go astray, saying: 'Let us go and worship *the idols of the nations* whom you did not know,'" 15. then you shall investigate and search out *witnesses* and ask thoroughly. Now if it be true and straightforward that the abominable deed was done among you, 16. you shall surely destroy by the edge of the sword[20] the inhabitants of that city, destroying it and everything in it as well as its animals, (putting them) to the edge of the sword. 17. You shall gather all its spoil into the center of the street[21] and you shall burn completely[22] with fire the city and its spoil before the Lord your God; it shall be a *desolate* mound[23] forever, and it shall not be rebuilt. 18. And nothing of the curse[24] shall adhere to your hands so that the Lord[25] shall turn from his great anger[26] and feel compassion for you and truly love you and make you multiply just as he promised your fathers, 19. if you heed *the Memra of*[27] the Lord your God to keep all his commandments[28] that I am prescribing for you today, doing what is proper[29] before the Lord your God.

Notes, Chapter 13

[17]Here and Nfmg *bswpʾ;* Onq. *btr* and Nf *ʾḥryt.*

[18]As in Onq., but Nf "the *Memra* of the Lord."

[19]HT "sons of Belial," but Onq. "wicked ones" *(ršʿ);* here *zydnyn* (*zyd* "to act with premeditation/insolence," Jastrow 391), and Nf "sons of evil counsels"; see Deut 15:9 (Ps.-J.) and Clarke (1984) 202 for other instances in Ps.-J.; see Drazin (1982) 154–155 for a discussion of Belial.

[20]See Exod 17:13 (Ps.-J.) "slaying them by the sword" and also Num 21:24 (Ps.-J.); see Clarke, *The Aramaic Bible* 4, 249 (Num 21:24).

[21]HT "open square" *(rḥwb):* here and Nf *plṭytʾ,* but Onq. *ptʾh* "open square"; see Grossfeld, *The Aramaic Bible* 9, 49 n. 12.

[22]HT "as a whole burnt offering" *(klyl),* but Tgs. *gmyr* "completely" (Jastrow 253).

[23]HT and Nfmg *tl* "heap" (RSV), "mound": here and Onq. *tl ḥwrb,* but Nf *ṣdy* "desolate." R. Jose (*b.Sanh.* 111b) "a heap forever"; see McNamara's note on this verse in *The Aramaic Bible* 5A, 77 n. 13.

[24]HT "devoted things" *(ḥrm):* Onq. and Nf *ḥrm* but Ps.-J. *šmtʾ* "curse/ban"; see n. 2 on 7:2 above.

[25]Nf "the *Memra* of the Lord shall turn."

[26]*Sifre Deut.* 144 says "as long as idolatry exists in the world fierce anger exists in the world; once idolatry is removed from the world, fierce anger will be removed from the world."

[27]HT "voice": Onq. as here, but Nf "voice of the *Memra* of."

[28]Here, Onq., and Nfmg the Aramaic *pyqwd,* but Nf *mṣwwth.*

[29]HT "in the eyes of": the Tgs. avoid an anthropomorphism: Onq. and here *kšr,* but Nf "what is good *(špr)* and right *(tqn)* before the Lord your God."

CHAPTER 14

1. So you are *like beloved* sons[1] before the Lord your God. You shall not cut[2] *your body* and do not make a bald spot *on the crown of hair* on your forehead because of *a* dead *person,* 2. for you are a holy people before the Lord your God and the Lord *your God*[3] has chosen to have you as *a well-beloved*[4] people for himself among all the nations that are on the face of the earth. 3. You shall not eat anything that is abominable *for you.* 4. Here[5] are the animals that you may eat: oxen *and* lambs *(born) of sheep, but not unclean ones; and kids*[6] *(born) of* goats, *but not mixed with unclean ones;* 5. deer, gazelles, roebucks, wild goats, ibex, wild oxen[7] and mountain sheep.[8] 6. All animals with cloven hoofs[9] *and having horns,* ruminating among the animals, them shall you eat. 7. But among these (beasts) that ruminate and have the cloven hoofs you shall not eat: *an embryo*[10] *that has two heads and two spinal columns and its kind is not seen to exist,* the camel, the hare,[11] and the rabbit[12] for they ruminate but their hoofs are not cloven, they are unclean for you; 8. and the pig, for it has a cloven hoof but there is no (animal) like it that has (the hoof) cloven and does not ruminate; it is unclean for you. You shall not eat any of their flesh nor draw near to their carcasses. 9. Among all that is found in the waters only these shall you eat: all that have fins for swimming and scales *on their skins. If they have fallen off but if one remains under its fins and one under its flipper and one under its tail,* you may eat them. 10. But all who do not have fins or scales you may not eat; it is unclean for you. 11. You may eat every clean bird, *the one that has a crop whose gizzard can be*

Notes, Chapter 14

[1]HT "you are the sons (of the Lord)" as also Onq.: here and Nf "you are beloved" *(ḥbybyn);* see *m.'Abot* 3:14 "beloved *(ḥbybym)* is Israel that they are called sons of God."

[2]HT "cut" (*gdd* I) and Onq. *hmm* "to mutilate oneself" (Jastrow 355) and Ps.-J. "cut *(gwd)* your body." Likewise the margin of the MS has a variant that I read as *hmm* (not *gyys* as Le Déaut IV, 129 n. 2). On the other hand Nf, contrary to Le Déaut's translation (IV, 128), reads "you shall not make individual bands" *(l' t'bdwn ḥbwrn ḥbwrn).* Ps.-J. *tgwdwn* suggests a root *gwd* "to band together," but the text of Ps.-J., following the HT, omits "foreign worship" as also does Onq., contrary to Nf; so Ps.-J. considers the root to be *gdd* "to cut" and therefore adds "your body." However, there is in Hebrew *gdd* II "to band together" and so Nf, using *'bd ḥbwrn,* and Nfmg, using the verb *gyys* from the noun of the same form "army/band" (Sokoloff 127) understands the phrase *ttgyyswn ḥbwrn ḥbwrn* as "you shall not band together to do evil." See *Sifre Deut.* 144 "do not split yourselves into several factions but rather be one faction," based on *'ydtw* "a single vault (of the sky)" and McNamara's note on this verse in *The Aramaic Bible* 5A, 78 n. 2, and Le Déaut IV, 129 n. 3.

[3]HT "the Lord," as also Onq., but here and Nf add "your God" as LXX and some Hebrew MSS.

[4]All Tgs.; *Sifre Deut.* 145 "more precious to the Holy One . . . than all the nature of the world."

[5]See Leviticus 11 (Ps.-J. and Nf) for the following discussion and *The Aramaic Bible* 3, 44-47 (McNamara) and 148-152 (Maher).

[6]HT *śh* can mean a young sheep (*'ymr* "lamb") or a young goat (*gdy* "kid"), hence the specification in the Tgs.; see McNamara's note, *The Aramaic Bible* 5A, 78 n. 5, and Grossfeld, *The Aramaic Bible* 9, 51 n. 4 for a discussion of the meaning of the Aramaic words.

[7]HT *t'w* "antelope" (RSV and Jewish Translation): here and Nf *twry br,* but Onq. *twrbl';* see *m.Kil.* 8.6, and McNamara's notes on these words in *The Aramaic Bible* 5A, 79 n. 11.

[8]The same vocabulary in v. 5 of the Tgs.*;* here and Onq. same order, but the order differs in Nf; see also *b.Ḥul.* 80a.

[9]Aramaic here *sdyq' ṭlpy';* Onq. "the claw is split *(ṭlp)* and has two split hoofs *(ṭlpyn trtyn)*" and Nf adds "dividing *(ṭlp)* the hoof in two parts."

[10]See *b.Ḥul.* 60b and *b.Nid.* 24a.

[11]Aramaic *'rnb'* in all the Tgs.

[12]Aramaic *ṭpz'* here and Onq., but Nf *ṭpsh;* see McNamara's note in *The Aramaic Bible* 5a, 79 n. 14.

peeled and the one that has a supplemental digit[13] *and does not seize*[14] *its prey*. 12.[15] But here are the ones that you may not eat: the eagle, and the black eagle and the osprey,[16] 13. *the black and white* kite, which is a vulture,[17] and the kite according to its kind, 14. every type of raven according to their kind, 15. the ostrich, the falcon,[18] the sea-mew,[19] and the hawk,[20] according to its kind, 16. the ibis,[21] seagull, the owl,[22] 17. *the white and black* pelican,[23] the gier eagles,[24] the cormorant,[25] 18. *the white and black* stork[26] according to its kind, the woodcock,[27] the bat, 19. *(Bees),*[28] *wasps, worms of vegetables and beans*[29] *that separate from food and flying* like birds are unclean[30] for you. 20. Every *locust*[31] that is clean you may eat. 21. Do not eat anything *that is damaged*[32] *in (an improper) sacrifice*. You shall give it to *the uncircumcised* stranger[33] in your cities[34] and they will eat it or sell it to a foreigner.[35] For you, you are a holy people before the Lord your God. You are not *permitted to* cook, *even so to eat, meat and* milk, *the two of them mixed together*.[36] 22. *Be careful* to tithe your fruit from what you produce *and gather* from the field year by year; *but not (to take) the fruits of one year in place of the fruits of another year*. 23. And you may eat *the second tithe*[37] before the Lord your God in the place where he will desire *his Shekinah to dwell;*[38] the tithes of your grain, your wine, and your oil,

Notes, Chapter 14

[13]See *Sifre Deut*. 149, "all birds of prey are unclean—just as the great vulture clearly has neither crop nor extra toe; has a craw that cannot be peeled . . . so is any other bird that shares these marks forbidden."

[14]Aramaic *drs* "tread/press" (Jastrow 324); see also Deut 28:33, 56 (Ps.-J.); the phrase is not found in the other Tgs.

[15]For the vocabulary dealing with the different kinds of birds in the following verse, see McNamara's notes in *The Aramaic Bible* 5A, 79–80 nn. 16–17. Leviticus 11:13-19 contains a different form of the list from that found here in Deut 14:12-18; see Emerton (1962) 204–211 on the species according to the Tgs. listed in vv. 12-18. Emerton observes that even in Talmudic literature there was uncertainty about the identification of some birds (see *b.Ḥul*. 63a and b).

[16]Aramaic *br nyzʾ*.

[17]Aramaic *ʾybw*.

[18]Aramaic *ḥṭpytʾ*.

[19]Aramaic *sypr šḥpʾ*.

[20]HT *ns:* here *br nṣṣʾ*.

[21]Aramaic *qpwpʾ*.

[22]Aramaic *ṣdyʾ*.

[23]Aramaic *qqʾ*.

[24]Aramaic *šrqrqʾ*.

[25]Aramaic *ʾwtyʾ*.

[26]Aramaic *dyytʾ* as Lev 11:19 (Ps.-J.); see Jastrow *dyyh,* 295, but *dyyrh* in Nf.

[27]Aramaic *nqr ṭwrʾ* in the Tgs.; see *b.Ḥul*. 63a.

[28]MS leaves a space at the beginning of this verse that the *editio princeps* supplies with *dybby* "bees."

[29]See *b.Ḥul*. 67b for another opinion.

[30]Aramaic *msʾbyn:* all Tgs.; Nf adds "they shall not be eaten."

[31]Aramaic *qwbʾ;* see *Sifre Deut*. 149 "this refers to clean locusts."

[32]See *Sifre Deut*. 149 "all winged swarming things are unclean."

[33]HT "alien" *(gēr):* Onq. *(twtb ʿrl),* here *(gywr ʿrl),* but Nf "a sojourner of the nations" *(twtbyyh ʿmmyʾ)*. The Tgs. consider a person who is not a proselyte, since this person can eat un-kosher food, to be unlike an Israelite and a convert. See *Sifre Deut*. 149–150 for a view of "the resident alien." Consider the view of redemption of a "stranger" in Lev 25:47-48 (Ps.-J.).

[34]HT "gates" but all Tgs. as here; see also here vv. 27-29.

[35]HT *nkry* "foreigner" (RSV), but Tgs. specify *br ʿmmyn* because HT *nkry* is not always a non-Israelite; see Deut 15:3; 23:21; 29:21 (Ps.-J.) for the same term.

[36]See McNamara's note on this phraseology in *The Aramaic Bible* 5A, 81 n. 37, the rabbinic support in *b.Ḥul*. 113a, 114a, 115b and *Sifre Deut*. 150 "mixing milk and meat," and Exod 23:19 (Ps.-J., Nf, and Frg. Tg.[P]); 34:26 (Ps.-J. and Nf).

[37]See *Sifre Deut*. 150 "this (seemingly) applies only to the second tithe."

[38]HT "name"; all Tgs. as here; see v. 24.

and *even* of the firstlings of your oxen and of your lambs in order that you learn to fear always before the Lord your God. 24. If the road be too much for you, if you be unable to carry the tithe to the place where the Lord your God chose his *Shekinah*[38] to dwell and it be far away from you, because the Lord your God has blessed you, 25. you shall convert (it) into money[39] and you shall enclose the coins[40] in your hand and you shall go to the place that the Lord your God has chosen. 26. So you shall give[41] the money in exchange for all that you desire: for oxen and for lambs, for *new and old*[42] wine, for everything that you ask. You shall eat there before the Lord your God and you shall rejoice, you and your household. 27. But do not abandon the Levite who is in your cities for he has no portion or inheritance among you. 28. At the end of (every) three years you shall bring out the full tithe of your harvest of that year and you shall store it in your cities.[43] 29. Then the Levite shall come, for he has no share or inheritance among you, and the stranger,[44] the orphan, and the widow who are in your cities; then they will eat and be satisfied in order that the Lord your God bless you in all your works that you will undertake.

CHAPTER 15

1. At the end of seven years you shall grant a remission of debt. 2. And this is *the instruction of the regulations concerning* the remission: every man possessing a loan that he has lent to his friend shall remit it; he shall not be permitted to press his friend to reclaim his loan from his *Israelite* brother when *the Court* has announced a remission before the Lord. 3. You may press[1] a claim on a foreigner;[2] but the legal claim[3] between you and your brother your hand shall remit. 4. However, if you apply *the commandments of the Law,*[4] there shall not be any needy among you, for the Lord shall surely bless you in the land that the Lord your God is

Notes, Chapter 14 (Cont.)

[39]HT "to turn it": Onq. as HT, but here pa *ḥll* "to redeem" (Jastrow 470) and Nf *prq* "redeem"; see also Deut 20:6 (Ps.-J.); *Sifre Deut.* 154 (on Deut 14:25): "hence we learn that the second tithe can only be redeemed with (silver) money."

[40]See *Sifre Deut.* 154 "meaning the kind of money that is usually bound up (that is, coins that can be held in the palm of the hand)."

[41]HT, here, and Onq. "give" (*ntn*), but Nf "buy" (pa *zbn*).

[42]HT *škr:* Tgs. "new and old" except Deut 10:9 (Onq. and Ps.-J.) where the question of intoxication is being addressed.

[43]The tithe of the third year is considered the tithe for the poor; see *Sifre Deut.* 156–157 (on Deut 14:28): "the year of the tithing (Deut 26:12) . . . this obviously refers to none but the poor man's tithe."

[44]HT "sojourner" *(gēr):* see the vocabulary distribution (*gywr* or *twtb*) in v. 21 above, but here all the Tgs. translate *gywr'* "alien" (Grossfeld), "sojourner" (McNamara), but Drazin (1982) 162 translates as "proselyte."

Notes, Chapter 15

[1]Aramaic *tdḥwq:* the imperfect may simply translate the HT, but it can also reflect the debate discussed by McNamara in this verse in *The Aramaic Bible* 5A, 84 n. 6.

[2]Aramaic *br ʿmmyn;* see *Sifre Deut.* 160 "whatsoever debt is owed to me . . . free to collect it at any time."

[3]Aramaic *dyn';* see *Sifre Deut.* 160.

[4]See *Sifre Deut.* 160 "so long as you do God's will."

giving you as an inheritance, 5. if only you will surely heed *the Memra of*[5] the Lord your God by keeping[6] all this entire commandment that I am prescribing for you today. 6. For the Lord your God is blessing you just as he spoke to you; you may seize[7] many nations but you may not be seized and you may dominate many nations but they may not dominate you. 7. *But if you do not apply the commandment of the Law*[8] then there shall be among you a needy (person), one of your brothers, in one of your cities that the Lord your God is giving you; do not harden your heart and do not withhold your hand from your needy brother; 8. rather you should surely open your hand to him and should surely lend him as in accordance with his necessity what he needs. 9. Take heed lest there be a malicious[9] word in your heart, saying: "The seventh year is approaching, the year of remission!" and your eyes look evilly on your needy brother and you do not give him anything. So he complains[10] against you before the Lord, it shall be a sin against you. 10. You shall surely give to him and your heart shall not do evil in giving to him, for because of this deed the Lord your God shall bless you in all your undertakings and in all the acquisitions of your hands. 11. For because *the house of Israel does not rest*[11] *in the commandments*[12] *of the Law,* the needy are not ceasing from the midst of the land. Therefore I am prescribing for you, saying: "You shall surely open your hands to your relations and to the poor who are around you and to the needy (in) your land." 12. If your Israelite[13] brother or a daughter of Israel be sold to you and serve you six years, at the approach of the seventh (year) you shall release[14] him as a free man from your service. 13. But when[15] you release him as a free man from your service you shall not release him empty (handed). 14. You shall surely set apart[16] for him from your sheep, from your threshing floor and from your wine press; you shall give him from that with which the Lord your God blessed you. 15. For you shall remember that you were slaves in the land of Egypt and that the Lord your God redeemed you. Therefore I am prescribing for you to do this deed today. 16. And it shall be when he says to you: "I shall not depart from you" because he loves you as well as the men of your house, for it was good for him that he has profited[17] with you 17. then you shall take a needle and in-

Notes, Chapter 15

[5]HT "the voice of the Lord": Onq. as here, but Nf "the voice of the *Memra* of the Lord."

[6]HT, Onq., and Nf "being careful to do."

[7]HT, Onq., and Nf "you shall lend" (ap *yzp*), but Ps.-J. suggests the result of making loans (*mšk* "to seize") rather than the action of lending itself.

[8]HT, Onq., and Nf add "within your land," but see v. 22 (Ps.-J.).

[9]HT "a word with a base thought" (Belial): here and Nf *zwn* "malicious" but Onq. "wicked" *(ršʿ).*

[10]Aramaic here *qbl;* Onq. *qrʾ,* but Nf *ṣwḥ/ṣbḥ* "to shout/clamor"; see McNamara's note on this phrase in *The Aramaic Bible* 5A, 85 n. 13.

[11]Aramaic *nyyḥyn (nwḥ);* Nf "keep" *(nṭr);* see Deut 17:18 (Ps.-J.).

[12]Nf "teaching of the Law and put in practice its ordinances"; see *Sifre Deut.* 163 "so long as you perform God's will there will be poor only among others, but when you do not perform God's will the poor will be among you."

[13]Also Onq., but Nf *ʿbryh* "Hebrew."

[14]Here and Onq. *pṭr,* but Nf *šlḥ* in the causative.

[15]Here *wʾrwm ʾyn,* but Onq. *wʾry* and Nf *wʾrwm.*

[16]HT "furnish him liberally" *(ʿnq):* Onq. *prš;* here *dḥd* "set aside some of each kind" (Jastrow 291); Nf *zwd* "endow/furnish" (Jastrow 384).

[17]Aramaic itp *hny.*

sert (it) into his ear, into the door *of the court;*[18] and he shall be your servant,[19] *serving*[20] *(you) until the jubilee (year).*[21] *Furthermore, you shall write a document of freedom for your maidservant and give (it) to her.*[22] 18. It shall not be difficult, in your eyes, to release him free from you for he has served you for six years with double the wages of a day worker. The Lord your God has blessed you because of him in everything that you did. 19. You shall sanctify before the Lord your God every male firstling that shall be born among your oxen and among your lambs. You shall not work with the firstlings of your oxen nor shall you shear the firstlings of your sheep. 20. You, you and the men of your house shall eat it, year by year, before the Lord your God, at the place that the Lord shall choose. 21. And if there shall be a blemish in it, lameness or blindness, anything evil, you shall not sacrifice it before the Lord your God. 22. You shall eat it in your cities,[23] what is unclean *to approach the sanctuary*[24] and what is clean *to approach the sanctuary,*[24] in the same way as (if it were) the flesh[25] of the gazelle and the deer. 23. Only you shall not eat its blood; you shall pour it as water on the earth.

CHAPTER 16

1. *Be careful to keep the times of your festivals, the intercalation of the years and to keep the equinox*[1] in the month of Abib to make the Passover in it before the Lord your God; for in the month of Abib the Lord your God brought you out from Egypt: *you shall eat it* at night.[2] 2. You shall sacrifice the Passover before the Lord your God in the evening, *both the sheep and oxen,*[3] *tomorrow, on that very day to rejoice in the festival* at the place that the Lord has chosen

Notes, Chapter 15 (Cont.)

[18]HT "door," but here specified.

[19]Onq. and here *ʿbd plḥ* "a laboring slave"; Nf *ʿbd mšʿbd* "a slave in bondage."

[20]See Exod 21:6 (Ps.-J. and Nfmg); see *Sifre Deut.* 165 "this applies to the one who is freed in the Jubilee year," and *Mekilta* on Exod 21:6 (III, 17) "until the Jubilee year."

[21]See *Sifre Deut.* 168.

[22]Onq. as here but Nf "the name of the Lord your God."

[23]HT "towns" (RSV; *šʿr*).

[24]See *Sifre Deut.* 171.

[25]Aramaic here and Onq. *kbšr tbyʾ*, but Nf *kbšr dtbyʾ*.

Notes, Chapter 16

[1]See *Sifre Deut.* 172, "Scripture discusses the festivals in three places . . . in Deuteronomy, in regard to the intercalation of the year."

[2]HT "by night," but this seems to contradict Num 33:3 where the HT text reads "they set out on the fifteenth day . . . on the day after the Passover." Onq. and Nf modify the biblical text by suggesting that the Lord "brought you out" and performed miracles and "redeemed you" at night. Ps.-J. is literal, unlike Onq. and Nf, but adds "you shall eat it (at night)."

[3]HT and Nf "from the flock or herd": both "sheep and oxen" raises a question since only "sheep" are to be used in the Passover celebration. *Mekilta* on Exod 12:6 (I, 32) quotes R. Akiba who resolves an apparent conflict between Deut 16:2 ("the flock and the herd") and Exod 12:5 ("from the sheep or from the goats") by quoting Exod 12:21 ("from the flock and not from the herd"). In *Sifre Deut.* 173 R. Ishmael says that in Deut 16:2 ("from the flock and from the herd") "the flock" refers to the Passover sacrifice while "the herd" refers to the festival sacrifice *(hāgîgāh). M.Šeqal.* 2.5 seems to agree with Ps.-J.

for *his Shekinah*[4] to dwell. 3. Do not eat leavened (bread) with *the Passover;* seven days shall you eat, *for his Name,* unleavened (bread), the bread of affliction, for in haste did you go out from the land of Egypt, so that you will remember all the days of your life the day of your departure from the land of Egypt. 4. *Be careful during the Passover* that leaven be not seen by you, in all your territories, for seven days. Nor should a trace of flesh that you sacrificed in the evening of the first day be kept over till the morning.[5] 5. You are not permitted to sacrifice the Passover in any one of your cities that the Lord your God has given you; 6. but in the place where the Lord your God has chosen *for his Shekinah* to dwell, there shall you sacrifice the Passover, and you shall eat it *in the evening at sunset until the middle of the night,* the time when your redemption from Egypt began. 7. Then you shall *roast*[6] and eat at the place that the Lord your God has chosen; then in the morning, at the end of the festival,[7] you shall turn and go to your city. 8. *On the first day you shall offer the (first) sheaf and you shall eat the unleavened (bread) of the old harvest;*[8] but during the six days *that remain you shall begin* to eat the unleavened bread *of the new harvest.*[8] On that seventh day you shall gather in praise[9] before the Lord your God; you shall not do work. 9. Seven weeks shall you count for yourselves from the time when you begin to put the scythe to harvest in the field; *after the harvesting of the (first) sheaf*[10] you shall begin to count seven weeks. 10. Then you shall celebrate the *joy of the* festival of Weeks before the Lord your God, in accordance with the freewill offering[11] of your hands just as the Lord your God blessed you. 11. So you shall rejoice *in the joy of the festival* before the Lord your God, you, your sons and your daughters, your male servants and your female servants, the Levites who are in your cities, the stranger, the orphan, and the widow who are among you in the place wherein the Lord your God has chosen *for his Shekinah*[12] to dwell. 12. But you shall remember that you were enslaved in Egypt so you shall do carefully these statutes. 13. You shall make for yourselves the festival of Booths during seven days, when you would have completed the ingathering of the harvest from your threshing floor and the wine from your wine presses. 14. Then you shall rejoice in *the joy of* your festival *with the ceremony of drawing (water) and the (sound of the) flute,* you, your sons and your daughters, your male servants[13] and your female servants, the Levite and the stranger,[14] the orphan and the widow who are in your cities. 15. Seven days shall you celebrate before the

Notes, Chapter 16

[4]"*Shekinah*" Onq. as here, but Nf "the Glory of his *Shekinah*."

[5]See Exod 23:18; 34:25 (Ps.-J.), and Maher, *The Aramaic Bible* 2, 229 n. 27 and 260.

[6]HT *bšl* "to boil," also Onq. and Nf, which contradicts Exod 12:8, 9 where it is said not to boil but to roast. Only Ps.-J. recognized the inconsistency and translates here *ṭwy* "to roast."

[7]See *Sifre Deut.* 177, "hence we learn that this requires an overnight stay (in Jerusalem)."

[8]See *Sifre Deut.* 177–178, "unleavened bread must be eaten all seven days, six (days) from the new crop and the seventh from the old." It is understood that "before the counting of the omer on the second night of Passover . . . the old crop may be used." Hammer (1986) explains (446 n. 5) that the "first day" is really the seventh day and hence the old crop, but the succeeding six days begin a new calculation and hence the new crop.

[9]HT "a solemn assembly"; Onq. "assembly" *(knyš)* and Nf "assembly of rejoicing" *(knyšt ḥdwh),* but here "praise" *(twšbtʾ).*

[10]See Lev 23:15-16, "the day on which you bring the sheaf . . ." and Maher, *The Aramaic Bible* 3, 192 n. 11.

[11]Aramaic *nysbt;* see note on Deut 12:17.

[12]HT "his name."

[13]Omitted in *editio princeps* and Ginsburger; the note in BHS is incorrect since the word does appear in MS.

[14]Aramaic *gywrʾ.*

Lord your God in the place that the Lord has chosen, for the Lord your God will bless you with all your harvest and in all the works of your hands and so you shall surely rejoice *in the prosperity*. 16. Three times a year shall all your males appear before the Lord your God in the place that he has chosen: at the festival of unleavened (bread), at the festival of Weeks, and at the festival of Booths. But you are not permitted to be seen before the Lord *your God* empty handed *of every precept*.[15] 17. A man (shall give) according to the measure of the gifts[16] of his hands, according to the blessing that the Lord your God would have given you. 18. You shall appoint *upright* judges and *efficient* commanders *for yourselves* in all your cities that the Lord your God is giving to you, in (each of) your tribes, and they will judge the people with a true judgment. 19. Do not pervert judgment and do not be partial and do not accept a bribe, for a bribe blinds the eyes of the wise man *who takes it, for it causes them to be foolish and confuses*[17] *just words in the mouth of judges at the hour of their judgment*.[17] 20. A *true* judgment *and a perfect judgment in truth* shall you pursue in order that you shall live and possess the land that the Lord your God is giving you. 21. *Just as you are not permitted* to plant an asherah at the side of the Lord your God's altar *so you are not permitted to associate in judgment a foolish (judge) with a wise (judge), to teach you what you should do for yourselves. 22. And just as you are not permitted* to erect a stela, *so you are not permitted to appoint as responsible*[18] *a willful man, whom* the Lord your God abominates.

CHAPTER 17

1. Do not sacrifice[1] before the Lord your God an ox or a lamb that has a blemish or any deficiency[2] *that would have been torn or ruptured*,[3] for it is an abomination before the Lord your God. 2. If there be found among you, in one of your cities that the Lord is giving to you, a man or a woman who does what is evil before the Lord your God by transgressing against his covenant, 3. *and he follows the evil inclination*[4] and worships *the idols of the nations* and bows

Notes, Chapter 16 (Cont.)

[15]HT reads only "empty handed," but Ps.-J. and Nf add "of every precept" *(mkl mṣwwtʾ)*; see Exod 23:15, where the exhortation is also "empty handed" but where only Nfmg reads *mn kd mṣwh*.

[16]Aramaic *mwḥbwt:* here as HT ("give as he is able"); Onq. "gift" *(ntn)*, but Nf "his acquisition," i.e., the occupation/stretching out *(ʾwšṭwt)* of his hands.

[17]HT "subverts" (pi *slp*): Onq. *glgl* ("corrupt," Grossfeld); Nf "carries away" (*ṭlṭl*, Sokoloff 225), and here *ʿrbb;* see Clarke (1984) 471; see also *Sifre Deut.* 183–184. Le Déaut IV, 147 n. 16 suggests that the text of Ps.-J. is corrupt according to Onq. and Nf; but consider Exod 23:8 (Ps.-J.) "confuses *(ʿrbb)* the words of the innocent in their mouths."

[18]Aramaic *prnsʾ* "administrator" (Jastrow 1231); see Clarke (1984) 486.

Notes, Chapter 17

[1]Aramaic *nks* here, Onq., and Nfmg, but Nf *qrb*.

[2]Aramaic *byš* here, Onq., and Nfmg, but Nf *psylh* "defective."

[3]Aramaic *gzyl wʾns,* describing physical conditions: *gzl* "to tear away" (Jastrow 230) and *ʾns* "to violate/force" referring to animals whose organs are dislocated (Jastrow 86); see *b.Sukk.* 30a.

[4]See *Sifre Deut.* 187.

down to them, or to the sun or to the moon or to all the host of the heaven that I have not prescribed for you, 4. and you have been informed or you have heard, then you will seek with care *the witnesses.*[5] And behold if the matter is true that this abomination has been done *among you,* 5. then you shall bring out that man or that woman who did this evil thing to the door *of your court,*[6] and you shall stone them, the man or the woman, until they die. 6. According to the word[7] of two witnesses or three witnesses shall they who are convicted[8] be killed; they shall not surely be slain by the word of a single witness. 7. The hand of the witnesses shall be the first against him to slay him and then the hand of all the people. Thus you shall eliminate *the doer of* evil[9] from among you. 8.[10] If a matter[11] is set aside[12] for judgment from among you between *impure* blood and *pure* blood,[13] between a criminal case and a civil case, between a plague *of leprosy*[14] and a plague *of ringworm,*[15] words of dissension *in your court,* then you shall arise and go up to the place that the Lord your God has chosen. 9. You shall come to the priests *who are from the tribe of* Levi and to the judge who is acting[16] in those days, and you shall inquire of them and they shall tell you the interpretation (applicable to) the case. 10. So you shall act according *to the word of the interpretation of the Law* that they indicated to you from that place which the Lord has chosen; and you shall do carefully according to all that they have taught you. 11. You shall do according to the word of the Law that they teach you and according to the interpretation of the case that they say to you; do not stray to the right or to the left from the advice that they have shown[17] you. 12. But the man acting presumptuously, in order not to obey the priests who stand to minister there before the Lord your God or even the judge, that man shall be slain and you shall eliminate from Israel *the one who does* evil. 13. Then all the people shall hear and fear and will not do evil again. 14. When you shall have entered the land that the Lord your God is giving to you and you shall possess it and live in it and you shall say: "Let us appoint a king over us like all the nations who are around us,"[18] 15. *you shall seek instruction from before the Lord, and according to this* shall you appoint over

Notes, Chapter 17

[5]See *Sifre Deut.* 188, "whence do we learn that conviction may not be based on the testimony of only one witness?"

[6]HT "gates" both here and Onq. understood as "entrance to the courts," but Nf "towards the interior" *(lgw).* In Deut 17:5; 21:19; 22:15, 24; 25:7 Nf (except 22:24) reads as Onq. and Ps.-J.; see *Sifre Deut.* 188.

[7]See *Sifre Deut.* 188.

[8]Nfmg "the condemned to death" *(qṭyl');* see *m.Sanh.* 9.4.

[9]See v. 12 below.

[10]See *Sifre Deut.* 189, "there were three courts there . . ."; see McNamara's note in *The Aramaic Bible* 5A, 91 n. 8 on how Nf clarifies the three cases.

[11]Aramaic *ptgm'* in all Tgs.

[12]HT "arises"; here and Onq. itp *prš,* but Nf itp *ksy* "be complicated."

[13]HT and Onq. omit and Nf "between blood virginity *(btwlyn)* and the blood of the slain." Ps.-J. contrasts "impure" *(s'wb)* and "pure" *(dky).*

[14]Aramaic *ṣwr'':* see Grossfeld, *The Aramaic Bible* 9, 55 n. 6. Quoting rabbinic sources, he notes that the Tgs. normally translate "plague" as "leprosy plague."

[15]Aramaic *nytq'* "causing baldness" (Sokoloff 363: *ntq* "baldness"); see Leviticus 13 (Ps.-J.) for an expanded discussion of *nytq'* and Clarke (1984) 398 for the sixteen occurrences of the word in Ps.-J.

[16]HT "who is in office"; here and Onq. *dy yhy bywm'* as HT, but Nf *mny* "appointed."

[17]Here and Onq. *ḥwy* "show," but Nf *tny* "recount."

[18]MS "me."

you a king.[19] *You are not permitted to appoint* over you a non-Israelite man[20] who is not one of your brothers. 16. Only he should not increase for himself *more than two* horses *lest his officers ride upon them and become exalted and neglect the matters of Law and commit a sin of (sending into) exile to Egypt.* For the Lord has said to you: "You shall not set out anew in this way."[21] 17. And he shall not multiply for himself *more than eighteen* wives, so that they will not lead his heart astray; nor multiply silver and gold for himself *that his heart shall not be exalted greatly, and that he not rebel against the God of the heavens.* 18. *But it shall be if he rests satisfied with the commandments of the Law,* he shall live *in safety* upon the throne of his kingdom. *The elders* shall write for him a copy[22] of that Law in a book, in the presence of the priests *who are from the tribe of* Levi. 19. He would have it with him to read, all the days of his life, in order to learn to fear *before* the Lord his God to observe all the words of this Law, and all the statutes to put them into practice; 20. in order that his heart not swell *with pride* more than his brothers and in order that he not go astray from the commandments, neither to the right nor to the left, in order that days over his kingdom be lengthened,[23] he and his sons, among Israel.

CHAPTER 18

1. The priests *who are from* the tribe of Levi[1] shall have no portion or inheritance *with their brothers;* the sacrifices of the Lord shall they eat for their inheritance.[2] 2. But he shall not have the inheritance *of field and vineyard* among his brothers; *the twenty-four gifts*[3] *of the priesthood*[4] *that the Lord has given him* are his inheritance just as the Lord promised[5] him.[6] 3. So

Notes, Chapter 17 (Cont.)

[19]Onq. has "one whom the Lord your God will choose, you should set over yourself a king from among your kinsmen," which Ps.-J. and Nf omit due to homoioteleuton on *mlkʾ*.

[20]HT "foreigner" *(nkry):* here *gbr ḥylwnyy;* Onq. as HT, and Nf *gbr ʿmmyn.*

[21]HT *ʿwd* and here *twb:* Nf *twb ʿd lʿlm* "never again for all times."

[22]Here and Onq. *pršgn* or *ptšgn* "copy (of the Law)," but Nf *tnyy* "readings (of the Law)" and Nfmg *šbḥ* "praises (of the Law)."

[23]Here passive of *ngd,* but in Onq. and Nf *ʾrk* "prolong."

Notes, Chapter 18

[1]HT "the Levitical priests, that is, all the tribe of Levi": Onq. as HT, but Nf "all the sons of the tribe of Levi." For Ps.-J. Ginsburger adds in brackets "all the tribe of Levi," as in HT and Nfi.

[2]Contrary to Le Déaut IV, 154 n. 2, I read in the MS *bʾḥsnthwn,* that is, not with a *waw* prefix and a *k* suffix as *editio princeps,* nor with a *waw* as in HT, Onq., and Nf (*wnḥltw* "and his inheritance") which raises exegetical questions. LXX reads without *kai*. Ps.-J. refers to the Levites rather than to God.

[3]Aramaic *mwhbtwtʾ,* but Onq. *(mtnn),* whereas Nf has *qrbn* "offering."

[4]See Lev 2:13 (Ps.-J.) and Maher, *The Aramaic Bible* 3, 126 n. 16; Num 18:20 (Onq.) and Grossfeld, *The Aramaic Bible* 8, 121 n. 10.

[5]Literally *mll* "spoken to" (also Onq. and Nf).

[6]Also Onq., but Nf "them."

this shall be the portion[7] due to the priests from the people, those who offer a sacrifice whether of oxen (or) of sheep: they shall give to the priest the *right* shoulder, the *lower* jaw, the *upper*[8] jaw, and the stomach. 4. You shall give him the first fruits of your grain, your wine, and your oil, and the first fruits *of the shearing of* your lambs, *as much as to replenish a belt,* 5. because the Lord your God has chosen him among all your tribes to stand and serve in the name of the Lord, he and his sons, always. 6. And when a Levite shall come from one of your cities, where he resides,[9] from all of Israel, he shall come in all the priestly band[10] that he himself takes pleasure in, to the place that the Lord has chosen; 7. and he shall minister in the Name of *the Memra of*[11] the Lord his God, as all his brother Levites who are ministering there before the Lord. 8. They shall eat equal portions besides *the surplus of the sacrifices that the priests eat, that Eleazar and Ithamar, their*[12] *ancestors, made them inherit.*[13] 9. When you are entering the land that the Lord your God is giving you, you shall not learn to do the abominations[14] of these nations. 10. There shall not be found among you those who pass their sons and daughters through fire, nor those who practice divination, nor quacks,[15] nor observers of omens, nor sorcerers, 11. nor charmers, nor spellbinders *of serpents, scorpions, and all kinds of reptiles,* nor necromancy seekers *with bones and the bone of Yidoa*[16] nor those who consult the dead. 12. Because all these deeds are abominable[17] before the Lord and it is because of these abominations[18] that the Lord[19] is banishing them before you. 13. You shall be perfect *in the fear of*[20] the

Notes, Chapter 18

[7]HT "due" *(mšpṭ):* Onq. "what is due" *(dḥzy),* whereas Ps.-J. makes the HT specific as "the portion" as well as "that it is due" *(ḥwlq' dḥmy);* Nf interprets always as "judicial ordinances" *(sdr dyn);* see McNamara's note on this verse in *The Aramaic Bible* 5A, 94 n. 3.

[8]HT "the shoulder, the two cheeks, and the stomach": Onq. translates literally except singular "cheek." The Aramaic word for "stomach" is *qybth.* Ps.-J. seems to translate the HT "two." The Aramaic word *rqyt'* is difficult and appears only here in Ps.-J. and Nf in this passage. Jastrow (1497) translates as "upper (jaws)" parallel to "lower *('r'y')* jaws." Ps.-J. then has the word for "stomach, the third body part," as in Onq. *(qybth).* On the other hand Nf does not have the word for "stomach" found in Onq. and Ps.-J. However, Sokoloff (529) interprets *rqyt'* as "stomach" in order to maintain the three body parts of the HT. McNamara, on the other hand, omits the third body part, interpreting *rqyt'* as "upper." Either Ps.-J. is attempting to translate the HT literally or Nf is incomplete, assuming that *rqyt'* means "upper" rather than as Sokoloff understands it; see *Sifre Deut.* 196–197, "shoulder—right shoulder" and *b.Ḥul.* 134b and Num 25:13 (Ps.-J.).

[9]HT "lives": here and Onq. *dwr,* but Nf *ytb.*

[10]Aramaic *krwk;* see Jastrow (665) "band, priestly section."

[11]Also Nf, but omitted in Onq.

[12]*Editio princeps* "your."

[13]Aramaic here *'wrytw,* Onq. *qwn* "establish" and Nf *'ḥsn* "to inherit"; see Grossfeld, *The Aramaic Bible* 9, 57 n. 6 for the rabbinic sources and McNamara's note on this phrase in *The Aramaic Bible* 5A, 94 n. 7. *B.Ta'an* 27a explains when the rotations *(mišmārôt)* were established. Nf supports Ps.-J. in an abbreviated form, but Nfmg and Frg. Tg.(V) support *Sifre Deut.* 199, that is, each will get his own weeks of service.

[14]Aramaic *mrḥq* here and Nf.

[15]Aramaic *ḥrwry* (or *ḥdwdy*) *'ynyn* of Lev 19:26 as well as here and Deut 18:14; see McNamara's note on this word in *The Aramaic Bible* 5A, 95 n. 9. Le Déaut IV, 157 translates "charlatans." The problem concerns first the root *ḥrr* or *ḥdd,* but also the second word in the phrase. Onq. reads a verb, *'nn* "to practice sorcery." It would appear that there is confusion between the root *'nn* and the noun *'ynyn* "eyes."

[16]According to Jastrow (564) it is the name of a bird (Maimonides) or an animal (Rashi) whose bone is used in witchcraft; see Lev 19:31; 20:6 (Ps.-J.), and Maher, *The Aramaic Bible* 3, 179 n. 70 and *m.Sanh.* 7.7 and *b.Sanh.* 65b.

[17]Aramaic *mrḥq.*

[18]Aramaic *tw'ybt'* Onq. and here, but Nf *mrḥq.*

[19]HT, Onq., and Nf add "your God."

[20]HT "blameless": Onq. as here "fear/reverence" *(dḥlt'),* but Nf "(perfect) in good works"; see n. 3 on Deut 27:6 below, and Maher, *The Aramaic Bible* 1B, 39 n. 18 on Gen 6:9 (Ps.-J.).

Lord your God. 14. For these peoples whom you are about to dispossess are obeying[21] quacks[22] and those who practice divinations; but you *are not like them*. Therefore the Lord has given you *priests who seek the Urim and Thummin and the upright prophets*. 15. The Lord your God will raise up a prophet for you from among you, from among your brothers, who is like me, *in the holy spirit;* you should obey[23] him. 16. It is according to everything that you asked before the Lord your God, at Horeb, on the day that *the tribes were gathered to receive the Law,* saying: "Let us no more hear the voice *of the Dibbur*[24] before the Lord our God and let us no more see this great fire lest we die." 17. So the Lord said to me:[25] "What they have spoken is proper.[26] 18. I shall raise up for them, from among their brothers, a prophet *in whom there is a holy spirit,* like you, and I shall put in his mouth the words *of my prophecy*[27] and he shall speak with them all that I am prescribing for him. 19. Then the man who shall not obey[28] the words *of my prophecy,*[27] which he speaks in my Name, *my Memra*[29] will take revenge[30] on him. 20. But a *false* prophet who would be wicked enough to speak, in my Name, a thing that I have not commanded him to say and who would speak in the name of *the idols of the nations,*[31] that prophet shall be slain by the sword."[32] 21. Now if you shall say in your thoughts:[33] "How shall we recognize the thing that the Lord has not spoken?" 22. Whatever the *false* prophet speaks in the name of the Lord is a thing that does not happen and shall not take place,[34] that is a thing that the Lord has not said; with presumption the *false* prophet has spoken it, do not fear him.

Notes, Chapter 18

[21]Aramaic *ṣwt* "to listen/obey"; Onq. and Nf *šmʿ*.

[22]See n. 15 on v. 10 above.

[23]Here and Onq. *qbl,* but Nf *šmʿ*.

[24]Literally *dybwrʾ,* but both Onq. and Nf read *mymrʾ* "*Memra*"*;* see Le Déaut's note on Gen 3:10 (I [1978] 92 n. 7), where he says that *dybwrʾ* (found in Nfmg and Frg. Tg.[P]) means the same as *mymrʾ* but is less frequently used; see Sysling (1991) 5 n. 33 for all the occurrences in the Tgs.

[25]Nf adds "—said Moses—."

[26]Aramaic *tqn;* Nf "right *(špr)* and proper *(tqn)*"*;* Nfmg "they have spoken well *(ṭbʾt)* in all they have spoken."

[27]HT "in his mouth": Onq. as here, but Nf as HT.

[28]HT "hear": Onq. as here *(qbl),* but Nf as HT; see n. 23 above.

[29]HT "I": here and Onq. "Name" and *"Memra,"* but Nf *"Memra"* and *"Memra."*

[30]Here and Nf *prʿ,* but Onq. *tbʿ* "seek."

[31]HT "other gods": Onq. as here, but Nf "other idols."

[32]HT "shall die": also Onq. and Nf (itp *qṭl*); see Grossfeld, *The Aramaic Bible* 9, 59 n. 11, and Deut 13:6 (Ps.-J.) for "by the sword."

[33]HT, Onq., and Nfmg "in your heart"; here *rʿywn* and Nf *ḥšb* "thoughts of your heart."

[34]HT "come true": Onq. as here (itp *qwm*) but Nf as HT *ʾtʾ*.

CHAPTER 19

1. When the Lord your God will have destroyed the nations whose land the Lord your God is giving to you, you shall dispossess (them) and live in their cities and their houses. 2. You shall set aside for yourselves three cities[1] in the midst of your land that the Lord your God is giving to you to possess. 3. You shall prepare a way for yourselves and you shall divide into three parts the territory of your land that the Lord your God shall cause you to inherit; it shall be to where[2] a murderer may flee. 4. So this is the regulation of the murderer who may flee there and live: the one who slays his brother unintentionally without bearing hate against him previously; 5. such a one who enters a forest with his friend to cut wood and his hand having grasped the hatchet to cut wood, the iron slipped[3] from the handle and touched his friend who died; he may flee to one of these appointed cities and live: 6. lest the avenger of blood, chasing after the murderer, *for his heart was filled with his anger against him,* should overtake him, for the road is long, and should slay him while he did not have the guilt of the judgment for murder,[4] for he did not hate him previously. 7. Therefore I am commanding you today: "set aside for yourselves three cities." 8. And if the Lord your God enlarge your border, just as he promised[5] your fathers, and gives you the entire land that he promised your fathers, 9. then you shall do carefully all this commandment that I am prescribing for you today, to love the Lord your God and to walk always in the ways *that are proper before him,* then you shall add for yourselves another three cities to these three. 10. But innocent blood shall not be shed in your land that the Lord your God is giving you as an inheritance lest[6] the guilt of the judgment for murder[7] be upon you. 11. But if there be a man, hating his friend, and he lies in wait for him *secretly,* then arises against him and slays him and he die, then he shall flee to one of these cities, 12. the *wise men*[8] of his city should send (for him) and bring him back from there and deliver him into the hand of the avenger of blood and so he be killed. 13. Your eye shall be without pity for him. You shall remove from Israel the shedders[9] of innocent blood and it shall go well with you. 14. Do not alter[10] your friends' boundary stone that was fixed earlier in your inheritance that you inherited in the land that the Lord your God is giving you to possess. 15. The testimony of a single one against a man shall not be valid *for any life offense or for any monetary debt*[11] or for any sin that he shall have commited. *It is by the Memra of the Lord to*

Notes, Chapter 19

[1]See Num 35:11.

[2]HT "any" *(kl),* as also Onq. and Nf.

[3]HT "slips" *(nšl):* Onq. itp *šlp,* but here and Nf *šmṭ.*

[4]HT "deserve to die" (RSV), *mšpṭ mwt:* Onq. and here *ḥwb dyn dqṭwl,* and Nf *sdr dyn dqṭwlyn* "judicial ordinance for manslaughter"; see also v. 10 and Deut 21:22; 22:8, 26 (Ps.-J.); Grossfeld, *The Aramaic Bible* 9, 59 n. 7.

[5]HT "he promised to give," also Onq. and Nf.

[6]HT, here, and Onq. *wyhy* "and there be," but Nf *dlʾ yhwy* "that there not be."

[7]See n. 4 on v. 6 above: here and Onq. have the same text but Nf *ḥwbt dšpykwt ʾdm zkyy* "guilt of shedding innocent blood."

[8]HT and Onq. "elders," but Nf as here. This is the usual vocabulary distribution in the Tgs.

[9]Here and Onq. *šdy,* but Nf *špq* and Nfmg "and (thus) shall you blot out from Israel the crime of the shedding *(špq)* of innocent blood."

[10]HT, Onq., here and Nfmg *šny,* but Nf *ʾrʿ* "attack."

[11]See *Sifre Deut.* 209.

deal severely with secrets. Against the word[12] *of a single witness shall he swear to deny what was testified against* him; but by the word of two witnesses or three witnesses shall the matter be valid. 16. When *false*[13] witnesses shall arise against a man to testify deviously[14] against him, 17. the two men who have the complaint[15] shall stand before the Lord, before the priests and the judges who shall be (acting) at that time. 18. And the judges shall interrogate thoroughly the witnesses whom they summoned and behold if it is false testimony *in the mouth of the witnesses,* and if they testified falsely against their brother, 19. you shall do to them just as they had planned to do against their brother. You shall eliminate[16] those who did the evil deed from among you. 20. Then *the wicked ones* who remain shall hear and shall fear and shall not continue to do again such an evil thing among you.[17] 21. Your eyes will be without pity: a life for a life, *the value*[18] *of any* eye for an eye, *the value of* a tooth for a tooth, *the value of* a hand for a hand, *the value of* a foot for a foot.

CHAPTER 20

1. When you go out to battle against your enemies[1] and you see horses and chariots, *proud and powerful* peoples, stronger than you, do not fear them: *for all of them are considered as one horse*[2] *and one chariot* before the Lord your God *whose Memra*[3] *is in support*[4] *of you* who brought you *redeemed*[5] from the land of Egypt. 2. And it shall be at the time when you are drawing near to engage in battle, the priest shall approach and speak with the people. 3. And he shall say to them: "Hear, Israel! This day you are approaching to battle against your enemies; do not be faint-hearted, do not be afraid and do not tremble[6] and do not be shaken before them. 4. For the Lord your God, *his Shekinah,*[7] is leading before you to battle with your

Notes, Chapter 19 (Cont.)

[12]Aramaic *mymr.*

[13]HT "malicious" (RSV): Tgs. *šqr* explained by the first part of v. 19 below.

[14]HT "accuse him of wrongdoing": Onq. and here *sṭy,* but Nf *sḥdy dšqr* "give false witness."

[15]HT "dispute": Onq. and Nf *dyn'* "judgment," but here *tygr'.*

[16]HT "purge" *(bʿr):* here and Onq. *ply,* but Nf as HT.

[17]HT "such evil among you."

[18]Here *dmy* "value/equivalent compensation" (Jastrow 313), but Nf *tšlwmy* "payment" (Sokoloff 593); see *Mekilta* on Exod 21:24 (III, 67).

Notes, Chapter 20

[1]Onq., here, and Nfmg *bʿly dbb* but in v. 14 below Onq. and here *sn'.* In v. 3 all Tgs. use *bʿly dbb.*

[2]See *Sifre Deut.* 212 and *Mekilta* on Exod 15:1 (II, 19).

[3]HT "the Lord your God is with you," as also Nf. The Tgs. seek often to avoid direct contact between God and human beings; this is achieved by the introduction of *"Memra"* as in Onq., here, and Nfmg

[4]Aramaic *sʿd:* here, Onq., and Nfmg

[5]"Redeemed" *(prq),* a standard addition in Nf, sometimes in Ps.-J. as here, but not in Onq.

[6]HT "tremble" *(ḥpz):* Onq. *tbʿ,* here *zwḥ,* and Nf *pḥd.*

[7]Sperber's text of Onq. reads *mymryh mdbr* "his *Memra* leads," but many other MSS of Onq. omit *mymryh;* Nf "the Glory of the *Shekinah*"; see Exod 12:42 (Nf "he revealed himself").

enemies to redeem you." 5. Then the commanders[8] will speak with the people, saying: "Who is the man who has built a new house but has not *affixed a doorpost inscription*[9] *on it to complete*[10] it? Let him go and return to his house lest he *make himself guilty and* be slain in battle and another man shall complete it for him. 6. And who is the man who planted a vineyard *but did not redeem*[11] *it from the priest nor make it for ordinary use*? Let him go and return to his house lest he *cause himself guilt that he cannot redeem it and he* be slain in battle and another man make it for ordinary use. 7. And who is the man who has become engaged to a woman but has not married her? Let him go and return to his house lest he *cause himself guilt that he has not rejoiced with his wife and he* be slain in battle and another man will marry her." 8. So the commanders will continue to speak with the people and they will say: "Who is the man who is afraid *because of his guilt*[12] and whose heart is broken? Let him go and return to his house *lest his brothers be implicated in his sins* and their heart be broken as his (own) heart." 9. And it shall be when they[13] cease to speak with the people, then they shall appoint the leaders[14] of the armies, at the head of the people. 10. When you shall approach a city to battle against it and *you send scouts toward it* to invite it to make peace 11. it shall be, if it (the city) shall answer you with words of peace and open *its gates* to you, then it shall be that all the people who are found in it shall pay tribute and shall serve you. 12. However, if it will not make peace with you but will make war with you, then you shall encircle it. 13. So the Lord your God shall hand it over into your power[15] and you shall destroy all its males by the edge of the sword. 14. However, the women and the children, the animals and all that shall be found in the city, all its spoils[16] shall you plunder for yourselves. You shall eat all the spoils of your enemies that the Lord your God has given to you. 15. So shall you do to all the cities that are distant from you, that are not part of the cities of these *seven* nations.[17] 16. Only from the cities of these nations that the Lord your God is giving you as an inheritance will you not keep alive any person, *neither as male servant nor maid servant.*[18] 17. For you shall completely destroy them, Hittites, Amorites, Canaanites, Perizites, Hivites, and Jebusites just as the Lord your God is prescribing for you, 18. in order that they not teach you to imitate all their abominations that they made for their idols and that you not sin before the Lord your God. 19. When you *have encircled* a city *all the days of the week* to battle against it, to subdue it *on the Sab-*

Notes, Chapter 20

[8]Aramaic *srky'* here, Onq., and Nf.

[9]Aramaic *mzwzt,* see Deut 6:9; 11:20 (Ps.-J. and Nf).

[10]HT "dedicate" *(ḥnk):* Aramaic *škll* here and Nf "complete/dedicate/adorn" (Sokoloff 550), but Onq. *ḥnk* as HT "dedicate." Sokoloff (550) signals "dedicate" for the meaning here; see McNamara's note on this verse in *The Aramaic Bible* 5A, 100 n. 4.

[11]Aramaic *prq* here, Nf, and Nfmg, but Onq. "has not yet begun to make general use of it"; see Lev 19:24 (Ps.-J. and Nf) and Maher, *The Aramaic Bible* 3, 178 n. 48.

[12]See *Sifre Deut.* 216, "because of some sin he committed in secret," which is the interpretation of R. Jose the Galilean.

[13]HT "officers"; also Onq. and Nf *(srky')*.

[14]Aramaic *rbrb,* as Onq. and Nf.

[15]Literally "hand."

[16]Aramaic *'d'h/'dyth* from *'dy* "spoils" (Jastrow 1043 and Sokoloff 396), also Nf. McNamara translates as "riches"; see Clarke (1984) 431 *('d'h)*.

[17]Onq. and Nf "these nations"; Nfmg "these nations of Canaan"; see v. 17 for a list of the nations and also Deut 13:8 (Ps.-J.).

[18]The addition is not in HT, Onq., Nf, or *editio princeps* of Ps.-J.

bath,[19] do not destroy its trees by swinging against them anything *of iron,* for from *its fruit* shall you eat. You shall not fell it, for a tree in the open field[20] is not like a man *who is able to hide*[21] *from you during* the siege.[22] 20. However, the tree that you know is not a tree *making fruits to eat,* you may destroy it and cut it off so that you may build siegeworks against the *rebellious* city that makes war against you until you subdue it.

CHAPTER 21

1. If a slain person is found on the land, *who is not buried by a mound of stones,*[1] in the land that the Lord your God is giving you to inherit, lying, *and not hanging on a tree,* in the field, *nor floating on the surface of water,*[2] and it not be known who slew him, 2. *two of* your wise men[3] and *three of* your judges *from the high court* shall go out and measure *in the four directions* (the distance) to the cities that are in the environs of the slain man. 3. And the city that is the closest to the slain man *shall be suspected;* and the elders[4] *of the high court*[5] *shall attempt absolution;*[6] *so the wise men,* the elders[4] of that city, will take a year-old heifer[7] of oxen, *that is not mixed,* that has not been used for work,[8] nor has ever pulled in a yoke. 4. Then the wise men[3] of that city shall bring the heifer *to the uncultivated*[9] *field* in which the work of the land will not have been done, nor been sown.[10] And they shall strike down the heifer mortally[11]

Notes, Chapter 20 (Cont.)

[19]According to Le Déaut IV, 169 n. 9, *b.Šabb.* 19a allows for the finishing of a battle on the Sabbath if it had begun three days previously; see also *Sifre Deut.* 219: one may not begin a battle on the Sabbath but "once a city has been surrounded, and the Sabbath arrives, the Sabbath need not suspend the war."

[20]Aramaic *ʾnpy brʾ* for HT *śdh* "field"; see Maher, *The Aramaic Bible* 1B, 22 n. 10 for a discussion of the phrase and targumic distribution; see also Introduction to this volume.

[21]Aramaic *ṭmr:* Onq. *ʿll* and Nf *ʿrg* "flee before you."

[22]Aramaic here and Onq. *ṣy(y)r,* but Nf *bšʿt ʿqtyh* "the hour of their distress."

Notes, Chapter 21

[1]Aramaic *ʾwgrʾ*.

[2]See *b.Sot.* 44b and *j.Sot.* 89.2 for the specification of the HT "lying in the open field."

[3]HT and Onq. "elders," but here and Nf usually "wise men"; see *Sifre Deut.* 221 "'thy elders' means two," and *m.Sot.* 9.1.

[4]HT and Onq. read "elders [Aramaic *sby*] of that city" and Nf reads *ḥkymy* "wise men"; Ps.-J. in the first occurrence in the verse reads as Onq., but Ps.-J. has a unique addition that seems to reflect both the HT and Onq. (also in Deut 17:18; 27:1; 29:9) and the usual targumic way of translating HT "elders": *ḥkymy sby;* see vv. 2, 6, etcetera.

[5]HT "city," here *by dynʾ rbʾ,* which is a standard amplification in Ps.-J. See Num 16:16; 30:3; 36:1; Deut 15:2; 16:19; 21:2, 3; 32:50, etc., and Clarke (1984) 159 *(dyn);* see *m.Sot.* 9.5.

[6]See *Sifre Deut.* 221, "the sages say: only one city must bring it; both cities need not bring two heifers"; *m.Para.* 1.1.

[7]HT "a heifer"; see *Sifre Deut.* 221 where R. Eliezer says "a heifer is not yet one year old."

[8]Aramaic *ʾtplḥ:* see McNamara's note on this verse in *The Aramaic Bible* 5A, 103 n. "f."

[9]HT "valley with running water" *(nḥl ʾytn):* Onq. and Nf *nḥl by(y)r* "untilled valley" and here *ḥqyl byyr; byyr* "barren/uncultivated" (Sokoloff 96); see Grossfeld, *The Aramaic Bible* 9, 62 n. 1 for a discussion of *ʾytn.*

[10]See Grossfeld, *The Aramaic Bible* 9, 62 n. 2 for a discussion of the rabbinic debate; see also *m.Sot.* 9.5.

[11]HT "break the neck": Onq. ap *nqp* "to knock down" (Jastrow 934; here MS ap *npq* "bring forth/exclude" (Jastrow 926). Ginsburger supports the reading in the MS but Rieder (incorrectly) says that the MS reads *nqp;* Nf here has *qṭl* "kill." In Exod 13:13 HT has "break the neck"; Nf has *qṭl,* but Nfmg "you shall kill *(qṭl)* with the head of an axe *(qwps)*"; Onq. and Ps.-J. have *npq* as here.

there *with an axe,*[12] *from behind, in the middle of the field.* 5. Then the priests, sons of Levi, shall approach: for it is them that *the Memra of*[13] the Lord your God has chosen for his service and to bless Israel in his name and it is by the word[14] of their mouth that every judgment be made, *and every plague of leprosy*[15] *to isolate (the sickness) or to pass final judgment.*[16] 6. So all the wise men of that city that is near the slain man shall wash their hands over the heifer that was stricken mortally[17] in the field. 7. Then they shall answer and say: *"It is revealed before the Lord that the one who has shed*[18] *this blood did not come between our hands nor have we absolved him*[19] and our eyes have not seen." 8. *The priests shall say:*[20] "Atone for your people, Israel, whom the Lord has redeemed, and place not the guilt for[21] innocent blood in the midst *of your people, Israel; but reveal who slew him in order that* it be atoned for them concerning the blood." *But immediately a swarm of parasite worms were coming out from the heifer's dung, spreading and going to the place of the murderer there and going up over him.*[22] *Then (the judges of) the court grab him and judge him.* 9. As for you, *house of Israel,* you shall remove from among you him who sheds[23] innocent blood if you wish to do what is right before the Lord. 10. When you shall go out to battle against your enemies and the Lord your God will hand them[24] over into your hand, then you shall take some of them[25] captives. 11. If you see among the captives a beautifully formed woman whom you desire that you wish to marry, 12. then you shall bring her into your house. She shall cut the hair of her head and trim[26] her nails, 13. and she shall change out of her dress of captivity. *Then you shall bathe her and make her a proselyte in your house.* She shall mourn *for the idols of* her father's and mother's[27] *house* and you shall wait *three* months *in order that you should know whether she is pregnant.* After this,[28] you may go to her, and provide for her and she will become your wife. 14. But it shall be if you do not desire her, then you shall send her away by herself *with a bill of divorce.*[29] But

Notes, Chapter 21

[12]Aramaic *qwps;* see *Sifre Deut.* 222 "with a butcher's hatchet"; *m.Sot.* 9.5.

[13]Nf "Name of the *Memra.*"

[14]Aramaic *mymr.*

[15]See note on Deut 17:8 (Ps.-J.) and Grossfeld, *The Aramaic Bible* 9, 55 n. 6 for a discussion of the rabbinic evidence for "plague" being considered "leprosy."

[16]See Lev 13:11 (Ps.-J.) and Maher, *The Aramaic Bible* 3, 154 n. 15.

[17]See n. 12 on v. 4 above.

[18]HT *špk,* but there is both a Ketib (singular) and a Qere (plural): Onq. and here have the singular of another root *šd',* while Nf has plural of *špk.*

[19]See *Sifre Deut.* 223, "this indicates that the dead too require atonement"; *m.Sot.* 9.6.

[20]See McNamara's note on this phrase in *The Aramaic Bible* 5A, 103 n. 12.

[21]HT, Onq., and here are the same, but Nf "guilt for the shedding of" explains more clearly the meaning of the cryptic HT.

[22]Le Déaut IV, 172 n. 6 says that this haggadah is unknown in midrashic literature.

[23]See n. 18 on v. 7. Onq. and here have the same vocabulary *(šd'),* but Nf only "remove *(b'r)* innocent blood."

[24]HT "him," but all Tgs. plural.

[25]Here and Nf *mnhwn* "some of them."

[26]Aramaic *tyṣmy:* the Aramaic root *ṣmy* appears only here in Ps.-J.; see McNamara's note on this word in *The Aramaic Bible* 5A, 104 n. 15, and also *Sifre Deut.* 224, "R. Eliezer considers 'do her nails' as meaning trimming (of them)."

[27]Jer 2:27 suggests the worship of a tree (father) and of a stone (mother).

[28]See *Sifre Deut.* 225, which suggests "prostitution" or "illicit intercourse."

[29]Aramaic *gyṭ;* see *Sifre Deut.* 225, "with a bill of divorcement."

you may not sell her for money. You may not trade[30] her after you have *slept*[31] with her. 15. If a man has two wives, one beloved by him and one despised by him, and they give birth to sons for him, both the beloved one and the despised one, but if the firstborn son be the despised one's, 16. and it shall be on the day of his distributing his inheritance, his goods for his sons, he does not have the right[32] to give the birthright portion to the son of his beloved instead of the son of the despised one, who is the firstborn. 17. But he should acknowledge[33] the birthright of the despised one's son to all, that he is the firstborn, giving him two portions[34] of all that is found in his estate: for he is the beginning of his strength and the birthright[35] is duly his. 18. If a man has a stubborn and rebellious son, who does not heed[36] the word[37] of his father or the word of his mother, (if after) they rebuke him he does not heed their instruction, 19. then let his father and his mother take hold of him and bring him out before the wise men of the city to the door *of the court*[38] *that is in their*[39] *district.* 20. They shall say to the city's wise men: *"We have transgressed the decree of the Memra of the Lord: because of this,* this son of ours, born to us, is stubborn and rebellious, not listening[40] to our word; a glutton with meat and a drunkard with wine."[41] 21. *And it shall be, if he fears and heeds the instruction (offered) to him and pleads for his life, they shall let him live. But if he rebels anew,* all the cities' men shall stone him so that he dies. You shall remove *the one who does* evil from among yourselves. All of Israel shall hear and be afraid. 22. When a man, being guilty of the judgment of death, *he should be sentenced to being stoned*[42] *and after this,* they shall hang him on a tree; 23. *the remains of his dead* body shall not remain on the tree overnight, but you shall surely bury him on that day for it is a disgrace before the Lord to hang a man, *unless his guilt caused it.*[43] *And because he was made in the image*[44] *of the Lord, you shall bury him at the setting of the sun so that the wild animals will not abuse him nor shall* you defile, *with the dead bodies of the guilty,* your land, that the Lord your God is giving you.[45]

Notes, Chapter 21

[30]HT "treat as a slave"; here, Onq., and Nf *tgr* "to trade."

[31]HT "humiliated her" as Onq., but Nf "have power over her" and here *šmš* "to have sexual intercourse" (Jastrow 1602).

[32]Aramaic *ršw;* see also Deut 12:17; 16:15; 17:15, etc.

[33]HT "acknowledge" (hip *nkr*): Onq. ap *prš,* here ap *ydʿ* and Nf *qrb ntn* "bring near to give."

[34]HT "double portion" *(py šnym):* Tgs. *tryn ḥwlqyn;* see Grossfeld, *The Aramaic Bible* 9, 63 n. 11.

[35]HT "right" *(mšpṭ):* Onq. and here *ḥzyʾ* "duty," but Nf *dynʾ*. Some MSS of Onq. provide both alternatives found in Ps.-J. and Nf.

[36]Aramaic *qbl:* see note on v. 20.

[37]HT "voice": Onq. and here *mymr,* but Nf as HT.

[38]HT "at the gate of the place," interpreted in the Tgs. as "court of Law"; see Grossfeld, *The Aramaic Bible* 9, 64 n. 13.

[39]Literally "its."

[40]HT "obey": Onq. *qbl* as in v. 18 above, here *ṣwy* but Nf *šmʿ*.

[41]Aramaic *grgr* and *šty;* see Grossfeld, *The Aramaic Bible* 9, 65 n. 14 for a discussion of the two terms; see also McNamara's note in *The Aramaic Bible* 5A, 105 n. 22. *Sifre Deut.* 231 expands the HT with "meat" and "wine" to describe a glutton.

[42]See *m.Sanh.* 6.4; *b.Sanh.* 45b.

[43]See Grossfeld, *The Aramaic Bible* 9, 65 n. 17 for a rabbinic discussion of this phrase.

[44]Aramaic *dywqnʾ:* Ps.-J.'s vocabulary for HT *dmwt* (Gen 5:1) and *ṣlm* (Gen 1:27; 9:6); see Lev 26:1 (Ps.-J.) and Maher, *The Aramaic Bible* 1B, 20 n. 44, who suggests the origin of the Aramaic word is *ʾyqwnʾ,* Greek *eikōn,* "image."

[45]HT, Onq., and Nf add "as an inheritance."

CHAPTER 22

1. You shall not see your neighbor's[1] ox or his lamb straying *and divert your attention*[2] *from them*: you shall surely return them to him. 2. *Even if your knowledge of your neighbor is not clear*[3] *to you* or you do not know him, you shall gather it into your house and it shall be provided for by you until the time when your neighbor shall reclaim it; then you shall return it to him. 3. Likewise shall you do concerning his donkey and so shall you do concerning his garment[4] and likewise shall you do about any loss of your neighbor's (other property) that may be lost by him and you find it. You have no right *to conceal*[5] *it from him. Announce it,*[6] *then you shall return it.* 4. You do not see your neighbor's donkey or his ox lying in the road *and close your eyes*[7] to them; you shall surely raise them for him. 5. A woman should not wear *a fringed cloak or phylacteries,*[8] which are male *ornaments,*[9] and a man *shall not shave his armpits or his pubic hair or his face to appear as a woman* for[10] it is an abomination before the Lord your God. 6. If you chance upon a *clean*[11] bird's nest *before you in the road,*[12] in any tree or on the ground with chicks or eggs and the mother sitting upon the chicks or upon the eggs, you shall not take the mother from upon[13] the young. 7. You shall surely send away the mother (first) and then take the young for yourself, in order that it may go well with you *in this world* and your days be lengthened *in the world to come.*[14] 8. When you build a new house you shall make a parapet railing[15] for your roof; hence you shall not be the cause of the guilt of murder[16] happening in your house lest one *whose lot it be*[17] fall from it. 9. You shall not plant

Notes, Chapter 22

[1]Literally "brother's."

[2]HT "hide oneself" (hitp of *ʿlm*) both here and in vv. 3 and 4: here and Nfmg pa *plg* "divert"; Onq. *kbš* "ignore" and Nf *ksy ʿyyn* "cover one's gaze." In v. 3 Onq., as here, *ksy,* but Nf *ksy ʿyyn.* In v. 4 Onq. *(kbš)* and Nf *(ksy),* but in Ps.-J. *kbš ʿyn,* a combination of Onq. and Nf.

[3]HT "if he is not near": here, Onq., and Nf *qrb* "to be near," but neither Onq. nor Nf has *dʿtʾ* "knowledge of" as subject; see *Sifre Deut.* (Neusner 1987) 2, 132, "or you do not know who he is."

[4]Aramaic *kswtyh* as Onq.; Nf *lbwšh,* but Nfmg *ʾsṭlytʾ* "cloak."

[5]See n. 2 above.

[6]See *b.B. Meṣ.* 26b and 27a.

[7]Here *kbš ʿyn;* see n. 2 above.

[8]The HT of this verse is explicitly expanded in Ps.-J.: (1) HT *kly* "(men's) garments" is translated as *tpylyn* in Ps.-J. but in Onq. and Nf as *zyyn* "armaments" and (2) HT *śmlt* "(women's) garments" is translated as "ornaments" according to R. Eliezer in *Sifre Deut.* 236, "a woman may not dress like a man and go among men, and a man may not adorn himself with women's finery and go among women"; *The Aramaic Bible* 9, 65 n. 2 for the rabbinic sources and McNamara's note on this verse in *The Aramaic Bible* 5A, 106 n. 3.

[9]HT *smltʾ* "(women's) garments"; here interpreted as ornaments *(tygwny gbr).*

[10]HT, Onq., and Nf add "whoever does these things"; see previous note.

[11]See *Sifre Deut.* 237: the question of an unclean bird sitting on the eggs of a clean bird and vice versa is discussed here and so Ps.-J. specifies "clean."

[12]Aramaic *ʾsrṭʾ* = *strata,* but Onq. and Nf *ʾrḥʾ* "the way/road."

[13]Here *mʿl,* but Onq. *ʿl* and Nf *ʿm.*

[14]The additional phrases found in Ps.-J. are found also in Nf. See similar phraseology in Gen 29:10; Num 31:50 (Ps.-J. and Nf) and Deut 6:25 (Ps.-J.).

[15]The Aramaic *tyʾq gypwpyn* seems to be synonymous and a conflation of other targumic witnesses: Onq. *tyqʾ* and Nfmg *gpwp* "railing," whereas Nf has *syyg* "fence"; see Drazin (1982) 205 n. 6 for identification of the tradition *(tyqʾ)* with Ibn Ezra.

[16]HT "guilt of blood"; Onq. and here *ḥwbt (ʾdm d) qṭwl,* and Nf *ḥwbt špykwt ʾdm zky* "guilt of shedding innocent blood."

[17]Also in Nf.

your vineyard with a mixture of seeds *lest the fruit of*[18] *the seed that you sowed along with the harvest of the vineyard* be condemned[19] to be burned. 10. You shall not plow with an ox and a donkey *or with any two (different) kinds of animals tied together.*[20] 11. You shall not dress *or warm yourself with a garment corded or spun or woven with* wool and linen[21] mixed[22] together. 12. *However, on a linen covering you are permitted to put woolen* fringe[23] threads on the four corners of your (prayer) cloak with which you wrap[24] yourselves by day. 13. If a man takes a virgin wife and goes to[25] her then afterwards he hate her, 14. and sets a protest of words against her and brings out against her an evil report[26] and says: "I have taken this woman and slept[27] with her but did not find the proof (of her virginity),"[28] 15. then the father and mother of the girl, *having taken the permission of the court,*[29] shall bring to the wise men of the city, at the gate *of the court, the bed sheet*[30] *with* the proof (of the virginity) *of the girl.* 16. And the father of the girl shall say to the wise men: "I betrothed my daughter to this man;[31] *after he had slept with her,* he hated her 17. and behold he put words of protestation saying: I did not find the proof (of the virginity) of your daughter, but here is the proof (of the virginity) of my daughter." So they shall spread out the bed sheet[32] before the wise men of the city. 18. Then the wise men of this city shall take the man and shall flog[33] him. 19. And they shall fine him one hundred sela[34] of silver and shall give it to the girl's father because he brought an evil report

Notes, Chapter 22

[18]See Grossfeld, *The Aramaic Bible* 9, 65 n. 5 for a full explanation of the confusion caused by the HT *hml'h* "full produce" and *hzr'* "the seed," the second word defining the first more exactly. The Tgs. treat the HT as a genitive construction *(d(y) m't zr'')*. Nf has different vocabulary, "produce of the seed" *(mlyth dzr'')*.

[19]HT *tqdš* "be fortified"; here itp *ḥwb* plus *yqydt'* "condemned to be burned"; Onq. itp *s'b* "defile" and Nf *'bd* "destroy"; see Grossfeld, *The Aramaic Bible* 9, 67 n. 6.

[20]*Sifre Deut.* 241 does not say that one cannot plow with asses or oxen but that "mixed breeds of any kind" are prohibited from being used together.

[21]Aramaic *kytn* as Onq. and Nfmg, but Nf incorrectly *kdn*.

[22]HT "mixed together" *(š'ṭnz)*; Onq. *ḥbr* "joined," but here and Nf *'rb;* see Grossfeld, *The Aramaic Bible* 9, 67 n. 7, and *Sifre Deut.* 241–242, which argues that the HT *š'ṭnz* derives from *šu'a* ("carded") and *ṭawuy* ("spun") and *nuz* ("woven").

[23]Aramaic *ṣyṣyyt'* here, but Onq. *krwspd* (Greek *keraspedon*) and Nf *tnyph* "border." *Ṣyṣyyt'* appears also in Num 15:38, 39; see Clarke, *The Aramaic Bible* 4, 232 n. 28; see *Sifre Deut.* 243, which specifies the number of threads and the location on the shawl.

[24]HT "cover yourself" *(ksy)*, also Onq. and Nfmg, but here and Nf itp *'ṭp* "wrap yourself."

[25]Here and Onq. *'ll*, but Nf *zmn* "to have sexual intercourse" (Sokoloff 179); see also v. 14.

[26]Here *ṭyb byš*, but Onq. and Nf *šm byš*.

[27]Here *šmš:* see note on 21:14; Onq. *'ll* and Nf *qrb*.

[28]HT *btwlym* "tokens of virginity": Onq. as HT, but here and Nf *shd;* see vv. 15, 17 where the vocabulary distribution is the same in the Tgs.; see *Sifre Deut.* 244, i.e., "charges of the lack of virginity" and McNamara, *The Aramaic Bible* 3, 82 n. 12.

[29]*Sifre Deut.* 244 states that the case must be heard before a court ("at the door of her father's house") in the locality of the father when the witnesses are from the father's house.

[30]Aramaic here and Onq. *šwšyp'* "cloth," i.e., "a bedsheet."

[31]HT, Onq., and Nf add "give for a wife" *(yhb l'th);* here pa *gdš* only. Ginsburger is incorrect in adding "for a wife" without Ps.-J. MS support.

[32]HT "garment" *(śmlh);* here, Onq., and Nf *šwšyp'*. R. Akiba and R. Ishmael dispute whether producing the bedsheet is literal or figurative. R. Akiba says literal; see *Mekilta* on Exod 22:2 (III, 102); *Gen. R.* 61.3; *Eccl. R.* 11.6. Compare the phraseology here with that in v. 15 above.

[33]HT "punish" (pi *ysr*): the Tgs. see punishment with lashes: Onq., here, and Nfmg ap *lgy* but Nf *rdy* "chastise"; see Grossfeld, *The Aramaic Bible* 9, 67 n. 12 for rabbinic evidence.

[34]*B.Bek.* 50a says "every silver piece *(ksp)* mentioned in the Pentateuch without qualification means a 'sela.'"

against a *pure* virgin of Israel. She shall be his wife. He shall not *have permission to* divorce her all his days.[35] 20. But if this matter be true (that) proof of the girl's[36] (virginity) were not found, 21. then they shall bring out the girl to the door of the father's house, the men of the city[37] shall stone[38] her with stones so that she will die for she has made a disgrace in Israel by bringing a *bad*[39] report of prostitution upon her father's house. You shall remove the one who does what[40] is evil from among you. 22. If a man is found sleeping with the wife of another man, then you shall slay the both of them, the man who slept with the woman along with the woman; *even if she be pregnant, you shall not tarry until she has given birth but in that hour you shall slay them, by strangulation with a scarf.*[41] Also you shall remove from Israel *the one who does what is* evil. 23. When a virgin girl shall be engaged to a man and another man find her in the city and sleeps with her, 24. then you shall bring the two of them to the door *of the court that is in* that city, and you shall stone them with stones,[42] so they shall be put to death, the girl because she did not cry for help in the city and the man because he slept[43] with his friend's wife. You shall remove *the one who does what is* evil from among you. 25. But if it is in the open field that the man should find the girl who is engaged, and the man overpowered her and slept with her, then the man who slept with her shall alone be slain. 26. And to the girl you shall do nothing evil; the girl shall not have the death sentence *but the man (her fiancé) shall send her away with a bill of divorce*. In effect, this matter is similar to a man who lies in wait for his friend and slays him: 27. for in the open field[44] he found her; the engaged girl cried for help but no one was found to save her. 28. If a man find a virgin girl who is not engaged and he seizes her and sleeps with her and they are found, 29. then the man who slept with her shall give the girl's father the value *of her shame,* fifty sela of silver; and she shall become his wife because he violated her; he shall not have permission to send her away *with a bill of divorce* all his days.

Notes, Chapter 22

[35]Onq. as here, but Nf "all the days of his life."

[36]HT "young woman": here and Onq. *ʾwlymh,* Nf *rbyth,* and Nfmg *ṭlyth* "young girl"; for "proof" *(shd)* see v. 14 above.

[37]HT, here, and Onq., but Nf "people."

[38]HT "stone her to death": Onq. and Nf *rqm* "kill by stoning" (Sokoloff 516), but here ap *nṭl* "to stone" (Jastrow 900).

[39]MS omits, but found in *editio princeps.*

[40]HT "the evil": here and Onq. *dbyš,* the *d* being a relative "that which is"; Nf *ʿbdy byšth* "doers of evil"; see also vv. 22, 24 for the same distribution.

[41]"Strangulation *(šnq)* with a scarf *(swdrʾ)*" is an expansion in Ps.-J. The Aramaic *swdrʾ* is derived from the Greek *soudarion* (Sokoloff 370); see also Exod 21:15, 16 (Ps.-J.); Lev 20:10 (Ps.-J.); Deut 22:22; 24:7 (Ps.-J.); see *Sifre Deut.* 247, "namely by strangulation."

[42]The vocabulary distribution is the same as in v. 21 above.

[43]HT "violated"; Onq. as HT, but here *šmš* and Nf *ṣʿr* "to grieve/torment" (Sokoloff 468).

[44]Aramaic here and Nf *ʾ(n)py brʾ;* Onq. *ḥqlʾ;* see Deut 20:19 (Ps.-J.) for the other instance of this translation for HT *śdh* in Deuteronomy and the Introduction to this volume for a discussion of HT *śdh* "field" and the vocabulary distribution in the Tgs.

CHAPTER 23

1. A man shall not take a wife whom his father took by force *or seduced,*[1] especially his father's wife, and he shall not expose[2] *the corner (of the garment) that has revealed* his father's *(shame).*[3] 2. He who is castrated[4] or whose testicles have been cut off is not permitted[5] *to take a wife from the assembly of the* Lord's *people.* 3. He who is born a bastard,[6] *who has in himself an evil blemish*[7] *that is found among the non-Israelite nations,* is not permitted *to take a proper wife* from the assembly of the Lord's *people.*[8] 4. The males[9] of the Ammonites and the Moabites are not permitted *to take a wife* from the assembly of the Lord's *people;* even the tenth generation shall not be permitted *to take a wife* from the assembly of the Lord's *people,* forever. 5. It is because they did not sustain[10] you with bread and water on the way during your exodus from Egypt and because he hired Balaam son of Peor from Pethor-*of-the-Dreams that was built in the land of Aram which is on the Euphrates*[11] to curse you. 6. But the Lord your God did not want to hear[12] from Balaam and so the Lord your God turned the curses *in his mouth* to blessings in your favor, for the Lord your God loves you. 7. You shall not seek their peace or their welfare all your days *because, even if they become proselytes, hatred is kept in their heart,* forever. 8. You shall not loathe the Edomite *who came to be a proselyte,* for he is your brother; you shall not loathe the Egyptians *who came to be proselytes,* because you were living[13] in their land. 9. Children who are born of them, (to) the third generation shall be permitted *to take (a wife)*[14] *from the people* of the Lord's assembly. 10. When you go out to prepare against your enemies you should beware of any evil matter: *idolatry, incest, and the*

Notes, Chapter 23

[1]See *Sifre Deut.* 251, "a woman whom he (the father) had raped or seduced."

[2]HT "uncover" *(glh)* as here and Onq. *gly* "reveal/uncover" (Sokoloff 129); Nfmg *prśm* "expose/reveal" (Sokoloff 449); Nf *bzy* "expose/reveal" (Sokoloff 89).

[3]Nf translates "the corner (of the garment) of his father's nakedness," suggesting more clearly the targumic interpretation of the HT "nor shall he uncover"; see Grossfeld, *The Aramaic Bible* 9, 69 n. 1.

[4]See *Sifre Deut.* 251 for a discussion of maiming and castrating.

[5]HT "he shall not enter," as Nf, but Onq. and here *dky* qualifies the HT as "being pure/permitted."

[6]HT "bastard" *(mmzr):* also Onq. and Nf *mmzr'* as if understood to be from *mwm* "defect" and *zr* "strange" (see *j.Qidd.* 3.64c and *b.Yeb* 78b), but here in Ps.-J. literally "he who is born of harlotry" *(dmtylyd mn znw).* LXX supports Ps.-J. but Aquila and Symmachus reflect HT, Onq., and Nf *(mamzēr).*

[7]Literally "a bad defect" *(mwm' byš'):* see *m.Qidd.* 3.13 where a bastard may become purified; see Grossfeld, *The Aramaic Bible* 9, 69 n. 2 for rabbinic evidence.

[8]HT "assembly" *(qhl)* of the Lord"; Onq. *qhl',* but Nf *qhl knyšth.*

[9]HT "no Ammonite or Moabite": see *Sifre Deut.* 253, which states that "Scripture is speaking here of males, not of females."

[10]Aramaic *zmn* here but Onq. *'r'* "join/meet" and Nf ap *qdm* are closer to the vocabulary of the HT pi *(qdm)* "confront."

[11]Also Onq., but Nf "(interpreter) of dreams from Aram-Naharaim"; see Nfmg and Num 22:5 (Ps.-J. and Nf), and McNamara and Clarke, *The Aramaic Bible* 4, 124 n. 6, 252 n. 9.

[12]Aramaic *qbl* here and Onq., but Nf *šm'.* For Balaam's activities see Num 31:8, 15-16 (Ps.-J.) and Clarke, *The Aramaic Bible* 4, 278–279.

[13]Aramaic *dyyryn;* see Clarke (1984) 153 *(dwr)* for the other instances in Ps.-J.

[14]HT "may enter the assembly" which is the translation in Onq.: Nf "may be reckoned in the assembly"; Ps.-J.'s translation is more complex, suggesting a conjugal relationship. Rieder supplied "wife" based on the usual meaning of Aramaic *nsb* "to take (a wife)"; see v. 2 above.

shedding of innocent blood.[15] 11. If there be among you a man who is not pure from an accident (caused by) fancies of the night,[16] he shall go outside the camp (and)[17] he shall not re-enter the center of the camp. 12.[18] 13. And a place[19] *shall be designated,* for you, outside the camp *and there you shall urinate.* 14. You shall have *a shovel*[20] fixed to your war weapons,[21] at the place where you shall tie your swords and you shall dig with it and you shall relieve yourself there, then you shall again cover your excrements. 15. For the Lord your God, *his Shekinah*[22] goes through[23] the center of your camps to save you and to hand over your enemies into your power; therefore the place of your camps shall be holy and nothing shocking[24] shall be seen among you so that *his Shekinah*[25] not go away from among you. 16. You shall not hand over *an uncircumcised*[26] *into the hands of an idol worshiper* who has been a refugee among you *to put under the protection of my Shekinah, for it is because of this he has fled from the worship of his idol.* 17. He shall dwell with you *and shall keep the commandments* among you; *teach him the Law, appoint for him a school in the place that he shall want* in one of your cities; *be busy with him so that it* may go well with him, do not scare him with words.[27] 18. *Do not desecrate* your daughters by (letting them) become prostitutes and a man, son of Israel *shall not desecrate himself with harlotry.*[28] 19. You shall not bring, as an offering in the sanctuary[29] of the Lord your God, the profit *of the gratification of a prostitute*[30] or the price of a dog for any vow, *even any of the offerings,*[31] for the two of them are an abomination before the Lord your God. 20. You shall not charge interest to your neighbor on the loan[32] that he borrowed

Notes, Chapter 23

[15]See Gen 13:13; 25:29; 28:20; 49:12 (Ps.-J.), Num 35:25 (Ps.-J.) and Clarke, *The Aramaic Bible* 4, 292; see Shecter (1969) 222–227; Maher, *The Aramaic Bible* 1B, 54 n. 9, 90 n. 39, and 100 n. 30 for a discussion of the (three) cardinal sins of Judaism: sexual immorality, murder, and idolatry.

[16]See Gen 49:3 "the beginning of the effusion of my heated imagination"; see Maher, *The Aramaic Bible* 1B, 157 n. 7.

[17]Here, Onq., and Nfmg follow HT and omit "and" which is found in Nf.

[18]MS omits v. 12 due to homoioteleuton on "the camp," also missing in Nf but added in the margin with the Hebrew lemma; Onq. "then toward evening he should bathe in water, and at sunset may re-enter the confines of the camp"; see Grossfeld, *The Aramaic Bible* 9, 68.

[19]HT *yd,* literally "hand," is interpreted as "here" (*ʾtr;* also LXX *topos*); see *Sifre Deut.* 256–257 ("hand means a place") on 1 Sam 15:12 and Num 2:17; Deut 2:37; Jer 6:13.

[20]HT *ytd* "stick" (RSV); Tgs. *sykʾ/syktʾ.*

[21]Aramaic *mʾny zynykwn.*

[22]Onq. as here, but Nf "the Glory of his *Shekinah.*"

[23]HT, Onq., and here "walks" *(hlk),* but Nf *dbr* "leads," and Nfmg "is dwelling" *(šry).*

[24]Aramaic *qlnʾ;* see Clarke (1984) 527 *(qln)* for the three instances in Ps.-J.

[25]Onq. "*Memra*"; Nf "the Glory of his *Shekinah.*"

[26]HT "slave," also Nf: presumably Ps.-J., using *rʿltʾ,* means an uncircumcised slave—hence heathen—which the *editio princeps* explains as "foreigner" *(nwkrʾ).* Nf reads "slave of the (heathen) nations" *(ʿbd ʿmmyn);* see Grossfeld, *The Aramaic Bible* 9, 69 n. 11 for rabbinic citations and *Sifre Deut.* 257 "if one sells a slave to a heathen . . . including a resident alien."

[27]See *Sifre Deut.* 258 "warning him with words."

[28]Ps.-J. and Nf more or less translate the HT literally, but Onq. deviates to discuss the prohibition of a mixed marriage between an Israelite and a slave; see Grossfeld, *The Aramaic Bible* 9, 70 n. 13 for rabbinic citations and Le Déaut IV, 189 n. 13.

[29]HT "house" is clarified here as sanctuary.

[30]HT *zwnh:* here *mtʿytʾ* "prostitute" (Jastrow 769), but Onq. and Nf use the root *znh.* Other examples of *mtʿytʾ* in Ps.-J. are in Gen 38:21 (twice), 22; 42:9, 12; Num 24:14, but the form in Gen 34:31 is *mtʿyyʾ;* see Clarke (1984) 248 *(tʿy)* for other occurrences in Ps.-J.

[31]See *Sifre Deut.* 259, and *b.Tem.* 29a, 30a has exchanged a lamb for a dog.

[32]Aramaic *mzpw* from *yzp,* but Nf *zpw* and Onq. *rbytʾ.*

from you,[33] or on the loan of money, or on the loan of food or on the loan of whatever interest can be charged. 21. You may charge interest on a loan to *a Gentile*[34] but to your brother you shall not lend with interest in order that the Lord your God bless you in every enterprise of your hands in the land that you are entering to possess. 22. When you make a vow before the Lord your God, do not delay in its fulfillment *(at the time of the) three holidays;* for the Lord your God shall surely seek it from you.[35] *In the offering there shall not be guilt or deficiency for it is considered as already in the treasury*[36] *of the Master of the Universe.*[37] So let there not be with you the guilt *of delaying (the fulfillment of) a vow.* 23. But if you abstain from making a vow, there shall be no guilt in you. 24. You shall fulfill an oath that comes from your lips. *The commandments that are proper*[38] *to be done,* you shall do; *but what is not proper to be done, you shall not do;* and just as you have vowed so you shall fulfill (your vow): *sin offerings, guilt offerings, burnt offerings, offerings of holy things shall you offer*[39] before the Lord your God; and free-will offerings shall you give *and the presents that you have promised for the Temple shall you give, and alms for the poor,* which you promised with your own mouth. 25. When you go *to work for wages*[40] in the vineyard of your neighbor you may eat *for your pleasure until you are satisfied;* but do not put (any) into your basket. 26. When you go *to work for wages*[40] in the harvest of your neighbor you may pluck the kernels with your hand but do not put a sickle to your neighbor's standing grain.

CHAPTER 24

1. When a man takes a wife and has sexual relations with her, but she does not find favor in his eyes because he finds *something offensive*[1] about her, he shall write her a bill of divorce[2]

Notes, Chapter 23 (Cont.)

[33]Aramaic ap *yzp;* see also *Sifre Deut.* 259 "this refers to borrowers."

[34]Literally "a son of the nations": *br ʿmmyn* in all the Tgs.

[35]MS reads incorrectly "them."

[36]Aramaic *hptyq:* two spellings appear in Ps.-J.: *h(y)ptyqʾ* Gen 47:14 and here, and *ʾpwtyq(y)ʾ* Gen 24:2, 10; Deut 32:34. Jastrow (103, 363) considers the two spellings to be based on the Greek *apothēkē* "storehouse/treasury," but Klein (1980) 2.17, 104 links the spelling *h(y)ptyqʾ* to the Greek *hypothēkē* "title deed" because of the initial *he* in the Aramaic.

[37]See *b.Ḥul.* 139a.

[38]Aramaic *kšr:* the same idiom is found in Ps.-J. of Gen 20:9; 34:7; Lev 4:2, 13, 22, 27; 5:17; see Maher, *The Aramaic Bible* 1B, 73 n. 6 for a discussion of the negative *(lʾ kšr).*

[39]*Sifre Deut.* 261 lists the specific offerings.

[40]HT "you go": here literally "to take wages *(ʾgr)* as a laborer *(pʿl)*"; Onq. itp *ʾgr* "become a hired laborer"; Nf *ʾrys* "day laborer" ("tenant farmer," Sokoloff 74); see also v. 26 and Grossfeld, *The Aramaic Bible* 9, 71 n. 18 for the rabbinic citations.

Notes, Chapter 24

[1]HT "indecency" (RSV), literally "nakedness"; Onq. and here *ʿbyrt* "transgression," but Nf *ʿryh* "nakedness." There seems to be reflected here the debate between the schools of Shammai and Hillel. The text here follows Shammai, who specifies the grounds for divorce; see *m.Ketub.* 7.6.

[2]HT "bill of divorce" *(spr krytwt). M.Giṭ.* 9.3 speaks of three terms for a bill of divorce, all of which are found in the Tgs.: Ps.-J. *spr tyrwkyn* (see also v. 3); Onq. *gṭ pyṭwryn;* Nf *ʾgrt šybwqyn;* see Drazin (1982) 217 n. 2.

before the court, and shall give it into her possession[3] and send her out of his house. 2. After she went from his house and went and became (a wife) to another man, 3. *and the heavens cried out against her*[4] that the latter man hates her, then he shall write her a bill of divorce[5] and give it into her possession and shall send her out from his house; or (if) they (the heavens) shall announce, concerning him, that the latter man who took her as his wife would die, 4. the first husband, who sent her away *in the beginning,* is not permitted to take her again[6] to be his wife after she was made unclean; for it is an abomination before the Lord, *but her children who are born by her shall not be (considered as) an abomination.*[7] You shall not have the right to make guilty, *from the sin of pestilence,* the land that the Lord your God is giving to you as an inheritance. 5. When a man shall take a new wife, *a virgin,*[8] he shall not go into the army, so that nothing evil shall befall him; he shall be free in his house for one year and shall rejoice with his wife that he has taken. 6. A man shall not take, as a pledge, a millstone or an upper millstone *for they are needed in making food for everyone.*[9] *A man shall not unite grooms and brides*[10] *by witchcraft for he will destroy the life that is destined to issue from them.*[11] 7. If a man is found kidnapping a person from among his brothers, among the children of Israel, whom he made a business transaction[12] as goods and has sold him, then that man shall be put to death *by strangulation with a scarf.*[13] You shall eliminate the one who does what is evil[14] from among you. 8. Take heed *not to cut off*[15] *flesh in which there are white spots*[16] *but to watch* especially to distinguish between the affliction of leprosy *and the affliction of ringworm,*[17] *between the unclean and the clean,*[18] according to all that the priests who are from *the tribe of* Levi shall teach you; you shall do carefully just as I have prescribed for them. 9. *Be careful not to suspect one against his friends in order not to be punished;* remember what the Lord

Notes, Chapter 24

[3]See *Sifre Deut.* 264; *b.Giṭ.* 77a.

[4]See *b.Giṭ.* 90a.

[5]See n. 2 above.

[6]See the question of remarriage in Num 11:26 (Ps.-J.).

[7]See *Sifre Deut.* 267, "she is an abomination but her child is not an abomination."

[8]Aramaic *btwltʾ;* see *Sifre Deut.* 267, "this refers only to a virgin"; *b.Sot.* 49a.

[9]HT "he would be taking a life in pledge" *(ḥbl):* the Tgs. explain the HT as saying that the taking of the millstones, which are essential for providing food, is as taking life; here and Onq. "because with them food is produced for every person" are similar; Nf *ḥbyl* "guilty" and Frg. Tgs.(PV) *mšk* "to take possession" (Jastrow 853) are similar to the HT; see McNamara's note on this verse in *The Aramaic Bible* 5A, 114 n. 6.

[10]See *Gen. R.* 166, and Lieberman (1962) 110.

[11]Although this expansion is not found in Onq. and only indirectly in Nf ("guilty of destroying lives"), it is in the Frg. Tg.(PV), with an eschatological dimension, "denies *(kpr)* life in the world to come": see Ginzberg, *Legends* 6.208; Cook (1986) 47–48, who discusses the complexity of the targumic texts, and Shinan (1994) 214.

[12]HT "treats them as a slave": here *prgmtyʾ* (Greek *pragmateia*) "the undertaking of a business transaction"; see Clarke (1984) 485 *(prgmtyʾ)* for the ten instances in Ps.-J.

[13]HT "that thief shall die" *(mwt);* Onq. and Nf agree with the HT using the verb *qṭl*. Only in Ps.-J. is the method of death specified as "strangulation *(šnq)* with a scarf *(swdrʾ)*"; see n. 41 on Deut 22:22 above, and *Sifre Deut.* 247.

[14]See Deut 17:12 (Ps.-J.) and *Sifre Deut.* 247 "death without specification, namely by strangulation."

[15]See *m.Neg.* 7.4.

[16]See Le Déaut IV, 195 n. 8 "not to suppress signs of impurity."

[17]Aramaic *nytqʾ;* see n. 15 on Deut 17:8; Lev 13:33 (Ps.-J.); see Maher, *The Aramaic Bible* 3, 156 nn. 24–26.

[18]See *Sifre Deut.* 268, "refers only to the time before the patient has been declared unclean" (hence clean).

your God did to Miriam *who suspected Moses*[19] *with a thing that was not in him and she was afflicted with leprosy and even delayed on the way* when you were going out from Egypt. 10. When you lend your friend a loan of any kind, you shall not enter his house to claim his pledge. 11. You shall stand in the street, and the man to whom you have made the loan shall bring out the pledge *to the street.*[20] 12. But if he is a poor[21] man, do not pass the night with his pledge[22] with you; 13. you shall surely return to him the pledge when the sun sets, so that he shall sleep with his cloak; and he shall bless you, so you shall earn merit *because the sun shall testify for you* before the Lord your God. 14. You shall not oppress[23] *your friends or hold back*[24] *the wages*[25] of the laborers, poor[26] and needy,[27] who are among your brothers or among the aliens[28] who sojourn in your land, in your cities.[29] 15. On the same day you shall pay him his wages[30] and the sun shall not set upon it; because he is poor and because of it he hopes to maintain his life.[31] So he shall not complain against you before the Lord and you be guilty. 16. Fathers shall not be put to death, neither *by the testimony*[32] *nor because of the sins of* the children; and children shall not be put to death, neither *by the testimony nor because of the sins of* fathers. A man shall be put to death because of his (own) sins *according to proper witnesses.* 17. You shall not pervert the right of the alien[33] or the orphan,[34] nor one of you take as a pledge the garment of the widow *so that evil neighbors shall not arise and bring against her an evil report when you return her pledge to her.*[35] 18. Remember that you were enslaved in the land of Egypt and *the Memra of* the Lord your God redeemed you from there. Therefore I am commanding you to do this thing. 19. When you cut your crop in your fields and you forget a sheaf

Notes, Chapter 24

[19]See Num 12:1 (Ps.-J.), Clarke, *The Aramaic Bible* 4, 222, and *Sifre Deut.* 269, "Miriam, who spoke only when Moses was not present. . . ."

[20]HT "outside" *(ḥwṣ)* is translated as *šwq'* (rather than *br'*) in many of the passages in Ps.-J. such as Gen 9:22; 39:12-18; Deut 25:5; see Clarke (1984) 565, and Maher, *The Aramaic Bible* 1B, 46 n. 16. Usually Onq. and Nf translate with *br'* but in this instance Nfmg also has *šwq'*.

[21]Aramaic *gbr mskyn.*

[22]That is, "a man's cloak"; see Exod 22:25-27.

[23]Here, Nfmg, and Frg. Tg.(V) *ṭlm;* Onq. *ʿšg* and Nf *ʿsy.*

[24]HT "oppress": here *šq'* "to deviate/hold back"; see preceding note for the vocabulary distribution in Onq. and Nf.

[25]Here and v. 15 *swṭr'* "wages" (Jastrow 963); see Exod 2:9; 22:30; Lev 19:13 (Ps.-J.); v. 15 below; Onq. and Nf *'gr'* (Sokoloff 34), and *Sifre Deut.* 270–271, which cites Lev 19:13 and Deut 24:15, "if one withholds the wages of a hired servant, he transgresses. . . ."

[26]Aramaic *ʿny'.*

[27]Aramaic *mskyn'.*

[28]Aramaic *gywr mtgyyr:* see Le Déaut IV, 197, and Drazin (1982) 220 n. 4, who translate *gywr* to designate a proselyte, but I have treated *gywr* as in most of the passages in Deuteronomy where the word is found as "sojourner/stranger/alien" as also McNamara in this passage in Nf.

[29]HT "gates": see also the note in McNamara, *The Aramaic Bible* 5A, 114 n. 13.

[30]See n. 25 above.

[31]Vulgate *"ex eo sustenant animam suam"*; see Le Déaut IV, 197 n. 14; see also *Sifre Deut.* 271, ". . . he who withholds the laborer's wages is considered by Scripture as if he had taken his life."

[32]HT "because of the children": here *bshdwt;* Onq. "on account of the testimony," i.e., "mouth" *(ʿl pwm),* and Nf "for the sins of the fathers" *(ʿl ḥwb);* see Grossfeld, *The Aramaic Bible* 9, 73 n. 8 for the rabbinic citations.

[33]Aramaic *gywr.*

[34]*Editio princeps* adds "and the widow" as in vv. 19, 20.

[35]See *Sifre Deut.* 272, "R. Simeon says 'when you take a pledge from a man you may not return it to a woman.'"

in the field, do not return to retrieve it; it shall be for the alien, the orphan, and the widow, so that *the Memra of* the Lord your God may bless you in *all* the works of your hands. 20. When you knock down[36] your olives, do not search[37] (for what is left) after you; it shall be for the alien, the orphan, and the widow. 21.[38] 22. So you shall remember that you were enslaved in the land of Egypt; therefore I am commanding you to do this *thing*.

CHAPTER 25

1. When there is a complaint between *two*[1] men and they approach the court in order that they may judge them, *they shall decide by majority* to acquit the innocent and to condemn the guilty, 2. it shall be if the guilty one is sentenced to be flogged then the judge shall make him lie down and he shall be flogged before him, according to the measure of his guilt by his judgment. 3. Forty (lashes) shall he be struck *but with one less*[2] shall he be flogged; (the full number) shall not be completed *lest he flog him more than these thirty-nine (lashes),*[3] excessively, and he be in danger and your brother be despised while you see him. 4. You shall not muzzle *the mouth of*[4] an ox at the time of its threshing (grain). *On the other hand, a sister-in-law who is found pleasing in the presence of someone affected by scabs but who is not suitable for him, you shall not muzzle her for him.* 5. When brothers *from the (same) father*[5] sojourn[6] *in this world at the same time and claim (the same) inheritance,* the wife of the dead one shall not be free in the street for a strange man. Her brother-in-law shall go to her and take her as his wife and act the levirate toward her. 6. And the firstborn to whom she gives birth shall take the place *in the inheritance*[7] in the name of the dead brother; so his name shall not be blotted out from Israel. 7. But if the man does not want[8] to marry his sister-in-law, then his sister-in-law shall go up to the gate[9] *of the court* before *five wise men of whom three shall be*

Notes, Chapter 24 (Cont.)

[36]HT "to beat" *(ḥbṭ):* also Onq.; here *šbt* and Nf "beat" (*šmṭ*).

[37]HT "go over the boughs again" *(p'r):* here *bqr,* Onq. "do not bother with what is (left)" *ply* "search/go over" (Jastrow 1181) and Nf "not eat the gleanings" *('kl 'wllwt);* Nfmg *bqr* and Frg. Tg.(V) and Frg. Tg.(N) itp *bqr.*

[38]MS omits due to homoioteleuton on "widow," but the scribe notes the Hebrew lemma in the margin.

Notes, Chapter 25

[1]HT "men," also Onq. and Nf, but Nfmg as here.

[2]See *m.Mak.* 3.10; *b.Mak.* 22b.

[3]See 2 Cor 11:24.

[4]Onq. as here for clarification.

[5]See *Sifre Deut.* 279, "considered the same as brothers of the same father"; *b.Yeb.* 17b argues that fathers, not mothers, establish the relationships of brotherhood.

[6]HT, Onq., and Nf add "and one of them dies, and leaves not a son," which MS omits.

[7]Onq. and Nf read only "to the name," but Ps.-J. combines both readings in contrast to *b.Yeb.* 24a, which understands the "inheritance" rather than the name; see Grossfeld, *The Aramaic Bible* 9, 73 n. 5.

[8]Aramaic *sby;* also Onq., but Nf itp *r'y;* see *m.Yeb.* 12.4, where it says that a man may refuse.

[9]HT "gate" in Tgs. is understood as the court; see Grossfeld, *The Aramaic Bible* 9, 64 n. 13.

judges and two shall be witnesses,[10] and she shall say *before them in language of the sanctuary:*[11] "My brother-in-law refuses to cause his brother's name to stand in Israel. He refuses to act the levirate with me." 8. So the wise men[12] of the city shall call him and speak *good advice*[13] with him and he shall arise *in the court* and say *in the language of the sanctuary*: "I do not choose[14] to marry[15] (her)." 9. Then his sister-in-law shall approach him before the wise men. *There would be a shoe on the brother-in-law's right foot, a heeled sandal*[16] *that ties with laces and in the opening of the sandal the laces were tied; and he would have placed his foot on the ground.* The woman shall arise *and untie*[17] *the laces* and remove his sandal from his foot. Then she shall spit before him[18] *so much spittle to be seen by the wise men.*[19] She shall answer and say:[20] "So it is fit to be done to the man who will not rebuild his brother's house." 10. *Then all who are standing there shall announce to him and* shall call his name in Israel "The Pulled-Off Sandal."[21] 11. If some men, *a man and his friend,* are fighting together, the wife of one of them shall approach to save her husband from the hand of his attacker and shall put out her hand and seize his genitals,[22] 12. then you shall cut off her hand,[23] just to the wrist; your eyes shall not show pity. 13. You shall not have *fraudulent* weights in your case, greater *weights with which to buy* and smaller *weights with which to sell.*[24] 14. You shall not have in your houses greater *measures*[25] *with which to buy* and smaller *measures*[25] *with which to sell.* 15. You shall have exact weights[26] and true balances, perfect measures[25] and true scales shall you have in order that your days may be increased upon the land that the Lord your God is giving you. 16. For everyone who commits these frauds, *everyone who acts falsely in business* is an abomination before the Lord your God. 17. Remember what *those of the house of* Amalek did to you on the way during your Exodus from Egypt:[27] 18. that they harmed you on the way *and everyone who thought to stray from my Memra* was slain among you: *The men of the tribe*

Notes, Chapter 25

[10]See *b.Yeb.* 101a.

[11]That is, in Hebrew; Nfmg gives the statement in Hebrew; see v. 8 below and *m.Yeb.* 12.6.

[12]HT and Onq. "elders," but here and Nf "wise men."

[13]See *Sifre Deut.* 282, "provided that she is suitable for him," i.e., he is not a child and she is not an elderly woman; *b.Yeb.* 44a.

[14]Aramaic *rʿynʾ;* Onq. and Nf also *rʿy.*

[15]HT *lqḥ,* but *nsb* in Tgs.

[16]Aramaic *sndlʾ dlyh ʿqybʾ,* that is, a shoe with a heel; Onq. *synyh* from *synʾ* (Jastrow 982), and Nf only *sndlʾ;* see *b.Yeb.* 103a.

[17]Aramaic *šry* as also Onq., but Nf *šlp;* see John 1:27 for the same idiom; see *b.Yeb.* 102a.

[18]HT "in his face": see Grossfeld, *The Aramaic Bible* 9, 75 n. 7 for rabbinic citations.

[19]See *Sifre Deut.* 282, "her spittle must be visible to the elders," *m.Yeb.* 12.6 and *b.Yeb.* 101a.

[20]In "the holy tongue," that is, Hebrew; see *Sifre Deut.* 283, "in the holy language"; *m.Sot.* 7.2.

[21]*Editio princeps,* Onq., and Nf add "house of" *(by);* see *Sifre Deut.* 283, where "R. Judah said 'It is a commandment for all that are standing there to say "him that had his shoe loosed."'"

[22]Literally "place of his shame"; Aramaic *bbyt bhttyh* in all the Tgs.

[23]See Deut 19:21 (Ps.-J.) "value of a hand for a hand" *(dmy ydʾ ḥwlp ydʾ)* and *Sifre Deut.* 284, "'save her' by cutting off her hand."

[24]Aramaic *zbn;* Nfmg and Frg. Tgs.(PV) agree with Ps.-J., whereas Nf has "for giving" *(yhb);* see also v. 14 for the same vocabulary distribution.

[25]HT "ephah": Tgs. *mk(y)ln.*

[26]HT "stone": Tgs. *mtglyn šlmyn.*

[27]See *Sifre Deut.* 286, based on Exod 25:17, "'as you came forth out of Egypt'—at the time of your redemption."

of the house of Dan[28] *in whose hand was strange worship. The clouds rejected them, and those of the house of Amalek entrapped them and mutilated their genitals which they cast up on high.*[29] *Then you, House of Israel, were wronged and weary from great enslavement by the Egyptians and from the fear of the sea waves that you crossed in their midst, but the house of Amalek was not afraid before the Lord.*[30] 19. And it shall be when the Lord your God gives you rest from all your enemies around you, in the land that the Lord your God is giving you as an inheritance to possess, you shall wipe out the memory of Amalek from under the heavens: *even to the days of the King Messiah* you shall not forget.[31]

CHAPTER 26

1. When you enter the land that the Lord your God is giving you as an inheritance, you shall possess it and live in it, 2. then you shall take from your first fruits[1] *that are ripening in the first place,* of all the fruit of the land[2] that the Lord your God is giving you; and you shall put them in a basket[3] and you shall go to the place[4] where the Lord your God shall choose to make *his Shekinah*[5] dwell. 3. *And you shall decorate*[6] *(the first fruit) in the baskets, hampers, and the paper cases*[7] and you shall go up to the priest *who will have been appointed as chief priest,* in those days, and you shall say to him: "We acknowledge on this day before the Lord your God that we have come into the land that the Lord promised to our fathers to give us." 4. Then the priest shall take the basket *of first fruits* from your hand *and shall take and bring and raise and lower (it) and afterwards* set it down before the altar of the Lord your God. 5. So you shall answer and say before the Lord your God: "Our father Jacob[8] *descended to Aram Naharaim at the beginning and (Laban) sought to destroy him but the Memra of the Lord saved him from his hands.* Afterwards, he went down to Egypt and he sojourned there with a small[9] number of

Notes, Chapter 25 (Cont.)

[28]See Exod 17:8 (Ps.-J.); Maher,: *The Aramaic Bible* 2, 210 n. 9; and Le Déaut II, 142 n. 7.
[29]See *Num. R.* 507.
[30]See Exod 17:13 (Ps.-J.); Ginzberg, *Legends* 3.60, 67.
[31]See Exod 17:16 (Ps.-J.); Maher, *The Aramaic Bible* 2, 211 n. 25; and *Mekilta* on Exod 17:16 (II, 160–161).

Notes, Chapter 26

[1]See *m.Bik.* 3.1.
[2]HT "that you harvest from your land," also Onq. and Nf but missing in both the MS and *editio princeps* of Ps.-J.
[3]HT "basket" *(ṭnʾ):* all Tgs. *slʾ;* see *y.Bik.* 81.7, v. 4 below, and Deut 28:15, 17.
[4]MS *ʾrʿʾ* "land," but better to read with HT, Onq., and Nf *ʾtr.*
[5]HT "his name": Onq. as here; Nf "the Glory of his *Shekinah.*"
[6]See *m.Bik.* 3.9.
[7]MS *pypyyryʾ* "papyrus"; "decorative frame" (Jastrow 1168). See Etheridge (1968) 634 for this translation.
[8]HT "A wandering Aramean was my father" (RSV) has been interpreted in many different ways. Also the identification of "my father" has had a variety of interpretations. Onq. and Nf identify it as "Laban, the Aramean," and here in Ps.-J. as "Jacob" (as in Rashi, Ibn Ezra); see *Sifre Deut.* 290, "this shows that our father Jacob . . ." and Gen 31:20 "Laban, the Aramean"; see Grossfeld, *The Aramaic Bible* 9, 75 n. 3 for a discussion of the rabbinic evidence.
[9]Aramaic *qlyl,* but Onq. and Nf *zʿyr.*

people. But there he became a great nation, strong and many. 6. And the Egyptians insulted us and afflicted us and put upon us heavy labor. 7. So we prayed before the Lord, the God of our fathers, and the Lord heard[10] our prayer;[11] and our affliction, our labor, and our oppression were revealed before him. 8. Then the Lord brought us out of Egypt by a strong hand and with an upraised arm, *in a great vision,*[12] with signs and wonders. 9. And he brought us to this place and gave us this land, a land *whose fruits are as rich*[13] *as* milk and *as sweet*[14] *as* honey. 10. And, now, behold, I have brought the first of the fruits of the ground which you have given me, O Lord." You shall place it before the Lord your God and you shall worship before the Lord your God. 11. Then you shall rejoice in all the good that the Lord your God shall have given you, as well as *the men of*[15] your house. *You shall enjoy and eat,* you and the Levites and the aliens among you. 12. When you have finished setting aside a tenth of all the tithes of your harvest, in the third year *of the year of release,*[16] *then you shall give the first tithe* to the Levites, *the second tithe, that is the tithe of the poor,*[17] to the alien, to the orphan, and to the widow, and they shall eat in your cities and be satisfied; 13. *but the third tithe*[18] *you shall bring up and eat* before the Lord your God and you shall say: "Behold we have separated from the house the holy things, especially we have given *the first tithe* to the Levites, *the second tithe* to the alien, to the orphan, and to the widow according to all your commandments that you have prescribed for me. I have not transgressed any one of your commandments nor have I forgotten (any). 14. I have not eaten any of it (the tithe) during the days of my mourning, nor levied any of it while being unclean,[19] nor have I given any of it *as a shroud for a dead body. We*[20] *have* listened to the voice of *the Memra of* the Lord, my God;[21] I have done everything that you have prescribed for me. 15. From the dwelling *of the house of your holy Shekinah,*[22] from the high heavens, examine and bless your people, Israel, as well as the land that you have given us just as you promised our fathers: a land *whose fruits are as rich as* milk and *as sweet as* honey." 16. Today the Lord your God is commanding you to do these statutes and judgments. You shall do them carefully with all your heart and with all your soul. 17. You have selected[23] the Lord, on this day, *as your unique choice*[24] *in the world, for so it is written: "Hear, Israel, the Lord your God,*

Notes, Chapter 26

[10]HT "heard": Onq. and here *qbl,* but Nf *šmʿ,* but v. 14 below HT "hear" is *qbl* in Onq. but in Ps.-J. and Nf *šmʿ.*

[11]Here and Onq., but Nf "the voice of our prayer" and Nfmg "and the *Memra* of the Lord heard the voice of our prayer"; see Maher, *The Aramaic Bible* 1B, 104 n. 7 for other instances.

[12]HT "great terror" (RSV), *mrʾ gdl:* all Tgs. *bḥzwnʾ rbʾ.*

[13]Aramaic here *šmynyn,* but Nf *nqyyn* "clear"; see comments in the Introduction.

[14]Aramaic here *ḥlyyn,* but Nf *tʿymyn;* see comments in the Introduction.

[15]The additional phrase is found in all Tgs.

[16]HT and Onq. read "which is the year of the tithe"; here *šmyṭytʾ;* Nf "which is the year of tithing for the poor"; Frg. Tgs.(PV) add "which is the year of the poor *(mskynyyʾ)* tithes."

[17]See *Sifre Deut.* 292, "poor man's tithe."

[18]Rieder "the second tithe"; see Deut 14:23 (Ps.-J. and Nf).

[19]See *Sifre Deut.* 293, "when I was unclean . . ." and *b.Yeb.* 74a.

[20]HT and Onq. "I," but Nf as here.

[21]Omitted in *editio princeps.*

[22]Onq. "your sacred dwelling place" *(mdwr qwdšk);* Nf "the dwelling place *(mdwr)* of the Glory of your *Shekinah.*"

[23]HT "you have declared" (hip *ʾmr*): Onq. and here *ḥṭb* "select" and Nf "the *Memra* of the Lord has made you king"; see v. 10 above and Grossfeld, *The Aramaic Bible* 9, 77 n. 10 for rabbinic citations.

[24]Aramaic *ḥṭybʾ ḥdʾ.*

the Lord is one" in order to be your God and to go in the ways *that are established before him* and to keep his statutes and his commandments and his judgments and to heed *his Memra.*[25] 18. And *the Memra of* the Lord selected[26] you, on this day, as a unique choice[27] *in the world, as it is written: "Who is as your nation Israel, a unique nation on earth?*[28] *in order to be his beloved nation* just as he spoke to you that you keep all his commandments, 19. to appoint you high and exalted above all the nations *in greatness* with a glorious name and in splendor, in order to be a holy nation before the Lord your God, just as he spoke."[29]

CHAPTER 27

1. Then Moses and the elders of Israel commanded the people saying: "Observe all the commandments that I am prescribing for you today. 2. And it shall be on the day that you cross over the Jordan to the land that the Lord your God is giving you, you shall erect for yourselves great stones and shall plaster them with lime, 3. then you shall write on them the words[1] of this Law, when you cross over, in order that you may enter the land that the Lord your God is giving you: a land *whose fruits are as rich as* milk *and producing*[2] honey just as the Lord, the God of your fathers spoke to you. 4. And it shall be at the time when you cross over the Jordan you shall erect, at Mount Ebal, these stones that I am prescribing for you and you shall plaster them with lime. 5. Then you shall build there an altar before the Lord your God, an altar of stone upon which you shall not wield iron (tools). 6. You shall build the altar of the Lord your God with perfect[3] stones; then you shall offer upon it burnt offerings before the Lord your God. 7. And you shall sacrifice sacrifices of holy things and shall eat there and rejoice before the Lord your God. 8. So you shall write on the stones all the words of this Law, *a writing engraved and distinct,*[4] *read in one language and translated into seventy languages.*"[5] 9. Then Moses and

Notes, Chapter 26 (Cont.)

[25]HT "his voice": Onq. as here, but Nf "the voice of his *Memra*"; see also Exod 19:13-16; 29:45. As in Exodus, here Israel has chosen the *Memra* of the Lord God as king and redeemer; see also Urbach (1975) 529 for a comment on Deut 26:13-18.

[26]Aramaic *ḥṭb;* see n. 23 above on v. 17.

[27]Aramaic *ḥṭybh ḥd';* see n. 24 above on v. 17.

[28]See 1 Chron 17:22 "a unique and chosen people on earth"; Maher, *The Aramaic Bible* 1B, 29 n. 49, where HT *'ḥd* "one" is interpreted as "unique."

[29]HT *dbr* "spoke": in the Tgs. *mll* literally "to speak," but Grossfeld, *The Aramaic Bible* 9, 76 translates as "promised" and McNamara for Neofiti *"declared."*

Notes, Chapter 27

[1]HT, Onq., and Nf "all the words"; see v. 8.

[2]MS Aramaic *'bdyn,* but normally the stylized phrase is "milk as sweet as"; see Deut 6:3; 11:9; 26:9, 15 (Ps.-J.), but Deut 31:20 (Ps.-J.) "producing milk and honey" as in Exod 3:8, 17; 13:5; 33:3; Lev 20:24; Num 13:27; 16:13, 14.

[3]HT "unhewn" (RSV), *šlmt:* Onq. and here as HT, but Nf adds "and precious" *('bnyn ṭbyn šlmn);* see n. 20 on Deut 13:18 above.

[4]Aramaic *prš* as Onq. and Nf; see McNamara's note on this verse in *The Aramaic Bible* 5A, 124 nn. 9–10.

[5]According to the number of nations in Genesis 10; see also Gen 11:7-8 (Ps.-J.) and Maher, *The Aramaic Bible* 1B, 50 nn. 12–14; Deut 32:8 (Ps.-J.); see also *m.Sot.* 7.5; *b.Sot.* 32a, and Ginzberg, *Legends* 5.194.

the priests, sons of Levi, spoke with all the people, saying: "Listen and hear, Israel. Today you have been chosen to become a nation before the Lord your God. 10. And you shall heed[6] *the Memra of*[7] the Lord your God; you shall do the commandments and statutes that I am prescribing for you today." 11. So Moses on that day commanded the people saying: 12. "These *tribes*[8] shall stand on Mount Gerizim to bless the people at their crossing over the Jordan: Simeon, Levi, Judah, Issachar, Joseph, and Benjamin. 13. And these *tribes*[9] shall stand on Mount Ebal (to administer) the curses: Reuben, Gad, Asher, Zebulon, Dan, and Naphthali." 14. Then the Levites shall call out in a loud voice and say to all the men of Israel: 15.[10] *"Six tribes*[11] *stood on Mount Gerizim and six on Mount Ebal while the ark, priests, and the Levites (were) in the middle." Those who were blessing were turning their faces toward Mount Gerizim and saying: "Blessed be the man who will not make an image, or a form, or any likeness that is an abomination before the Lord, the work of an artisan's hands and who will not put it in a hidden place." Those who were cursing were turning their faces towards Mount Ebal and saying:* "Cursed be the man who will make an image, *or a form, or any likeness that is* an abomination before the Lord, the work of an artisan's hands and who puts it in a hidden place." All of them *were answering as one and* saying: "Amen. 16. Cursed be he who disregards the honor of his father or his mother!" All of them *were answering as one and* saying: "Amen. 17. Cursed be he who changes[12] his friend's border!" All of them *were answering as one and* saying: "Amen. 18. Cursed be he who misdirects the stranger[13] on the way, who is like a blind man!"[14] All of them *were answering as one and* saying: "Amen. 19. Cursed be he who perverts the right of the sojourner, the orphan, and the widow!" All of them *were answering as one and* saying: "Amen. 20. Cursed be he who has sexual relations with his father's wife for he uncovers the skirt that his father has uncovered!" All of them *were answering as one and* saying: "Amen. 21. Cursed be he who has sexual relations with any animal!" All of them *were answering as one and* saying "Amen. 22. Cursed be he who has sexual relations with his sister, his father's daughter or his mother's daughter!" All of them *were answering as one and* saying: "Amen. 23. Cursed be he who has sexual relations with his mother-in-law!" All of them *were answering as one and* saying: "Amen. 24. Cursed be he who wounds his neighbor in secret with calumny!"[15] All of them *were answering as one and* saying: "Amen. 25. Cursed be he who accepts a bribe to slay a man, shedding innocent blood!" All of them *were answering as one and* saying: "Amen." 26. *The twelve tribes, one by one, were saying the blessings in*

Notes, Chapter 27

[6]Aramaic *qbl* here and Onq., but Nf *šmʿ*, which is the usual vocabulary distribution in the Tgs. for HT "hear."

[7]HT "the voice"; Onq. as here, but Nf "the voice of the *Memra*."

[8]Omitted in HT, Onq., and Nf.

[9]See preceding note.

[10]Deut 27:15-26, by rabbinic tradition, is to be recited in Hebrew only; see Alexander (1976) 186, 188, and *m.Sot.* 7.2.

[11]See *m.Sot.* 7.5.

[12]HT "removes" (RSV): Onq. and here *šny,* but Nf *ʾrʿ* "attack," and the LXX "remove."

[13]Aramaic *ʾksnyʾ* (Greek *zēnos,* "hired soldier," Jastrow 64) only here in Ps.-J., but also in Nfmg Lev 19:14. Onq. and Nf as HT.

[14]Onq. and Nf add "on the road."

[15]Literally "triple tongued" *(lyšn tlytʾy)* as in Nfmg; see Gen 1:16; 49:23 (Ps.-J. and Nf); Lev 9:2, 3; 19:16 (Ps.-J. and Nf) suggesting the one who speaks (the slander), the one who hears (the calumny), and the one who is the victim; see Le Déaut I, 78 n. 12, and Maher, *The Aramaic Bible* 1B, 18 n. 29 "a slanderous tongue"; see *b.Sot.* 37a.

their entirety and the curses in their entirety. Those who were blessing were turning their faces for every single word (of the formula) toward Mount Gerizim and saying: "Blessed be the man who shall keep the words of this Law by performing them;" those who were cursing were turning their faces toward Mount Ebal and saying: "Cursed be the man who does not keep the words of this Law by performing them." All of them *were answering as one and* saying: "Amen." *These words were spoken at Sinai and repeated in the Tent of Meeting and pronounced a third time in the plains of Moab: twelve words from the words of every tribe and, concerning each single commandment, thirty-six statutes*[16] *were decreed upon it.*

CHAPTER 28

1. And it shall be that if you surely obey[1] *the Memra*[2] *of* the Lord your God to do carefully all his commandments that I am prescribing for you today then the Lord your God will set you up high and exalt you over all the nations of the earth. 2. And he will put upon you all these blessings and they will adhere to you when you obey *the Memra of* the Lord your God. 3. Blessed shall you be in the city and blessed shall you be in the field. 4. Blessed shall be *the children*[3] *of your womb* and the fruits of your land, the herds of your oxen and *the flocks of* your sheep. 5. Blessed[4] shall be the baskets *of your first fruits and the first loaves of* your kneading troughs. 6. Blessed shall you be when you enter *your schools*[5] and blessed shall you be when you depart *from your businesses.*[6] 7. *The Memra*[7] *of* the Lord will cause your enemies, who arise against you *to do evil,* to be broken[8] before you; they shall come out against you *to fight* by a single road, but by seven roads *shall they go astray,*[9] fleeing from before you.[10] 8. The Lord will assign for you a blessing, on your treasuries and on all the effort of your hands; he will bless you in the land that the Lord your God is giving you. 9. *The Memra of* the Lord will establish you before him as a holy nation, just as he promised you if you keep the Lord

Notes, Chapter 27 (Cont.)

[16]Aramaic *qyymyn:* each commandment was sanctioned on three occasions by each tribe, hence "thirty-six".

Notes, Chapter 28

[1]Aramaic *qbl* here and Onq., but Nf *šmʿ*.

[2]Also Onq. and Nf; see also vv. 2, 15, 45, 62 in Onq. and Nf where the same phraseology is used. In other places in the chapter Onq. and Nf have only "Lord."

[3]HT *pry btn:* Onq. *wldʾ dmʿk* (singular), here *wwldy mʿkwn;* also in vv. 11, 18, 53; Nf "my people, children of Israel."

[4]Aramaic *bryk:* Onq. and here singular; Onq. consistently singular as HT but Ps.-J. and Nf usually plural; see McNamara's note on this phrase in *The Aramaic Bible* 5a, 126 n. 4; see n. 24 below for number distribution of *lwṭ*.

[5]See Maher, *The Aramaic Bible* 1B, 81 n. 34 for a discussion of places where "school" appears in Tgs.

[6]HT "when you come in . . . when you go out": Aramaic *prgmṭyykwn;* see n. 12 on Deut 24:7 above, and nn. 27–28 on v. 19 below as well as *tyʾṭrwn (thēatron),* "theater," and *qwrqst (circus),* "circus"; see *Deut. R.* 136 and Le Déaut IV, 224 n. 18.

[7]Nfmg as here, but Onq. and Nf omit; see n. 2 above on v. 1.

[8]Aramaic *tbr;* Nf *tbr qdl,* "broken necks."

[9]Aramaic *ṭʿy;* omitted in Onq. and Nf but found in Nfmg

[10]Aramaic *ʿrqyn* omitted in Onq. and Nf, but Nfmg "they shall go astray" *(ʿrq);* see the same distribution in v. 25 below.

your God's commandments, and walk in the paths *that are proper*[11] *before him.* 10. Then all the nations of the earth shall see that the Lord's name *is inscribed already on the tefillim that is (you carry) on you*[12] and they will be afraid of you. 11. So *the Memra of* the Lord will spare you for good in *(that which concerns) the children of your womb,* and the offspring of your animals, and the fruit of your ground, on the land that the Lord promised to your fathers.[13] 12.[14] *There are four keys in the hands of the Master of the universe and that are not handed over into the hand of any dignitary:*[15] *the key of life, of graves, of food, and of rain. And so Moses, the prophet, said:* "Thus will the Lord open for you his good treasures *that are with him in* the heavens to give in its time the rain on your land, *the early (rain) in Marheshwan and the later (rains) in Nisan,*[16] to bless all the works of your hands. Then you shall lend to many nations but you will not need to borrow. 13. Then *the Memra of* the Lord will appoint you *as kings but not as commoners*[17] and so you shall be *exalted* but shall not be *rejected,* if you obey the Lord your God's commandments that I am prescribing for you today to do carefully, 14. and if you will not deviate to the right or to the left from any of the words that I am prescribing for you today by going after *the idols of the nations,*[18] worshiping them." 15. *When Moses,*[19] *the prophet, began to say these following words of reproof, the land was shaken, the heavens trembled, the sun and the moon darkened, and the stars suppressed their light. The patriarchs*[20] *shouted from their graves, while all the creatures were silent, and the trees did not move their branches. The patriarchs answered and said: "Woe to our children when they sin and bring these curses upon them! How will they be able to endure them? Perhaps destruction shall work against them, and our merit will not be a protection for them and (perhaps) no man shall arise who will pray on their behalf?" A celestial voice*[21] *fell from the heavens on high*[22] *and said thus: "Do not fear, patriarchs, for even if the merit of all the generations shall cease, your*[23] *merit shall not cease and the covenant that I established with you shall not be annulled, but it*

Notes, Chapter 28

[11]Aramaic *tqn*.

[12]MS and *editio princeps hqyq mzmn btpylyn dʿlk*. Ginsburger reads *ʿlk* instead of *dʿlk*.

[13]HT adds "to give you," as also Onq. and Nf.

[14]The following midrash is found in Nf, Nfmg, Frg. Tgs.(PV) at Gen 30:22 (Ps.-J.); see Maher, *The Aramaic Bible* 1B, 106 n. 23, and Sysling (1991) 137, 144, 152–153, 259, 264 for a full discussion of the midrash; see *Gen. R.* 670 and *Deut. R.* 137.

[15]Aramaic *ṭypsrʾ;* Akkadian *ṭupšarru* "high official" (Dalman 174; Kaufman [1974] 138 n. 6, and Köhler-Baumgartner [1974] 362 for HT references in Jer 51:27 and Nah 3:17); "divine key-keeper" (Jastrow 548); in Gen 30:22 Nf reads "to angel of Seraph."

[16]See Deut 11:14 (Ps.-J.).

[17]Aramaic *hdywṭ:* HT "make you the head, and not the tail"; Onq. "top . . . bottom," but Nf as here; see vv. 43 and 44 below.

[18]Aramaic *tysṭwn tʿwwt ʿmmyʾ* as Onq. and Nf; see Clarke (1984) 407 *(sṭy)*. Onq. and Nf agree with Ps.-J. in the translation of HT *swr*. The phrase "idols of the nations" is the usual translation in Ps.-J. for HT "other gods."

[19]See Marmorstein (1905) 153: "We see that the Targumist held the view that the merits of the fathers operate for the benefit of the children forever," and Le Déaut (1970) 54.

[20]Literally "the fathers of the world."

[21]Aramaic *brt qlʾ* (Bath Qol).

[22]A phrase found often in Ps.-J. as noted by Maher, *The Aramaic Bible* 1B, 51 n. 19.

[23]MS reads incorrectly "their." The idea that the merits of the patriarchs and/or the covenant will save them finds echoes both in Deut 1:1 (Ps.-J.) for the idea of merits and in the HT (Exod 2:24; 6:5; Lev 26:42; Deut 4:31) for the idea of covenant.

shall protect them." Moses, the prophet, answered and said: "Even though I rebuke them, it is only a conditional rebuke, saying: That if you do not obey *the Memra of* the Lord your God in not doing carefully all the commandments and statutes that I am prescribing for you today, then all of these curses shall come upon you and shall overtake you. 16. Cursed[24] shall you be in the city and cursed shall you be[25] in the field. 17. Cursed[24] shall be the baskets *of your first fruits and the first loaves of* your kneading troughs. 18. Cursed[24] shall be *the children of your* womb and the fruits of *your* land, *the herds of your* oxen and *the flocks of your* sheep. 19. Cursed[24] shall you be when you enter *your theaters and your circuses,*[26] *negating the words of the Law,* and cursed shall you be when you depart *for your businesses.*[27] 20. *The Memra of* the Lord will send curses against you to curse *your wealth* and confusion *to disturb your peace* and wrath *against all undertakings* in which you engage until you are destroyed and until you perish quickly because of the evilness of your deeds for having abandoned *my Fear.*[28] 21. *The Memra of* the Lord will cause the plague[29] to take hold of you until it will destroy you from upon the land you are entering to possess. 22. *The Memra of* the Lord will smite you with consumption, with fever, with sickness *of the bones that burns the marrow,* with imaginings *of fear, pain of the heart,* with ruffians, with mildew, and with the blight *of Macedonia* that will pursue you *on your couches* until you perish. 23.[30] The heavens that are above you shall be as bronze *that oozes but does not give sufficient dew or rain* for you, and the earth that is under you shall be like iron *that does not ooze because it cannot provide moisture*[31] *for the trees, and the herbs*[32] *and fine fruits and vegetables.*[33] 24. So the Lord will send, after the rains that come down on your land, *a wind that offers*[34] dust and ashes *upon the grasses of your fields;* from the heavens *punishment* will descend upon you until you shall be destroyed. 25. *The Memra of* the Lord will shatter[35] you before your enemies; by one road shall you come out before them *to fight* but by seven roads *shall you go astray,* decamping before them and you shall be an abomination[36] to all the kingdoms of the earth. 26. So your dead bodies shall be thrown[37] as food for all the birds of the heavens and for the animals of the earth and there shall be no one to chase them *from your dead bodies*. 27. *The Memra of* the Lord will smite you with boils *by*

Notes, Chapter 28

[24]Aramaic *lwṭ;* there is oscillation between singular and plural in vv. 16-19.

[25]Nf adds *bmh d'yt lkwn* "what you have," which is not found in Onq. or here; vv. 16-19 are expanded with the same phrase in Nf.

[26]Aramaic *ty'ṭrwn* and *qwrqst;* see n. 6 on v. 6.

[27]See n. 6 on v. 6 above.

[28]Aramaic *dḥlty* here and Onq., but Nf "the teaching of my Law," and Nfmg "it."

[29]Aramaic *mwt';* Nf *mwtn';* see Sysling (1991) 216 n. 29.

[30]For the imagery of this verse see Grossfeld, *The Aramaic Bible* 8, 63 n. 17 on Lev 26:19 (Onq.).

[31]Aramaic *mrṭb',* from the root *rṭb* "to drip moisture" (Jastrow 1470).

[32]Aramaic *'ysprmqy* "smelling herbs" (Jastrow 97).

[33]For the imagery of this verse, see Lev 26:19 (Onq., Ps.-J., and Nf), Maher, *The Aramaic Bible* 3, 206 n. 43, and Deut 11:17 (Nf).

[34]*B.Ta'an.* 3b.

[35]Aramaic *tbr;* see Grossfeld, *The Aramaic Bible* 8, 63 n. 16 on *tbr* and Lev 26:17 (Onq.); see also v. 7 above.

[36]Aramaic *ryḥwq,* from *rḥq* "to reject/be an abomination" (Jastrow 1469); here and Nf, but Onq. *zy'* "horror," and Nfmg *lwṭ* "curse."

[37]Aramaic *šqr* here and Onq., but Nf omits the verb and has only *mzwn* "food."

which the Egyptians were affected, and with hemorrhoids[38] *that blind the sight,*[39] and with an itch *and with scabs*[40] from which you will be unable to be healed. 28. *The Memra of* the Lord will smite you with madness[41] *that makes the mind dull* and with blindness and stupefaction[42] of the heart. 29. *Then you will specify good advice for the relief of your anguish, but there will be no one among you to show the truth,* just as the blind goes gropingly in darkness, *for there are no passersby on the way to show (them) their direction on the way.*[43] So you shall not be successful in your way but shall be oppressed and restrained every day and there will be no one who can rescue (you). 30. You will become engaged to a woman, but another man will have sexual relations with her; you will build a house, but will not live in it; you will plant a vineyard, but will not benefit from it. 31. Your oxen will be sacrificed and you will see (it) and you will not eat any of it; your donkeys will be robbed before you and will not return to you; your sheep will be handed over to your enemies and no one will rescue (you). 32. Your sons and your daughters will be handed over to *a strange* nation and your eyes will see and grow dark because of them every day; but in your hands *there will be no good works that will strengthen your hands in prayer before your Father,*[44] *who is in Heaven*[45] who can rescue you. 33. The fruit of your land and of all your labor, a nation whom you do not know will destroy (it), so you will be continually oppressed and trodden. 34. But you will become demented[46] *from the punishment* and from the sights of your eyes that you will see *you will be shaken.* 35. *The Memra of* the Lord will destroy you *with severe boils* on the knees, *because you knelt to a matter of transgression,* and upon your thighs, *that (were used to) run to it. If you do not return to the Law* you will be unable to be healed, *but you will be affected by it* from the soles of your feet to the top of your heads. 36. The Lord will exile[47] you as well as your king whom you have appointed over you, in a nation that neither you nor your fathers have known, *and you will bring chests*[48] to the worshipers of idols of wood and stone. 37. *And if your heart will plan to worship their idols* you will become *idiots,*[49] bywords and jests,[50] among[51] the nations among whom the Lord will scatter you. 38. You shall take out much seed to the field but little will you gather, for the locusts will nibble it. 39. You shall plant and cultivate vineyards but wine you shall not drink *nor shall you press to put in reserve* for worms will destroy it. 40.

Notes, Chapter 28

[38]Aramaic *ṭhwry'* here, Onq., and Nf, which translates the HT Qere.

[39]This phrase *(msmyyn ḥzwt'),* which is additional in Ps.-J., is interpreting the HT as *'pl* "to obscure/make dark"; see Le Déaut IV, 227 n. 28 for additional comments.

[40]Aramaic *ḥykwk';* Onq. and Nf *ḥrs.*

[41]HT "madness" *(šg'wn):* Onq. and Nf *ṭpšwt',* but here *šwwyywt',* but in Deut 10:16 Ps.-J. has *ṭpšwt'.*

[42]Aramaic *šy'mmwt.*

[43]A reference to *b.Meg.* 24b "people to direct (the blind) on the way."

[44]Ginsburger "before the Lord, your Father"; Nf "and God will be on hand to redeem you."

[45]See Sysling (1991) 175.

[46]Rather than a root *šwy,* which seems inappropriate here, follow Onq. *šṭy* "to become demented"; Nf follows the HT *šg'.*

[47]HT "bring you," but the Tgs. interpret as "exile" *(gly).*

[48]Aramaic *'rwnyn* "chests," in which were placed various tithes for the gods; see v. 64 below.

[49]Aramaic *šy'mwm;* Onq. and Nf *ṣdw.*

[50]Aramaic *tynwyyn;* also Nf, but Onq. *šw'y.*

[51]HT, Onq., and Nf "among all" *(bkl 'mmy')* instead of *byny 'mmy'* as here.

You shall have olives in all your territory but with oil shall you not anoint, for your olives shall fall off. 41. You shall give birth to sons and daughters but you shall have nothing from them, for they will go into captivity. 42. All your trees and the fruit of your land shall the locusts[52] destroy.[53] 43. *The uncircumcised who resides*[54] among you shall rise up over you, higher and higher, while you shall sink under him, lower and lower.[55] 44. He will lend to you but you will not lend to them;[56] he will be the ruler while you will be *the commoners*.[57] 45. So all these curses will come upon you and will pursue you and adhere to you until you are destroyed, because you have not obeyed *the Memra of* the Lord your God to keep his commandments and his statutes that he prescribed for you. 46. They will be as signs and wonders *against* you and your children forever. 47. Because you did not worship before the Lord your God with joy and with the cheerfulness[58] of your heart for an abundance of all good, 48. you will serve your enemies whom *the Memra of* the Lord will send against you in hunger, in thirst, in nakedness, and in lacking all good. They will put iron yokes on your necks until the time when one has destroyed you. 49. *The Memra of* the Lord your God will cause a nation (to come) from afar, from the ends of the earth, swiftly as an eagle flies, a nation whose language you shall not know,[59] 50. a nation arrogant in appearance who does not have any regard for the old or protection for the young. 51. So they will destroy[60] the offspring of your animals and the fruit of your land until you have been destroyed; because they will not leave for you either grain, oil, wine, calves of your herds, or the flocks of your sheep, until the time when they will have destroyed you. 52. And they will besiege you in all your cities until the time when your high and fortified gates[61] on which you are trusting to be saved[62] by them[63] shall fall throughout all your land. They will besiege you in all your cities,[64] in all your land that the Lord your God gave you. 53. The children of your womb *will be destroyed*,[65] because you will eat, *because of famine*, the flesh of your sons and your daughters, whom the Lord your God gave you, in pain and in trouble with which your enemies will oppress you. 54. The most tender and refined man among you will only look with an evil eye upon his brother, and upon the wife who sleeps on

Notes, Chapter 28

[52]HT "locusts" (*ṣlṣl*): Onq. *sq'h*, here *ḥlnwn'*; Nf *ḥlzwn'* and Nfmg *ḥylzwnh* (according to the correction by Díez Macho). The MS *ḥlwn'* Jastrow (471) and Dalman (149) read as *ḥlzwn'* as in Nf, but it is clearly *ḥlnwn'* in my edition as the correction in the notes for the Nfmg; see McNamara's note in *The Aramaic Bible* 5A, 132 n. 40 for a different interpretation of the vocabulary here.

[53]Aramaic here and Nf *šyṣy*, but Onq. *hsn* "take over."

[54]See Grossfeld, *The Aramaic Bible* 8, 59 n. 10 for a discussion of the sojourner as uncircumcised, and rabbinic citations.

[55]See v. 13 above.

[56]MS reads incorrectly *lkwn* "you."

[57]Aramaic *hdywṭ*: HT contrasts "head" and "tail"; Onq. contrasts "strong" and "weak"; here and Nf contrast "ruler" and "commoner" (*hdywṭ*); see n. 17 above.

[58]HT "gladness" (*ṭwb*) of heart": Onq. as here, but Nf as HT.

[59]HT "understand" (*šmʿ*): Tgs. also *šmʿ*.

[60]HT, Onq., and Nf "eat," but here the verb *gmr*; see v. 53 below for the same vocabulary distribution.

[61]HT, Onq., and Nf "walls," but here *'bwl'* "city gateway."

[62]Aramaic itp *šyzb* here and Onq., but Nf *rḥṣ* "trust."

[63]MS incorrectly *bkwn*.

[64]Aramaic *qyrwykwn*.

[65]See n. 60 above on v. 51 for the same vocabulary distribution.

his bosom[66] and upon the rest of his children who are left, 55. for not giving to one of them any of the flesh of his children which he will eat, because nothing remains for him, in the pain and trouble with which your enemies will oppress you, in all your cities.[67] 56. The most tender and refined woman among you, who did not raise the sole of her foot *to tread on* the earth, out of refinement and tenderness, will look with an evil eye upon the husband who sleeps on her bosom[68] and upon her daughter, 57. and upon the fetal afterbirth that comes out[69] *of her womb at the time of birth,* and upon her son to whom she will have given birth, because lacking everything she shall eat in need in hiding, in the pain and the trouble with which your enemies will oppress you, in your cities. 58. If you will not do carefully all the commandments of this Law that is written in this book: to fear this glorious and fearful Name, the Lord your God, 59. then *the Memra of* the Lord *will hide from you the holy spirit*[70] when the plagues *will come* upon you and plagues upon your children, many and strong plagues, *that will not leave you,* and evil and strong sufferings *that will remain long upon your bodies.* 60. He will bring back on you all the sufferings that he sent against the Egyptians[71] and they will adhere[72] to you. 61. As well every affliction and every plague that is not written in this book of the Law shall *the Memra of* the Lord bring up against you until you are destroyed. 62. So you shall only remain as a small nation[73] even though you have been as numerous as the stars of the heavens for you did not obey *the Memra of* the Lord your God. 63. And it shall be just as *the Memra of*[74] the Lord rejoiced over you doing good to you and multiplying you, so *the Memra of* the Lord will rejoice (in sending) foreign nations against you to cause you to perish and to destroy you; and you shall be uprooted from upon the land that you are entering to possess. 64. Then the Lord will scatter you among all the nations from one end of the earth to the other end *of the earth* and you *will be carriers of the chests*[75] *for worshipers of the idols* of wood and of stone that you had not known.[76] 65. *But if your opinion be divided worshiping their idols, then I will send enmity*[77] *between you and those nations;* and you shall not rest and there will be no resting place for the sole(s) of your feet. *The Memra of* the Lord will give you there a frightened heart, darkness of the eyes, and a despairing soul. 66. Then your life will be constantly suspended, and you will be afraid day and night, and you will not be sure of your (own) life. 67. In the morning you will be saying: 'Oh that it would be evening!' *Because troubles lengthen before your eyes the hours of the day.* And in the evening you will say 'Oh that it

Notes, Chapter 28

[66]Aramaic here *ʿwbyh:* HT "wife of his bosom"; Onq. "wife of his covenant," and Nf "wife of his bosom" *(ʾtt ḥwbh);* see note on Deut 13:7; 28:56.

[67]HT "gate."

[68]HT, Onq., and Nf add "upon her son"; see note on Deut 13:7, but omitted in MS.

[69]Onq. "the youngest of her children that emerges from her."

[70]Onq. and Nf "the Lord will make wonderful (ap *prš*). . . ."

[71]HT, Onq., and Nf add "which you were afraid of."

[72]Here *ʾdq,* not *dbq* "cling" as in Onq. and Nf.

[73]Aramaic *ʾwmʾ glyl;* Onq. *ʿm zʿyr,* and Nf "a people *(ʿm)* (few) in number."

[74]Onq. as HT "the Lord" and Nf "the voice of the Memra."

[75]See v. 36 above.

[76]HT, Onq., and Nf add "neither you nor your fathers."

[77]HT, Onq., and Nf "no ease" *(lʾ nwḥ),* but here *bbw* expresses in the MS (but omitted in *editio princeps*) the opposite to "no ease"; see Clarke (1984) 147 *(dbb)* for the other instances of *bbw* in Ps.-J.

would be morning!' for troubles lengthen before your eyes the hours of the night, because of the terrors of your heart, of which you shall be afraid, and because of the seeing of your eyes, *by which you see punishment and are afraid.* 68. *The Memra of* the Lord will exile[78] you to Egypt in ships[79] *through the Reed Sea, on the way that you have crossed and I said to you: 'You shall not see it any more.'* There you shall be sold *to your enemies for an expensive price as artisans, and after this for a cheap price* as slaves and maid servants *until you will be worthless for free labor,* but there is no one to gather[80] (you)." 69. These are the words of the covenant that the Lord prescribed for Moses to make with the children of Israel in the land of Moab in addition to the covenant that he made with them at Horeb.

CHAPTER 29

1. So Moses summoned[1] and said to them: "You saw all *the plagues*[2] that *the Memra of* the Lord did before your eyes in the land of Egypt, to Pharaoh, to all his servants as well as to *all the inhabitants of* his land, 2. great miracles[3] that you saw with your eyes, these great signs and wonders. 3. But *the Memra of* the Lord did not give you *a heart to forget but rather* to know, and eyes *to make signs but rather* to see, and ears *to close but rather* to listen. *However, you have forgotten the Law of your heart, you have made signs with your eyes and you have closed your ears to the time of this day.* 4. So I led you for forty years in the desert; your clothes did not become worn out[4] on your bodies and your sandals *were not taken off*[5] from your feet. 5. You did not eat bread *(made) from grain* and wine *and juice*[6] you did not drink; *so my Law took refuge*[7] *in your schools*[8] *so that you might occupy yourselves with it* (study) and know that I am the Lord your God. 6. Then you came to this place. Sihon, King of Heshbon, and Og, King of Mathnan,[9] came out before us to fight and we defeated[10] them. 7. And

Notes, Chapter 28 (Cont.)

[78]HT "return": Onq. ap *twb* "return"; Nf *ḥzr* "bring you back," but here *gly*.

[79]HT "ships"; here *ʾylpyʾ;* Onq. *spynn* "ships"; Frg. Tg.(V) *lbrnyyʾ* "Liburnian"; Nf *blbrnyyh wbʾlpyyh* "Liburnian ships," which suggests a conflation of the readings found in Ps.-J. and the Frg. Tg.

[80]MS incorrectly *mnyš,* but *editio princeps mknyš;* HT, Onq. *qny* "buy," but Nf *zbn* "buy."

Notes, Chapter 29

[1]HT, Onq., and Nf "all Israel."

[2]HT, Onq., and Nf "all that (the Lord did)" but here the text is specific: Aramaic *mḥwwtʾ* "plagues" (Levy II, 23), which Sokoloff (299) takes from *mḥh;* see also v. 21.

[3]HT "trials": here and Onq. *nysyn,* but Nf *nsyyh* "trials."

[4]MS reads incorrectly *blm* "to muzzle," but read with Onq. and Nf *bly* "to become worn"; see the preceding note.

[5]Here itp *ṭlʿ;* Ps.-J. like Onq. *(ʿdy)* varies the vocabulary but Nf has the same verb *(bly)* in both instances in the verse.

[6]HT "strong drink"; here Aramaic *m(y)rt* (the only occurrence in Ps.-J.), Onq. and Nf "old wine."

[7]Aramaic *mstrʾ,* itp of *str* I "to hide oneself" (Jastrow 1033).

[8]See Deut 28:6 (Ps.-J.) and Maher, *The Aramaic Bible* 1B, 81 n. 34 for other witnesses of *(byt) mdryš* in the Tgs.

[9]HT "Bashan": see Num 21:33 (Clarke, *The Aramaic Bible* 4, 250 n. 65) for an explanation of the consonantal shift. See Clarke (1984) 673 for all the instances of "*Mathnan*" in Ps.-J.

[10]HT "defeated them" *(nkh):* here and Onq. *mḥʾ,* but Nf *qṭl.*

we captured their land and we gave it as a possession to *the tribe of*[11] Reuben and to *the tribe of*[11] Gad and to the half tribe of Manasseh. 8. So keep my words[12] and do them in order that you will succeed[13] in all that you do." 9. *Moses, the prophet, said: "It is no secret that I have done these abominations against you* but when you, all of you, are placed[14] today before the Lord your God, the chiefs *of your Sanhedrin,* and *the officers*[15] *of* your tribes, your elders[16] and your commanders,[17] all the men of Israel, 10. your children *and* your wives as well as your aliens who are found in the midst of your camps: the hewers[18] of your wood and the drawers of your water, 11. to make you enter into[19] the covenant of the Lord your God *and to make you take heed of the oath* that the Lord your God has established[20] with you today, 12. in order to establish you[21] today as a *proven*[22] nation and he will become your God[23] just as he spoke to you and just as he promised your fathers, Abraham, Isaac, and Jacob. 13. But it is not with you alone that I am establishing[24] this covenant *and attesting to this oath*: 14. *but with all the generations who have existed from the days of old,*[25] all of them, who are standing now with us today before the Lord our God; *and all the generations who will exist*[26] *until the end of all the ages,*[27] *all of them,* standing here with us today. 15. As for you, you know *the number of years* during which we lived in the land of Egypt *and the mighty deeds that he did for* us among the nations through which you passed. 16. And you saw their abominations *and* their idols of wood and stone *that were raised up in the streets and the idols* of silver and gold that were put *with them in the houses, locking the doors*[28] *after them so that they would not be stolen.* 17. Take heed that there not be among you, *now or after this,* a man or a woman or a clan or a tribe whose heart is turned today to be estranged[29] from *the Fear*[30] *of* the Lord our

Notes, Chapter 29

[11]Nf "the tribe of the house of"; see Deut 3:12 where Ps.-J. has the expanded phrase.

[12]HT, Onq., and Nf "the words of this covenant," but Nfmg has "(the words) of the praise of this Law" *(šbḥ ʾwryyth hdh).*

[13]Tgs. *ṣlḥ;* see Drazin (1982) 250 n. 7 for a discussion of this vocabulary in the Bible.

[14]HT "stand" as Onq. *qym,* but here *ʿtd* and Nf both words.

[15]HT "heads" *(rʾšy);* here *ʾmrkly* (see Clarke [1984] 50 *[ʾmrkwl])* for the thirty-eight occurrences of the word in Ps.-J. The word is of Persian origin: *hamarakara/ ʾamarkal;* see J. C. Greenfield (1970) 180–186.

[16]HT, Onq., and here "elders," but Nf "wise men."

[17]HT "officers" *(šṭr):* here *srk* (see Clarke [1984] 416 for the fourteen occurrences in Ps.-J.). This seems to be vocabulary influenced by Onq. and Nf.

[18]Aramaic *qṭʿ* here and Nfmg, but Nf *qss* "cut down" (Sokoloff 501) and Onq. *lqṭ* "gatherers."

[19]Ap of *ʿll* here and Onq., but Nf *ʿbr.*

[20]HT literally "to cut a covenant" *(krt):* here and Onq. *gzr,* but Nf pa of *qwm* "to establish" (Sokoloff 481); see v. 13 for the same vocabulary distribution.

[21]Ginsburger adds "for him," which Rieder says is found in the Basel printed edition as in the MS, but the MS does not have the word; Nf "a holy people."

[22]Aramaic *ʿwmʾ bryrʾ;* Onq. *ʾm* ("people"), and Nf "a holy people"; see Deut 1:23 (Ps.-J.).

[23]Literally "a God to you"; Nf "redeemer God."

[24]Here and Onq. *gzr,* and Nf pa of *qwm;* see n. 20 above on v. 11.

[25]The phrase is found also in Nf; see next note.

[26]Aramaic *qwm;* see *b.Sanh.* 90b; this expression is found also in Nf.

[27]Singular in MS.

[28]Aramaic *dšʾ* found here and Onq.; see Clarke (1984) 176 for the five occurrences in Ps.-J. Kaufman (1973) 326 n. 58 does not consider it a Palestinian word. See McNamara's observation in *The Aramaic Bible* 5A, 137 nn. 15–16 on the possible meaning because Nf's text is incomplete.

[29]HT *pnh* "turns away": Onq. as HT, but here *pnh* is combined with *tʿy* "to go astray" and Nf *ṣty* "turn aside."

[30]Aramaic *dḥltʾ;* also Onq., but Nf "*Memra* of."

God by worshiping the idols of these nations; lest there be *an error of idolatry*[31] *among you, anyone whose heart is thinking about pursuing his sin: for the beginning of sin is sweet but its end is bitter like the poisonous wormwood.*[32] 18. And if it shall be in hearing the words of this oath he despairs[33] in his mind, saying: 'I shall have peace when I follow the power of the evil inclination in my heart'[34] *in order to add*[35] *my sin of forgetfulness to (the sins of) wilfulness,*[36] 19. it shall not be pleasing before the Lord to forgive[37] him. For the anger of the Lord and his wrath will be increased[38] against that man and all the words of the curses that are written in this book[39] will take effect against him. Then the Lord will erase *the remembrance of* his name from beneath the heavens. 20. And the Lord will separate him, *for his evil,* from all the tribes of Israel according to all the curses of the covenant that are written in this book.[39] 21. Then the later generations shall say, (those) of your children who shall arise after you and *the children of Gentiles,*[40] who will come from a distant land, and when they see the plagues of that land and the suffering that the Lord sent against it, 22. with sulphur and salt, with a consuming fire,[41] the entire land will be burned, it will be unfit for seeding, and it will no longer grow plants, and no herbs will be produced in it; *it will be swallowed* as the destruction of Sodom and Gomorrah, Admah and Zeboiim that *the Memra of* the Lord destroyed with his anger and his wrath, 23. all the nations will say: 'Why did the Lord do thus to this land? How intense is the strength of this great anger!' 24. So they will reply: 'Because they abandoned the covenant of the Lord, the God of their fathers, that he made with them when he brought them out from the land of Egypt, 25. and they followed *the evil inclination* and worshiped[42] *the idols of the Gentiles,*[43] gods[44] that they did not know and who had not been assigned[45] to them, 26. so the

Notes, Chapter 29

[31]Literally "error of the root" *(šryš),* understood as the root of idolatry, that is, the idol itself; see Lev 25:47 (Ps.-J.), and Maher, *The Aramaic Bible* 3, 202 n. 56 for an explanation of the expression.

[32]HT "a root bearing bitter and poisonous fruit": the various Tgs. expand on the HT because they interpret "root" to symbolize "man"; Onq. "perchance there is a man among you with sinful or presumptuous thoughts"; Nf "let there not be among you a man whose heart meditates on sin, since he is likened to a root fixed in the ground, for the beginning of sin is as sweet as honey but its end is as bitter as the wormwood of death." The HT "poisonous fruit" is interpreted as "wormwood"; here *ʾqdnʾ* (Jastrow 11) and Nf *lʿnyth;* see Clarke [1984] 5 for the only example of the word in Ps.-J. Bacher cites this verse to suggest that the Onq. paraphrase is best understood by studying the earlier and longer text found in Ps.-J.

[33]HT "blesses himself in his heart": here itp of *yʾš* "to be careless/to despair of meaning" (Jastrow 560); Onq. *ḥšb* "think to himself"; Nf itp *pyys* "be appeased" (Sokoloff 430); see Grossfeld, *The Aramaic Bible* 9, 83 n. 11 for a discussion of the translation in the ancient versions.

[34]See Gen 8:21 (Onq. and Ps.-J.), and Grossfeld, *The Aramaic Bible* 9, 85 n. 12.

[35]HT "would lead to the sweeping away" (infinitive *spwt*) is understood in the Tgs. from the root *ysp* "to add."

[36]HT "the moist and the dry": all the Tgs. specify as sins of omission and willfulness.

[37]HT "pardon" *(slḥ):* Tgs. *šbq.*

[38]HT "would smoke against" *(ʿšn):* the HT being figurative, all the Tgs. specify with *tqp.*

[39]Nf adds "of the Law."

[40]Aramaic *br ʿmmyn,* also in other Tgs.

[41]Aramaic *mṣlhb;* see n. 21 on Num 1:51 (Ps.-J.) in Clarke, *The Aramaic Bible* 4, 192 n. 21.

[42]HT, Onq., and Nf have "and bowed down to them," which the MS omits but it is found bracketed in Ginsburger and Rieder. It is presumably added by them on the basis of the HT and the other targumic witnesses.

[43]Aramaic *tʿwwt ʿmmyn:* see n. 18 on Deut 28:14.

[44]MS *dtlq* as an error for *dḥltʾ.*

[45]HT "allotted to them" *(ḥlq):* here itp *plg* and Onq. "which could not do any good for them" *(ʾṭyb)* and Nf *bdr* "which were not distributed to them."

Lord's anger increased against that land, bringing upon it all the curses that were written in this book, 27. and the Lord cast them away[46] from their land with anger, wrath, and great strength and threw (them) *into exile* to another land, until today.' 28. Hidden things are revealed before the Lord our God and he avenges because of them. But revealed things are transmitted to us and to our children for ever *to do by them justice* in order to keep all the words of that Law."

CHAPTER 30

1. "When all these things, blessing and *their opposite,*[1] that I have set before you, shall happen to you, you shall repent in your heart in order *to return to my worship* among all *the exiles (among)* the nations where the Lord[2] exiled you. 2. *Blessed be you who are the righteous ones, who repent. For if after having sinned you repent,*[3] *your repentance*[4] *reaches to the throne of the Glory*[5] *of the Lord your God.* If you heed his *Memra*[6] according to all that I am prescribing for you today, you and your children, with all your heart and with all your soul, 3. his *Memra* will accept with pleasure[7] your repentance[8] and will be gracious to you and will return and gather you from all the nations where the Lord[9] scattered you. 4. Even though your dispersal will be to the ends of the heavens, from there will *the Memra of* the Lord gather you *through the mediation of Elijah,*[10] *the great priest,* and from there *he will bring you near through the mediation of the King Messiah.* 5. Then *the Memra of* the Lord your God will bring you to the land that your fathers inherited[11] *and he will do good to you* and increase you more than your fathers. 6. So the Lord your God will remove the obduracy[12] of your heart and the obduracy of the heart of your children, *because he will abolish from the world the evil*

Notes, Chapter 29 (Cont.)

[46]HT "uprooted" (RSV), *wytšm:* here and Onq. *ṭlṭl,* but Nf *tlš* "uproot/tear out."

Notes, Chapter 30

[1]Aramaic here *ḥylwp* and v. 19 for the same idiom; see also Deut 11:26-29; 27:12-13 (Ps.-J.).

[2]HT and Nf add "your God."

[3]See vv. 6, 16, 20, which also express the result of repentance.

[4]See *b.Yoma* 86a.

[5]A frequent phrase in Ps.-J.; see Maher, *The Aramaic Bible* 1B, 22 n. 12 and Clarke (1984) 296 for the eight occurrences in Ps.-J.

[6]HT "his voice": here and Onq. *"Memra,"* but Nf "voice of his *Memra*"; see vv. 8, 10, and elsewhere.

[7]Aramaic here *rʿwʾ.*

[8]Aramaic here and Nf *tywbt;* Onq. "your exile" (*glwtk*).

[9]Nf adds "your God," as does HT, but Onq. as here.

[10]According to Exod 6:18 (Ps.-J.) Phinehas is called "Elijah, the high priest"; see also Exod 4:13; 40:10; Num 21:32; 25:7-8, 11-12 (Ps.-J.), and LAB 48:1-2; Ginzberg, *Legends* 6.316–317; Hayward (1978) 22–34; and Maher, *The Aramaic Bible* 2, 171 n. 16 and 176 n. 14.

[11]HT, Onq., and Nf add "that you may possess it."

[12]See Deut 10:16 (Ps.-J. and Nf) for the same idiom, "obduracy *(ṭpš)* of the heart," as here, but Nf "circumcise *(gzr)* your heart" in place of "remove" *(ʿdy).* Nf has no "obduracy."

inclination,[13] *and he will create the good inclination that will persuade you* to love[14] the Lord your God with all your heart and with all your soul in order that *you will prolong* your life *forever.* 7. Then *the Memra of* the Lord your God will send these curses against your enemies, who oppressed you *in your exile, and against those hating you who pursued you until they despoiled you.* 8. As for you, you shall again heed[15] *the Memra of*[16] the Lord and shall do all the commandments that I am prescribing for you today. 9. And the Lord your God shall spare you for good *because you shall succeed* with all the works of your hands, with the children of your wombs,[17] and with the fruits of your land for (your) good. For *the Memra of* the Lord will again rejoice *because of you,* for good toward you, just as he rejoiced with your fathers, 10. if you heed[15] *the Memra of* the Lord your God by keeping his commandments and his statutes that are written in this book of Law, and if you return to *the Fear of*[18] the Lord your God with all your heart and with all your soul. 11. For this commandment that I am prescribing for you today is neither hidden[19] from you nor is it far from you. 12.[20] It[21] is not in the heavens, (that you should) say, 'Who will go up for us into the heavens[22] and take it for us and proclaim it to us that we may observe it?' 13. Nor is it yonder, beyond the *Great* Sea, (that you should) say: 'Who will cross over, for us, to the other side of the *Great*[23] Sea and take it for us and proclaim it to us so that we may observe it?' 14. But *the matter*[24] is close to you *in your schoolhouse;*[25] *open your mouth so that you may study it,*[26] *purify* your heart to observe it. 15. See that I have arranged[27] before you today *the way of* life *through which is the recompense of* the good reward *for the righteous and the way of* death *through which is the retribution of*[28] the evil reward *for the wicked.* 16. That, as for me, I am prescribing for you today to love the Lord your God[29] and to walk in ways *that are right*[30] *before him* and to keep his commandments, his statutes and his judgments. Then you will live and you will increase. The Lord your God will bless you in the land that you are entering to possess. 17. But if your heart will make evil

Notes, Chapter 30

[13]See *Num. R.* 707; *Exod. R.* 479.

[14]Nf adds "the teaching of the Law of."

[15]Here and Onq. *qbl,* but Nf *šmʿ.*

[16]HT "voice" and Nf "the voice of the *Memra* of."

[17]HT and Nf "fruit of your body, fruit of your cattle, fruit of your land"; Onq. and Ps.-J. retain "fruit" only in the third phrase and Ps.-J. fails to translate "fruit of your cattle." For "fruit of your body" here and Onq. *mʿh* "womb."

[18]Aramaic *dḥlyʾ;* Onq. as here, but Nf omits and has only "the Lord your God."

[19]HT "is not too hard for you": Onq. "is not too removed *(prš)* from you"; here and Nf "hidden" *(ksy);* see Deut 17:8 (Ps.-J.) for similar vocabulary distribution.

[20]On the expansion in vv. 12-13 see *Deut. R.* 8.6 on Deut 30:11-12 and McNamara's notes on these verses in *The Aramaic Bible* 5A, 141 nn. 11–12.

[21]Nf "the Law."

[22]See Exod 24:2, 15-18; "when Moses ascended to the mountain" may be understood as Moses going up to the heavens to obtain the Law.

[23]HT "the Sea": Onq. as HT; see McNamara's note on this word in *The Aramaic Bible* 5A, 141 n. 15.

[24]Aramaic *pytgmʾ,* as also Onq. and Nf.

[25]See Maher, *The Aramaic Bible* 1B, 81 n. 34 for a discussion of *byt mdryšʾ* in the Tgs.

[26]MS "them," implying the commandments, but here following "it" in v. 12.

[27]HT *ntn:* Onq. *yhb,* but here and Nf *sdr.*

[28]See *Gen. R.* 175.

[29]Nf "teaching of the Law of the Lord your God"; Onq. and Nfmg as here.

[30]Aramaic *tqn* in Onq., Ps.-J., and Nf.

plans[31] and you will no longer obey (me), if you will stray and bow down to *the idols of the nations*[32] and worship them, 18. I declare to you today that you will surely be destroyed and you will not prolong (your) days in the land that you are crossing the Jordan to enter (and) to possess. 19. *Those who are passing from the world*[33] *do not bear witness that* I take witness against you today, instead the heavens and the earth (take witness): I have arranged before you life and death, a blessing and *its opposite.*[34] Choose then the way of life, *which is the Law,*[35] so that you may live *in the life of the world to come,*[36] you and your children,[37] 20. by loving the Lord your God,[38] by heeding his *Memra,*[39] and by drawing near[40] to *his Fear. For the Law with which you are occupying (yourselves)* is your life *in this world* and the prolongation of your days *in the world to come. And you will be gathered at the end of the exile and* you shall live upon the land that the Lord promised to your fathers, Abraham, Isaac, and Jacob to give to them."

CHAPTER 31

1. So Moses *went to the Tent of Instruction*[1] and spoke these words with all Israel. 2. And he said to them: "Today I am one hundred and twenty years old: I am no longer able to come and go[2] and *the Memra*[3] *of* the Lord said to me: 'You shall not cross over this Jordan.' 3. The Lord your God *and his Shekinah*[4] shall cross before you; he will destroy these nations[5] and you shall dispossess them. Joshua shall go before you just as the Lord has spoken. 4. Then the Lord shall exact just punishment from them just as he did to Sihon and Og, kings of the Amorites, and to the nations of their land whom he destroyed. 5. So *the Memra of* the Lord will hand them over before you and you will do to them according to every commandment that I prescribed for you. 6. Be strong and courageous, do not fear nor be alarmed before them, for the

Notes, Chapter 30 (Cont.)

[31]HT *pnh:* Onq. as HT, but here *hrhr* and Nf *sṭy* "turn aside."

[32]Aramaic *ṭ'wwt 'mmyn* here and Onq., but Nf "other idols"; see n. 18 on Deut 28:14.

[33]See Gen 15:2 (Ps.-J.) for the same idiom; see Maher, *The Aramaic Bible* 1B, 60 n. 7.

[34]See n. 1 on v. 1 above.

[35]See Gen 3:24 (Ps.-J. and Nf) where it is stated that the Law was created before the world, and also Maher, *The Aramaic Bible* 1B, 30 n. 57; Num 22:28 (Ps.-J.) where it is stated that the tablets of the Law were one of the things created after the world (Clarke, *The Aramaic Bible* 4, 254).

[36]Onq. and Nf omit the phrase; see Sysling (1991) 192 n. 24.

[37]HT "your seed": Tgs. usually translate HT as "children/sons."

[38]Onq. and here, but Nf "the teaching of the Law of."

[39]Onq. as here, but Nf "the voice of his *Memra.*"

[40]Onq. as here *(qrb),* but Nf "cleaving *(dbq)* to him."

Notes, Chapter 31

[1]Aramaic *byt 'wlpn',* the "tent" as "schoolhouse"; see Exod 18:7; 33:7; Deut 32:44 (Ps.-J.).

[2]Here, Onq., and Nf *npq w'll.*

[3]Also Nf, but not Onq.

[4]Nf "the Glory of his *Shekinah*"; see also vv. 6, 8, 17.

[5]HT, Onq., and Nf add "from before you."

Lord your God, *his Shekinah,*[6] marches before you. He shall not forsake you nor be far from you."[7] 7. So Moses summoned Joshua *from the midst of the people* and said to him in the presence of all Israel: "Be strong and courageous for you *have been appointed to* enter,[8] with this people, the land that *the Memra of* the Lord promised to their fathers to give them. And you shall divide it for them. 8. So *the Memra*[9] *of* the Lord, *his Shekinah*[10] is marching before you and his *Memra*[11] will be your support. He will not forsake you nor will he be far from you.[12] Do not fear or be alarmed." 9. Then Moses wrote this law and gave it to the priests, the sons of Levi, who were carrying the ark of the Lord's covenant, and to all the wise men of Israel. 10. And Moses commanded them, saying: "At the end of seven years, at the exact time of the year of release, at the Feast of Booths, 11. when all Israel comes to appear[13] before the Lord your God, at the place that he will have chosen, you shall read this Law before all Israel, in their hearing.[14] 12. Assemble the people: men *to learn,* the women *to hear instruction,* and the children *to accept for themselves the reward that is coming to them,* and the aliens who are in your cities[15] *who shall see the Glory of the Law* so that all of them shall fear before *the Memra of*[16] the Lord your God, and do carefully all the words of this Law. 13. And their children who do not yet know will listen and learn to fear before the Lord your God, all the days that you exist upon the land that you are crossing the Jordan to possess." 14. *In (the case of) three righteous men their death was told in the future because they had not reached the number of days of their fathers, and each one of them was appointed in his time as a community leader:*[17] *Jacob our father, David the king, and Moses the prophet.*[18] *For so it is written,* and the Lord spoke to Moses: "Behold your day of death is approaching. Call Joshua and present yourselves at the Tent of Meeting that I may put him in charge." So Moses and Joshua went and presented themselves at the Tent of Meeting. 15. Then *the Glory of* the Lord's *Shekinah* was revealed[19] at the Tent in a pillar of cloud; and the pillar of cloud stood at the door of the Tent, *and Moses*

Notes, Chapter 31

[6]Onq. and Nf "his *Memra*"; for Nf see n. 3 above.

[7]HT and Nf "let alone (ap *rpy*) and forsake *(šbq),* but here and Onq., since they had already used *šbq* for the first verb, used *rḥq* for the second; see v. 8 below for the same verbal distribution.

[8]In the HT there is a Qere and a Ketibh reading *tbw'* "go/enter" (Masoretic text and LXX), or *tby'* "bring" (Syriac and Vulgate): Díez Macho reads in Nf *ty'l* as an ap "to bring," but both Onq. and Ps.-J. read a simple peal "to go/enter." Grossfeld (1972) 533–534 and (1976) 30–34 notes that some MSS for Onq. also read a causative *(t'yl);* see also Grossfeld, *The Aramaic Bible* 9, 86 note c.

[9]Here and Nf, but Onq. as HT "the Lord"; see nn. 3 and 6 above.

[10]Nf "the Glory of his *Shekinah.*"

[11]HT "he" is often translated in the Tgs. as "*Memra*"; see here and Onq.

[12]See n. 7 on v. 6.

[13]Here passive of the itp of *ḥm'* "to be seen," i.e., "to appear" as a passive to avoid direct contact with God; see McNamara's note on this word in *The Aramaic Bible* 5A, 143 n. 6.

[14]HT "in their ears"; Tgs. *šm'.*

[15]HT "within your gates": Onq. as here, but Nf "in your land"; see McNamara's note on this verse in *The Aramaic Bible* 5A, 144 n. 8.

[16]HT, Onq., and Nf omit "the *Memra* of."

[17]Aramaic *prns'* "community leader" (Sokoloff 448); see n. 31 on Deut 16:22 above, and Gen 30:30; 49:24 (Ps.-J.); Gen 40:12 (Frg. Tg.[V]).

[18]See *Gen. R.* 887.

[19]HT "the Lord appeared": Onq. "the Lord revealed himself" (itp *gly*); Nf "the *Memra* of the Lord revealed itself" (itp *gly*).

and Joshua stood on the outside.[20] 16.[21] Then the Lord said to Moses: "Behold, you are about to lie in the dust with your fathers *and your soul shall be deposited*[22] *in the treasury of eternal life with your fathers. Then the wicked ones* of this people shall arise and shall stray after *the idols of the nations*[23] wherein they are entering. Then they will forsake my *Fear*[24] and will *change*[25] my covenant that I have established with them. 17. So my anger will increase against them on that day and I shall keep them at a distance[26] and I shall remove[27] *my Shekinah*[28] from them; they will become *plunder,* many *distressful* evils will happen to them. So they will say at that time: '*By oath,*[29] it is because *the Shekinah*[30] *of* my God no longer dwells in my midst that these evils are happening to me.' 18. So I, I shall surely remove[31] *my Shekinah*[32] from them, at that time, *until they be weakened and accept the punishments for their sins* because of all the evils done when they turned (to follow) *after the idols of the nations.*[33] 19. So therefore, write for yourselves this song. Teach it to the Israelites, put it in their mouths in order that this song be before me as a witness against the Israelites 20. when I have brought them to the land, (a land) producing milk and honey,[34] that I promised[35] to their fathers. So they shall have eaten and been satisfied and grown fat, then they shall turn *to the idols of the nations*[33] and shall worship them and shall cause anger[36] before me and shall change[37] my covenant. 21. And it shall be when many and *distressful* evils happen to them, that this song[38] shall bear witness[39] before them as testimony: *for it has been revealed*[40] *before me that* it will not be forgotten from the

Notes, Chapter 31

[20]See *b.Yoma* 4b.

[21]See Sysling (1991) 187, 190–192, 209, 260 for a detailed discussion of this verse.

[22]Aramaic *gnyz': * for the reserve of souls; see *Sifre Deut.* 297: Moses "is assured of the world to come."

[23]Aramaic *yt'wn t'wwt 'mmyn;* see n. 18 on Deut 28:14, and v. 20 below. Here HT *pnh* is translated in the Tgs. by *ṭ'y.* See Maher (1994) 284–286 on HT *pnh.*

[24]Aramaic *dḥlty;* also in Onq., but Nf as HT "me."

[25]HT "forsake" *('zb)* and break *(prr)* my covenant": Onq. as here *(šny),* but Nf ap *pss* "break" (Jastrow 1198); but see *šny* in Lev 26:15 (Onq.): Grossfeld, *The Aramaic Bible* 8, 61 n. 14, and Gen 17:14 (Ps.-J.): Maher, *The Aramaic Bible* 1B, 64 n. 12.

[26]Aramaic ap *rḥq;* see n. 7 on v. 6 above.

[27]Aramaic ap *slq;* also Onq., but Nf *hpk* "to turn away."

[28]Onq. as here, but Nf "Glory of my *Shekinah.*"

[29]Aramaic *šbw'h* is omitted in Onq. and Nf.

[30]HT "my face": see also the next verse for the same change in the Tgs.; see Deut 33:20 where Ps.-J. translates literally.

[31]Aramaic *slq* here and Onq., but Nf "my *Memra* will surely hide *(ṭmr)* my face."

[32]Onq. and here, but Nf "my *Memra.*"

[33]Aramaic *'tpnyyw t'wwt 'mmyn:* Onq. as here, but Nf "having gone astray *(sṭy)* after other idols"; see also n. 23 in v. 16 above, and n. 18 in Deut 28:14.

[34]Onq. as here, but Nf "producing good fruits, clear as milk and sweet and tasty as honey"; see the Introduction to this volume.

[35]HT adds "to give," but Onq. and Nf as here (pa *qwm*).

[36]HT "despise" *(n's):* here, Onq., and Nf *rgz,* as in Deut 32:19 (Ps.-J.); see Grossfeld, *The Aramaic Bible* 8, 107 n. 8 and Clarke, *The Aramaic Bible* 4, 227 n. 10 on Num 14:11.

[37]HT "break" *(prr):* Onq. and here "change" *(šny),* but Nf *pss;* see n. 25 on v. 16 above.

[38]Onq. as here, but Nf "praiseworthy song *(šbḥ šyrth)* shall answer *('nh)* before me as a witness."

[39]Here ap *shd,* but Nf *'nh* and Onq. ap *twb;* see preceding note.

[40]Here *gly* is used impersonally, but Onq. refers to "a song of praise" *(twšbḥth)* and Nf to "a praiseworthy song" *(šbḥ šyrth).*

mouth of their children.[41] Also their evil inclination that they are doing today *has been revealed before me,* even before I have brought them to the land that I have promised." 22. So Moses wrote this song[42] and taught it to the Israelites. 23. Then he commanded Joshua son of Nun and said: "Be strong and courageous, for you will bring the Israelites to the land that I have promised them and my *Memra*[43] will be your support." 24. And when Moses finished writing the words of this Law *on parchment,* as far as its completion, 25. Moses commanded the Levites, carriers of the ark of the Lord's covenant, saying: 26. "Take *this* book of the Law and put it *in the box,* at *the right* side of the ark of the covenant of the Lord your God, and it shall be there as a witness for you. 27. For your rebelliousness and your stubbornness have been revealed before me. Behold, while I am alive among you today, you have been rebelling before the Lord; and therefore, how much more so[44] after I die. 28. Gather before me all the wise men[45] of your tribes and your commanders[46] and I shall speak all these words in their hearing[47] and shall call heaven and earth to witness against them. 29. For I know that after I die you shall surely corrupt your deeds and shall stray from the path that I prescribed for you. Then evil shall happen to you at the end of days for you will do what is evil before the Lord to cause anger before him."[48] 30. So Moses spoke in the hearing of all the assembly of Israel, until their completion, the words of this song.

CHAPTER 32[1]

1. *Now when*[2] *the time had arrived for Moses the prophet to be gathered*[3] *from the midst of the world, he said in his heart: "I will not call witnesses to witness against this people who taste death*[4] *in this world. Behold, I will call witnesses to witness against them who do not taste*

Notes, Chapter 31 (Cont.)

[41]HT "descendants" *(zr')* is translated as "children" in the Tgs.; see Grossfeld, *The Aramaic Bible* 6, 47 n. 8, and McNamara's note on this verse in *The Aramaic Bible* 5A, 145 n. 19.

[42]HT and Nf add "on that day."

[43]Also Onq. and Nf; see nn. 3 and 6 above.

[44]Here *dkn,* but Frg. Tg.(V) *kmh wkmh.*

[45]HT and Onq. "elders," but Nf as here. Normally Ps.-J. translates the HT as "elders."

[46]Aramaic *srk'* also in all Tgs.

[47]HT "in their ears": Nf as here, but Onq. "before *(qdm)* them"; see Klein (1979) 502–507, and Ribera (1983) 114–115.

[48]HT, Onq., and Nf add "through the work of their hands."

Notes, Chapter 32

[1]A detailed discussion of this chapter is found in Cook (1986) 54–106. The paraphrase in this chapter is found in Nf as well as Frg. Tg.(P) vv. 1-7, 10, 13-14, 18-19, 24, 31, 33-35, 37-38, 42, and Frg. Tg.(V) vv. 1-52.

[2]Aramaic *hwh dy,* but Nf and the Frg. Tgs. read *kywn dy;* Le Déaut IV, 261 n. 1 observes that in the triennial liturgical calendar Isa 1:2 is read with Deut 32:1; see also McNamara's note on the paraphrase in this chapter in *The Aramaic Bible* 5A, 146 n. 2.

[3]Aramaic *mtknš'* here and Nf, but Frg. Tgs.(VP) *mstlq'* "be taken up"; see Deut 31:14 (Ps.-J.) for the same idea.

[4]Nf "cup of death"; see McNamara's note on this phrase in *The Aramaic Bible* 5A, 147 n. 4.

death in this world,[5] *but their end is to be renewed*[6] *in the world to come." Isaiah*[7] *the prophet, when he prophesied in the congregation of Israel, ascribed hearing to the heavens and listening to the earth because he was close to the earth and far from the heavens. But Moses the prophet, when he was prophesying in the congregation of Israel, ascribed hearing to the earth and listening to the heavens because he was close to the heavens and far from the earth. For so it is written:* "Give ear, O heavens, and I shall speak and, O earth, listen to my mouth's discourse. 2. Let my teaching[8] *strike*[9] *the rebellious* as *torrential* rain, *but let (it) be received with pleasantness* like the dew[10] *by those who accept the teaching. May my discourse*[11] *(be) like the fruitfulness of the winds of rain that blow*[12] on the plants *in the month of Marheshwan and as the later* rains *drop*[13] *that saturate the growing* plants *of the earth in the month of Nisan."* 3. *Woe to the wicked who recall the holy Name with blasphemies! Because Moses, who was the teacher of Israel, (found) it impossible to recall the holy Name until he taught his mouth,*[14] *at the beginning of the song with eighty-five*[15] *letters that were twenty-one words.*[16] *After this he said: "So in* the Name of the Lord *I pray;*[17] *and you, people of the house of Israel,* give glory and greatness[18] *before* our God." 4. *Moses the prophet said: "When I ascended Mount Sinai, I saw the Master of all the Ages,*[19] *the Lord, dividing the day into four parts: three hours occupied*[20] *with (the study of) the Law, three occupied with judgment, three coupling*[21] *man and*

Notes, Chapter 32

[5]See Deut 4:26 (Ps.-J.).

[6]Aramaic here itp *ḥdt,* but Nf and Frg. Tgs. *bly* "to wear out."

[7]Echoes of Isa 1:2, "hear, O heavens, and listen, O earth," suggesting the idea of heaven and earth as witnesses; found also in Isa 51:6; 65:17; see also *Sifre Deut.* 302 for a discussion of whether Moses was closer to heaven and farther from the earth or the reverse.

[8]Frg. Tgs.(PV) "the teaching of my Law."

[9]HT "drop" (*ʿrp* II): Onq. "be delightful" *(bsm)* as in Nf, here *nqp,* but the Frg. Tgs.(PV) possibly read *ʿrb* "sweet" according to Cook (1986) 59, but Klein (1980) reads *ybsm;* see *Sifre Deut.* 304, where R. Jose the Galilean says the HT means "'kill' . . . so the words of Torah atone for all transgressions," and R. Eliezer in *b.Taʿan.* 31a "'just as rain is sweet,' rain has the power to give each tree its distinct sweetness."

[10]Targum Jonathan to Isa 5:6 and Mic 2:6 interpret "rain" as prophecy.

[11]Aramaic here *mmlly dyly:* Cook (1986) divides the verse in the HT "may my discourse be like," but Nf and Frg. Tgs.(PV) read "may the word *(mymr)* of my mouth be favorably accepted by them like the dew."

[12]HT *sʿyrym* "gentle rain"; Onq. and Nf *nšb* and here *ntb.* Drazin (1982) 269 n. 5 quotes Rashi who interprets the HT as "storm": "just as the storm rain strengthens the grass and helps it strengthen and grow, so Torah matures those who learn it"; see Grossfeld, *The Aramaic Bible* 9, 89 n. 3 for other rabbinic refinements.

[13]HT *rbybyn* "showers" (RSV) is understood as copious rains by Ibn Ezra. The Tgs. *rsysyn lqwšyn* "rain droplets"; see Grossfeld, *The Aramaic Bible* 9, 89 n. 4.

[14]Aramaic spelling of *pwm* is not a Palestinian form; see Kutscher (1976) 20–22.

[15]MS reads incorrectly "eighty and fifty"; see Nf and Frg. Tgs.(PV) for the correct text as well as here.

[16]In HT twenty-one words (eighty-five letters) precede the first mention of the name YHWH in Deut 32:1-3; see McNamara's note on this idea in *The Aramaic Bible* 5A, 149 n. 14, and *Sifre Deut.* 308 "Moses did not mention the name of the Holy One . . . until after he had spoken twenty-one words."

[17]HT "proclaim," but Tgs. *ṣly* "pray."

[18]Aramaic *rbwtʾ;* see *Mekilta* on Exod 13:3 (I, 138), referring to the one who recites the benediction: "Praised be the Lord . . . praised be his Name" etc.

[19]Aramaic *rbwn kl ʿlmyʾ;* see Maher, *The Aramaic Bible* 1B, 69 n. 42 for a discussion of other occurrences of the phrase in the Tgs.

[20]Frg. Tg.(P) "toiled and occupied."

[21]Aramaic *mbrzg* (a denominative verb of *br zwg* "wife/consort") and Nf *mzwwg* are based on the verb *zwg;* see Deut 34:6 (Ps.-J.); both Ps.-J. and Nf *zwg.*

wife, dividing[22] *high from low, and three providing sustenance*[23] *for all creation."*[24] *For so it is written: "the Mighty One*[25] whose deeds are perfect because all his ways are just, the faithful God[26] *before whom no evil emerges,*[27] because he is pure and true." 5.[28] The *dear* children have corrupted *their good deeds,*[29] *a blemish* is found in them: an insidious generation *who have changed their deeds; and so shall the order of the earth's judgments be changed against them.* 6. *Is it possible that for the Name of the Memra* of *the Lord you are recompensing* this nation who was foolish,[30] *and, having received the Law,* has not become wise? Is it not your Father who acquired you; him who created you and adorned[31] you? 7. Remember the days of old, consider the years of each and every generation, *read the books of the Law*[32] and they will inform you *and the books of the prophets*[33] and they will speak to you. 8. When the Most High gave *the world as* an inheritance to the peoples *who came from the sons of Noah,* when he divided *the writings and languages among mankind,*[34] *in the generation of the division,*[35] *at that time, he cast lots*[36] *on seventy*[37] *angels, the leaders of nations,*[38] *with whom it was revealed to see the city; and at that time* he established the borders of the nations according to the sum of the number of *the seventy souls of Israel who went down to Egypt.*[39] 9. And when the holy people fell by lot *of the Master of the World, Michael*[40] *opened his mouth and said: "Thus the portion of good of the Name of the Memra of the Lord (is) his people."*[41] *Gabriel opened his mouth in*

Notes, Chapter 32

[22]Aramaic *mrwmm w m'yk* here and Nf *mrym wmmk.*

[23]Aramaic *prns* (Jastrow 1231; Greek *pronoeō*); see Clarke (1984) 486.

[24]Aramaic here *bryyt',* but Nf and Frg. Tgs.(PV) *'lm'* "world."

[25]HT "the Rock": see vv. 15, 18, 30-31, 37 below.

[26]HT "a God of faithfulness" (RSV) changed to "the" to avoid any suggestion of plurality.

[27]The Tgs. attempt to avoid any suggestion that God is evil.

[28]The phrase "they have dealt corruptly with him" in the HT is obscure and Drazin (1982) 271 n. 5 observes the various ways the obscurity has been clarified.

[29]HT "they have dealt corruptly with him": Frg. Tgs.(PV) "the children have corrupted their deed" as here but Onq. "they have corrupted themselves"; the Pal. Tgs. generally understood the reference as to "the children." Also the HT "blemish" *(mūmām)* is interpreted as not becoming wise although they had received the Law. Onq. interpreted "blemish" as idolatry; see Grossfeld, *The Aramaic Bible,* 9, 90 nn. 10–13.

[30]HT "foolish": Nf "stupid and unwise nation," and Frg. Tg.(V) "O foolish and witless nation."

[31]Aramaic *škll* "perfect/adorn"; see Akkadian *šuklulu,* although the verb may be a shapel form; see Rabin (1969) 150, and Kaufman (1974) 104.

[32]HT "father": Nf "your fathers who are greater than you in the Law."

[33]HT and Onq. "elders": Nf "wise men"; but Ps.-J. "the prophets"; see *Sifre Deut.* 316 "'ask thy father' . . . refers to the prophets."

[34]See Gen 11:7-8 (HT and Ps.-J.), *Sifre Deut.* 317 "he specified the area of each nation" (an idea based on the HT "he set the borders of the people") and *PRE* 177 "seventy nations and seventy languages," and Maher, *The Aramaic Bible* 1B, 50 n. 14.

[35]That is, the generation in the time of the Tower of Babel; see Shinan (1985) 77–78 for a discussion of the unity of this midrash in Ps.-J.

[36]Aramaic *pyst'.*

[37]See Gen 11:7-8 (Ps.-J.) and Deut 27:8 (Ps.-J. and Nf); see Maher, *The Aramaic Bible* 1B, 50 nn. 12–14 for other references to the idea of "seventy nations," and Ginzberg, *Legends* 5.194-195.

[38]HT "numbers of the sons of God": here both the idea of the angels and of the leaders of the people is expressed.

[39]See Gen 11:8 (Ps.-J.) and Shinan (1985) 77–78; Russell (1954) 248; and Cook (1986) 67–68, who discusses links between Ps.-J. and Ishodad of Merv (C. van den Eynde [1958] 180).

[40]Michael "the great prince": see Dan 10:13, 20, 21; 12:1, and Ps.-J. on Gen 32:25; 38:25; Exod 24:1; Num 13:13; here and Deut 34:3, 6; see Maher, *The Aramaic Bible* 1B, 114 n. 18.

[41]HT and MS *'mw* "his people": according to *PRE* 177 "Jacob is the lot," but *editio princeps 'myh* "with him"; see Etheridge (1968) 663 "with him."

praise and said: "Those of the house of Jacob are the lot of his inheritance. 10. He found them camped in the desert, in the desolation of a place *where demons and jackals*[42] *howl, and a parched place.*[43] He has surrounded[44] them with *the seven clouds of his Glory,*[45] *he has taught them his Law,*[46] he has kept[47] them *just as the eyelid*[48] *protects the pupils of his*[49] eye. 11. As an eagle who awakens[50] and cares[51] for its nest and is anxious[52] about its young[53] *so his Shekinah* awakens Israel's camp and the shadow of his *Shekinah* covers them with shade. And just as the eagle spreads its wings *over its young,* and bears them and carries them upon its wings,[54] *so he bore them and carried them and settled them in the strong fortified places*[55] *of the land of Israel.* 12.[56] *The Memra* of the Lord settled them *by themselves in their land*[57] and did not cause *the followers of* a strange worship to dwell among them. 13. He settled them in *the fortified places*[58] of the land of *Israel;* and *fed*[59] them delicacies of the produce of its fields. He nourished them with honey *from its fruit that grows* upon the rocks and oil *from its olives that spring forth* on the hard rocks. 14. *He gave them* thick cream[60] of cows *from the spoil of their kings* and milk from the firstlings of the sheep *from the prey of their rulers,* with the choice fatlings[61] and rams, fat offsprings of sheep of Mathnan[62] and goats." *Moses, the prophet, said: "If the people of the house of Israel keep the commandments of the Law, it was told to me in*

Notes, Chapter 32

[42]Aramaic *wyrwdyn;* see Tg. *yrwryn* in Isa 13:22; 34:13; 35:7 (Stenning [1949] 47, 113, 115); Dalman (1967) 187 "jackal," but Jastrow (594) *yrwd* "wild ass" or "Yarod," which is a "bird of solitary habit, mentioned in connection with the ostrich."

[43]Aramaic *byt ṣḥwtʾ;* Nf adds here the many benefits (manna, water, quail, etc.) given by the Lord to the Israelites during the forty years in the wilderness; see McNamara's note on this verse in *The Aramaic Bible* 5A, 151 n. 26.

[44]HT "encircled": Onq. and Nf "settled them," ap of *šry,* while here ap of *gyn* or *gnn* (Jastrow 239).

[45]There are only three references in Ps.-J. where the number of clouds is specified (here, Exod 12:37, and Num 33:5); see *Sifre Deut.* 320 "the cloud of glory encompassed them" and Maher, *The Aramaic Bible* 1B, 22 n. 11 for other references for the phrase in the Tgs.

[46]HT "he cared for them" (RSV), *byn* "instruct/discern": Onq. "taught them the *Memras* of the Law," and Nf "he taught them the ten *Memras*"; see also *Sifre Deut.* 320 "through the Ten Commandments."

[47]Aramaic *nṭr* in all the Tgs.

[48]Aramaic *škynh* here and Nf; Ginzburger *škynʾ.*

[49]Onq. "their," that is, the human eye, to avoid an anthropomorphism.

[50]HT "stir up": Onq., Nf, and Frg. Tg.(V) translate as pa of *ʿrr.* Ps.-J. uses three verbs: *ʿrr,* ap *ḥwš,* and *ḥpp.*

[51]Aramaic ap *ḥwš.*

[52]Aramaic *ḥpp;* also Nf and Frg. Tg.(V).

[53]HT *gwzl* "young": here *tsylʾ* "a young dove" (Jastrow 1682), which Ps.-J. interprets as a young eagle.

[54]Aramaic *ʾybr:* Onq., Nf, and Frg. Tg.(V) "upon the strength *(tqwp)* of its wings."

[55]Aramaic *krk.*

[56]HT "The Lord alone *(bdd)* did lead him": (1) all the Tgs. consider *bdd,* which applies to God in the HT, as referring rather to Israel being alone. Unlike the interpretation in both Onq. and Nf, I consider the action in the past as in the following verses; see McNamara's note on this verse in *The Aramaic Bible* 5A, 152 n. 33.

[57]See Num 23:9 "a people dwelling alone."

[58]HT "high places": Onq. "powerful ones," here *krk* and Nf "high places"; see Grossfeld, *The Aramaic Bible* 9, 92 n. 25 for additional observations.

[59]HT "he ate": LXX, Samaritan, Peshitta, and Nf as here, ap *ʾkl;* see *PRE* 332.

[60]Aramaic *lwwʾy šmyny,* literally "fat *(šmyn)* milk *(lwwʾy)*"; see Gen 18:8 (Ps.-J. and Nf) for the same idiom, and Maher, *The Aramaic Bible* 1B, 66 n. 11.

[61]Aramaic *ptymyn* (Jastrow 1155).

[62]HT "Bashan"; here and Nf translate literally, but Onq. sees the wealth of the Amorite kings; see Grossfeld, *The Aramaic Bible* 9, 92 n. 28.

a prophecy that the grains of their wheat shall be as the kidneys of oxen[63] *and that from one (grape) cluster they shall draw one kor*[64] *of red wine.* 15. *But the house of Israel*[65] was rich *and became arrogant and were extremely successful; they acquired possessions,*[66] and forsook the worship of the God who created them *and provoked the anger of the Mighty One*[67] *who had redeemed*[68] *them.*[69] 16. They made him jealous by idolatry,[70] with their abominations they provoked him to anger. 17. They sacrificed *to idols*[71] *comparable* to demons *who were of no value, idols*[72] that they did not know, new deities[73] recently made[74] and with which your fathers *had no business.*[75] 18. You have forgotten *the Fear of the Mighty One*[76] who created you, you forgot *the Memra* of the God who has made you *with many cavities.*[77] 19. *So it was revealed before* the Lord, *and he was angry,*[78] because *his beloved children, those called* sons and daughters *in his Name,* provoked him to anger. 20. Then he said: 'I shall surely withdraw the face *of my good pleasure* from them, let me[79] see what shall be their end; for they are a fickle-minded generation, children who have no faithfulness. 21. They have made me jealous with what is no god,[80] they have provoked me *to anger with their vanities.*[81] As for me, I will cause them to experience jealousy by a nation that is no nation: *with the Babylonians,* a foolish people, I shall provoke[82] them to anger. 22. *For an east wind, strong as* fire, *came out from*

Notes, Chapter 32

[63]See *Sifre Deut.* 324 "each grain of wheat . . . as large as the two kidneys of a large bull."

[64]HT *ḥmr* "wine" is read as "homer," a measure, i.e., "*kor*" (equal to 450 liters), as also Nf, but not Onq. In Onq. the wine becomes "the (blood of) their warriors"; see Deut 15:23 (HT) for that idiom and *Sifre Deut.* 325 where "you will bring in (the vine) in a wagon . . . then repeatedly drink (wine) from it as if one drinks it out of a large jar."

[65]HT "Jeshurun" is interpreted here as a poetic name for Israel. Both words contain the root *yšr* "upright"; see also Deut 33:5, 26 (Ps.-J.) and Isa 44:2 for the only other instances in the HT, and Grossfeld, *The Aramaic Bible* 9, 93 n. 30.

[66]HT "you waxed fat, you grew thick, you became sleek"; Onq. "it became prosperous as well as powerful, and acquired property"; Nf "they prospered and acquired many possessions."

[67]HT "the Rock."

[68]HT "salvation"; Onq. interprets *yšʿ* as *gʾl,* while here and Nf *prq.*

[69]Nf "forgot the *Memra* of the Lord who had created them and denied the fear of the Strong One who had redeemed them in the hour of their affliction."

[70]HT "strange gods"; Onq. "worshiping idols"; here *pwlḥnʾ nwkryyʾ;* Nf "by their abominations" *(mrḥqthwn),* while Frg. Tg.(V) "with their idols."

[71]Aramaic *tʿwwn;* Onq. *šdyn* "demons"; Nf "idols of demons."

[72]*Sifre Deut.* 327: "but they worshiped things that could neither benefit them nor harm them."

[73]Aramaic *dḥln ḥdtn.*

[74]HT "that had come in of late" (RSV); Nf "had been created since then *(mn kdwn)*"; see Grossfeld, *The Aramaic Bible* 9, 94 n. 37.

[75]HT "never dreaded": here, Onq., Nf, and Frg. Tg.(V) itp of *ʿsq* "deal with" (Sokoloff 414); *Sifre Deut.* 318 "your ancestors did not evaluate them to see if they were of any use or not."

[76]HT "the Rock"; Aramaic *dḥlt tqypʾ,* Onq. and here. "Fear" is added to prevent the suggestion that one could forget God.

[77]HT "gave you birth" *(mḥllk)* from the root *ḥwl,* but Ps.-J., Nf, and Frg. Tg.(V) *mḥ(y)lyn* from *ḥll* I "to pierce," hence "cavities." Onq. "who made *(ʿbd)* you"; see *Sifre Deut.* 328 where the rabbis differ in the interpretation of the HT *(mḥllk)* but R. Judah says "God made you full of cavities" *(meḥillim),* and see also McNamara on this word in *The Aramaic Bible* 5A, 154 n. 51.

[78]Onq. *tqyp rwgzyh* "his anger was intensified."

[79]Aramaic *nḥmy;* Le Déaut IV, 271 n. 36 reads as 1 c. plural and Cook (1986) takes the form to be Galilean 1 c. singular; see Nf *ʾḥmy* and Onq. *gly qdmy.*

[80]Aramaic *dlʾ ʾlqʾ;* Onq. *dlʾ dḥlʾ* "which is not fearful"; Nf *ʾlh dlʾ ʾlh;* and Frg. Tg.(V) "idols" *(tʿwwn).*

[81]Aramaic *hbl;* Onq. *tʿwthwn* "their idols"; Nf and Frg. Tg.(V) *rḥqtyhwn* "their abominations."

[82]Aramaic *nrgwz* is a Galilean 1 c. singular: correct to *nrgz* as an aphel; Onq. *ʾrgyzynwn* "I will provoke them"; Nf and Frg. Tg.(V) *ʾkʿs* "I will arouse."

before[83] *me,* and flamed in the ardor of my anger, and it burned[84] to the depths of Sheol and it brought the land to an end and its produce[85] and set on fire the foundations[86] of the mountains. 23. *So when they were put in Babylon they were worshiping their idols: therefore I ordered by my Memra*[87] to amass[88] evils upon them; *I shall destroy them with plague*-arrows *of my punishment.*[89] 24. *From the midst of the Babylonian captivity I shall exile them to Media and to Elam. Those of the house of Agag shall oppress them, who are comparable to demons*[90] *swollen*[91] with hunger *and like destroyer demons consumed by birds*[92] *and like midday demons afflicted by evil*[93] *spirits and demons of the night inflated with evil spirits.* I shall send against them *the Greeks who bite with their* teeth *like wild* animals, *and I shall exile them by means of the Edomites*[94] *who are filled* with poison *like* venomous serpents,[95] reptiles of the dust. 25. *The scourge of* the sword *shall consume a nation that is exiled outside the land of Israel, and I shall send against those who remain in the land of Israel* in the midst of their bedchambers[96] *where they sleep, the fear of death.*[97] *After that*[98] *even* their young men and their young women shall be destroyed, their nursing children along with their men and their elders. 26. I have ordered *by my Memra, to withhold from them my holy spirit; I shall spare only a few of them, as a man who reaps his field and leaves only one corner*[99] *(of the field).* I shall blot[100] out their memory *from the book of the genealogy of man,* 27. but that the anger of the enemy is feared,[101] lest their oppressors *vaunt themselves*[102] *against* me and lest they say: "our hands have *taken revenge*[103] *for us from our enemies;* but none of this *was decreed*[104] from before[105] the Lord;"

Notes, Chapter 32

[83]See *Sifre Deut.* 330: "when punishment issues forth from before me, it always issues from the nostril."

[84]Aramaic ap of *yqd;* also Nf, but Onq. shaphel of *yṣʾ* "to destroy."

[85]Aramaic *ʿllt*ʾ, read as *ʿllth* with all Tgs. for the 3d singular suffix.

[86]Aramaic *yswd;* also Nf, but Onq. *syp* "base" (Grossfeld).

[87]Also Nf and Frg. Tg.(V).

[88]Aramaic *knš;* Onq. *ʾsp* "amass," and Nf ap *ʾtʾ* "bring."

[89]Here a double specification of the meaning of "arrow" in the HT; also a parallel to Gen 15:12 (Ps.-J.), where Abraham is given a preview of the experience of his descendants at the hands of the world powers. See Gordon (1994) 48 n. 20.

[90]See Num 6:24 (Ps.-J.), and Clarke, *The Aramaic Bible* 4, 205 where the various demons are mentioned.

[91]HT "wasted"; Tgs. *npḥ* "swollen."

[92]HT *ršp* "burning heat"; Tgs. interpret with Job 5:7 as "birds."

[93]Aramaic *rwwhyn byšyn;* HT *mryry* "poisonous pestilence" (RSV) or "the demon *(qṭb)* Meriri."

[94]*Editio princeps* "Arameans"; see Gen 15:12 (Ps.-J.) and Maher, *The Aramaic Bible* 1B, 60 n. 20 where the other instances of the censor's work are listed and the reference to the four evil kingdoms.

[95]All Tgs. and *Sifre Deut.* 331 "crawl in the dust," but "Rabbi (Judah the Prince), however, says that this refers to snakes, who rule only over dust."

[96]Aramaic *qyṭwn* (Greek *koitōn*); see Gen 43:30 and Maher, *The Aramaic Bible* 1B, 143 n. 14 and Exod 7:28 (Ps.-J.).

[97]HT *ʾymh* "fear," which the Tgs. qualify as "fear of death."

[98]Aramaic *ʾylk ʾylk* "after that" (Jastrow 49).

[99]See Lev 19:9 (Ps.-J.), and Maher, *The Aramaic Bible* 3, 176 n. 12. The HT "I will scatter them afar" (RSV) is an uncertain translation of *ʾpʾyhm*. Here the Aramaic *ʾ(w)mn* suggests the idea of the part of the field left unharvested. Nf translates the HT as "to blot out" (shaphel of *yṣʾ*), and the Frg. Tg.(V) "through my *Memra* to bring wrath upon them."

[100]HT "make cease" (hip *šbt*); all the Tgs. *bṭl*.

[101]HT *ʾgwr,* which the LXX translates as "fear"; Onq. *knš* "gather," and Nf and Frg. Tg.(V) *tqp* "grow strong."

[102]Aramaic itp *rbb* (Jastrow 1446); Frg. Tg.(V) itp *gbr* "overpower."

[103]Aramaic here, Nf, and Frg. Tg.(V) itp *prʿ;* Onq. *tqp*.

[104]Aramaic itp *gzr*.

[105]Aramaic *qdm* is introduced to avoid God acting directly as in HT "the Lord has not wrought all this"; see Gen 45:8 (Onq. and Ps.-J.) for the same idiom; see Grossfeld, *The Aramaic Bible* 9, 97 n. 58.

28.[106] for they are a nation *lost* to *good* advice and they have no intelligence. 29. If they were wise men *they would have considered*[107] *the Law,* and they would understand what would be *their destiny.*[108] 30. How will a single enemy pursue a thousand *of them,* and two will put to flight myriads *of them,* except because *their Mighty One*[109] has delivered[110] them and the Lord has surrendered them (to their enemies).[111] 31. For *the idols of the nations* are not like *the Mighty One*[112] *of Israel. For the Mighty One of Israel brings upon them punishment when they sin;*[113] *but when they spread* their hands in prayer, he answers and saves them. But the idols of the nations have no value. It is because we have provoked him to anger and we have not returned to his worship that our enemies *have become our witnesses and our judges.* 32.[114] *For the deeds*[115] *of these people*[116] *are similar to the deeds of the people of* Sodom *and their evil plan*[117] *is as the plan of the people of* Gomorrah. *Their thoughts are as evil as the poison*[118] *of venomous serpents;*[119] *therefore their retributions shall be to be deprived and to be bitter to them.*[120] 33. *As* the gall[121] of serpents *when they are drunk with their wine, therefore let the cup of the curse that they drink on the day of their punishment be bitter.*[122] As the venom[123] of adders *so are they themselves cruel.* 34. *Are not their deeds, which they do in secret, all revealed before* me, sealed[124] *and arranged* in my storehouses?[125] 35. Punishment is *before* me and I will repay (them) at the time when their feet[126] stumble *into exile.*[127] For the day of their shattering[128] is coming closer, and the evil *that is designated to them* comes quickly.' 36. For

Notes, Chapter 32

[106]Verses 28-38: according to *Sifre Deut.* 334 R. Judah considers that the HT "void of counsel" refers to the Israelites, as do also the Tgs., but R. Nehemiah attributes the phrase to "the nations of the world."

[107]HT *skl* "understood"; here itp *skl,* but Nf and Frg. Tg.(V) *ʾlp* "learn." Both Ps.-J. and Nf consider the HT as referring to the Law.

[108]Aramaic *swp* "end" here and Onq., but Nf "in their future" *(bʾḥrywthwn).*

[109]HT "the Rock."

[110]HT "sold" *(mkr):* here and Onq. *msr;* Nf and Frg. Tg.(V) *šbq* "to abandon."

[111]HT "give them up" (hip *sqr*): here and Onq. ap *šlm,* but Nf and Frg. Tg.(V) read "the *Memra* of the Lord handed them over *(msr)* into the hands of their enemies."

[112]HT "the Rock"; Onq. "for their strength *(tqp)* is not like our strength"; Nf and Frg. Tg.(V) "for the security *(rḥz)* of the nation is not like our security."

[113]See *Sifre Deut.* 336 "R. Nehemiah applied it to the nations of the world. . . ."

[114]See Grossfeld, *The Aramaic Bible* 9, 98 n. 61 for a discussion of this verse.

[115]Onq. *pwrʿ* "punishment," but Nf and Frg. Tg.(V) as here.

[116]I.e., Israel.

[117]Aramaic here *ʿsthwn byšm;* Onq. *lqwt* "chastisement," but Nf and Frg. Tg. V *ḥšb* "thoughts."

[118]Aramaic *ryš,* which can mean "poison" as well as "head"; see Le Déaut IV, 275 n. 46.

[119]HT "their grapes are grapes of poison"; Onq. "their plagues are as harmful as the heads/poison of serpents"; Nf, Frg. Tg.(V) "their works are evil works."

[120]Aramaic here, Nfmg, and Frg. Tg.(V) *tkl* "bereft of children" (Jastrow 1668), and *mrr;* see *Num. R.*

[121]HT "poison" *(ḥmh);* here *mryrtʾ,* but Nf "anger" *(ḥmh);* Onq. conflates the text of Ps.-J.

[122]Nf adds "at the time that they drink."

[123]HT "poison/venom" *(ryš);* here *ryšy:* see n. 118 above.

[124]Aramaic *ḥtm;* see McNamara's note on this phrase in *The Aramaic Bible* 5A, 157 n. 79 for a different interpretation of the HT.

[125]Aramaic *ʾpwtyqyy;* Nf and Frg. Tg.(V) add "for the day of great judgment"; see *Sifre Deut.* 337 "When will all these receive (their just due)? On the morrow. . . ."

[126]HT "vengeance," also Nf and Frg. Tg.(V), but Onq. as here.

[127]The text originally, according to *PRE* 235, has to do with the fact that Jacob was born holding Esau's heel (feet); Onq. "go into exile from their land"; Nf and Frg. Tg.(V) do not mention exile.

[128]HT "calamity" is expressed in the Tgs. by pa *šbr* "to shatter."

the Memra of the Lord judges mercifully *the case of* his people *Israel,*[129] and there will be pity *before him for the evil that he will decree upon* his servants.[130] For it is revealed before him that *at the time when they will have sinned, the scourge of the enemy will be strong against them, and that assistance will have been removed from their hands, and that the faithful doers of good* deeds will be cut off[131] and that they will be exiled and forsaken.[132] 37. *The enemy*[133] will say: "Where is *the Fear*[134] *of Israel, the Mighty One*[135] in whom they trusted? 38. Those who were eating the fat of their sacrifices, drinking the wine of their libations, let them now[136] arise and assist[137] you! Let him be a shield over you *with his Memra.*" 39.[138] *When the Memra of the Lord shall reveal itself to redeem his people, he will say to all the nations:* "See, now, that I am *the one who is, was, and I am the one who shall be in the future,*[139] and there is no other god besides me; I *by my Memra* put to death and bring back to life. I smote *the people of the house of Israel* and it is I who will heal them *at the end of days.* There will be no one to save from my hand, *Gog and his soldiers who came to fight against them.*[140] 40. For I have raised my hands toward the heavens[141] *in an oath* and I have said: '*As* I exist, *so I shall not abolish my oath,*[142] *forever.* 41.[143] When my sword be *sharp as lightning* and my hand[144] be established in judgment, I shall return the punishment[145] on the oppressors *of my people* and, to their enemies, *I shall repay the wages of their evil deeds.* 42. I shall make my arrows drunk from the blood *of their slain* while my sword shall destroy their flesh with the blood of the slain and of the captives, *from the beginning of the punishment of my people's* enemies.'[146] 43. Nations praise his people, *the house of Israel!* For he has avenged[147] and kept the blood[148] of

Notes, Chapter 32

[129]HT and Onq. "his people," but here, Nf, and Frg. Tg.(V) the HT is interpreted as Israel.

[130]Onq. "the punishment *(prʿ)* of his righteous servants will be carried out *(prʿ)*"; Nf and Frg. Tg.(V) "will take pity (itp *nḥm*)." Nf adds "on the humiliation *(ʿwlb)* of his righteous servants who are just."

[131]Aramaic here *psq;* Onq. *tqp* "overpower," and Nf and Frg. Tg.(V) *šbq* "be abandoned" and "hidden away" *(rṭš).*

[132]Onq. and Nf appear to be shortened versions of the text of Ps.-J.; much of the tenor of this verse is recorded in *Sifre Deut.* 338–339, where the first part of the verse is interpreted as referring to the nations and the last half to Israel.

[133]HT "he"; *Sifre Deut.* 339 debates whether it refers to Israel (R. Judah) or to the nations of the world (R. Nehemiah).

[134]HT "their gods"; Onq. and here *dḥltʾ,* but Nf "God of Israel"; see McNamara's note on this word in *The Aramaic Bible* 5A, 158 n. 88.

[135]HT "the Rock."

[136]Aramaic here *kdwn,* but Onq. and Nf *kʿn.*

[137]HT "help"; here and Onq. *sʿd,* but Nf *prq* "redeem."

[138]This verse is interpreted as describing the resurrection of the dead; see Sysling (1991) 247–248, 265, and Hayward (1981) 28; see also *PRE* 252.

[139]See Exod 3:14 (Ps.-J.) "I am who I am and who will be." The translation of *ʾhyh* is variously interpreted in the Tgs. and ancient versions; see Grossfeld, *The Aramaic Bible* 7, 8 n. 16, where he discusses whether the phrase is left in Hebrew or translated; see also Shechter (1969) 123–125.

[140]See Exod 40:11 (Ps.-J.) and Maher, *The Aramaic Bible* 2, 273 n. 27 for rabbinic references.

[141]Here as HT; Onq. adds "the place of my *Shekinah* in heaven."

[142]The oath is omitted in Onq. but is found here, Nf, and Frg. Tg.(V).

[143]God as a warrior: see Exod 15:3; Isa 42:13; 59:17.

[144]See *Mekilta* on Exod 16:3 (II, 100–101).

[145]Aramaic *pwr ʿnwtʾ* Onq. and here, but Nf and Frg. Tg.(V) *nqmtʾ* "revenge."

[146]Nf and Frg. Tg.(V) specify "the warriors, the generals."

[147]HT "avenges"; Onq. and here *prʿ,* but Nf *tbʿ* "seek"; see Cook (1986) 103 for our translation.

[148]HT "the blood of (his servants)": Onq. *pwr ʿnwtʾ* "punishment," but Nf *ʿwlbn wdm* "humiliation and blood," and Frg. Tg.(V) only *ʿwlbn.*

his servants *that was shed;* and returned the revenge *of the punishment* upon his enemies, *and he, by his Memra,*[149] will make atonement *for the sins of* his land and of his people." 44. So Moses came *from the Tent of Instruction* and spoke in the hearing[150] of the people all the words of this song, he and Joshua son of Nun. 45. When Moses ended speaking with all Israel all these words, 46. then he said to them: "Set your heart to all the words that I attest today against you. You shall prescribe them for your children *in order* to do carefully all the words of this Law. 47. For *there is no* empty[151] word *in the Law except for those who transgress against it,* because *it is* your life; and through this word you shall lengthen (your) days in the land that you are crossing the Jordan to possess." 48. Then, this same day[152] *on the seventh of the month of Adar,*[153] the Lord spoke with Moses, *saying:* 49. *"And it was when the Memra* of the Lord said to him: 'Ascend this Mount of Abrayyah,[154] Mount Nebo,'[155] *he thought in his heart and said: 'Perhaps this ascending is like the ascending of Mount Sinai.' He then said: 'I will go and sanctify the people.' The Memra of* the Lord said to him: *'It is not how all appears! But ascend* and see the land of Canaan that I am giving to the Israelites as an inheritance. 50. Then rest on the mountain that you are ascending and be gathered to your people, *even you,* just as Aaron, your brother, died on Mount *Amanus*[156] and he was gathered to his people.' *Immediately Moses opened his mouth in prayer and so he said: 'Master of the World, I beg of you, let me not be compared to a man who has an only son who was taken captive. He went to redeem him with much money; he taught him wisdom and skill; he betrothed a woman to him; put up for him a kingly dining hall, built him a marriage house, prepared for him a marriage bed on which he wreathed for him a canopy. He invited honored friends*[157] *for him, baked his bread, prepared his feast, mixed his wine. When (the moment)*[158] *arrived for his son to rejoice with his wife, his marriage friends sought to begin the meal; that man was required at the court, before the king,*[159] *and was condemned to death, and they did not want to postpone it (his execution), so that he might see the enjoyment of his son. So have I worked for this people! I brought them out from Egypt by your Memra, I taught them your Law, I built for them a Tent for your Name. When the time*[160] *to cross the Jordan to possess the land arrived, I am condemned to death. Would that it be satisfactory before you, suspend (the sentence) for me that I may cross the Jordan and see the good of Israel; and after this, I shall die.'* 51. *The Master of the World answered him and so said:* 'Because you acted defiantly against *my Memra* in the midst of the

Notes, Chapter 32

[149]Nf "in his good mercies" *(rḥmwy ṭbyh).*

[150]HT "in the ear"; Onq. "before"; here and Nf "in the hearing" *(šmʿ).*

[151]HT "no trifle" *(dbr rq);* also Onq., but Nf *ryqn;* here *rqyn.*

[152]HT "that very day" *(bʿsm hywm);* Aramaic here *bkrn ywmʾ hdyn: krn* is the transliteration of the Greek adverbial form *kairon.* It is used thirteen times in this phrase in Ps.-J.; see Clarke (1984) 305.

[153]See Deut 34:5 (Ps.-J.).

[154]HT "Abarim"; MS *ʿbrʾy;* see also Num 21:11 (Ps.-J. and Nf); 27:12; 33:44 (Ps.-J.); see Clarke, *The Aramaic Bible* 4, 248 n. 23, 270 n. 17, and 286 n. 38.

[155]Onq., Nf, and Frg. Tg.(V) "which is in the land of Moab, which is opposite Jericho."

[156]See Num 20:22 (Ps.-J.); see Clarke, *The Aramaic Bible* 4, 245 n. 21.

[157]Aramaic *šwšbyn* "special friend" or *šybbʾ* "neighbor" (Jastrow 1543, 1556).

[158]MS *kywwn dmtʾ,* but Ginsburger supplies *kywwn mtʾ zymnʾ* (see n. 160 below).

[159]The midrashic expansion here is based on a parable of kings that is common in rabbinic literature but as Shinan (1994) 209 notes there is no rabbinic parallel for this exact expansion in Ps.-J., nor does it appear in the other Tgs.

[160]Aramaic here *kd mtʾ zymnʾ;* see n. 158 above.

Israelites, at the Waters of Contention[161] *at Reqem,* in the Sin desert, because you did not sanctify me in the midst of the Israelites; 52. Therefore, before (you) you shall see the land but there you shall not enter, to the land that I am giving to the Israelites.' "

CHAPTER 33

1. So this[1] is *the series of* blessings with which Moses, *the Lord's prophet,*[2] blessed the children of Israel before he died. 2.[3] And he said: "the Lord was revealed[4] from Sinai *to give the Law to his people, the house of Israel. The splendor of the Glory of his Shekinah*[5] *shone* from Gabla[6] *to give it to the sons of Esau but they did not accept it.*[7] He shone[8] *in the splendor*[9] *of Glory* from the Mountain of Paran[10] *to give it (the Law) to the sons of Ishmael but they did not accept it.*[11] He was again revealed[12] *in holiness to his people, the house of Israel, and with him*[13] were many myriads[14] of holy angels.[15] *The writing of* his right *hand, and* the Law from the

Notes, Chapter 32 (Cont.)

[161]HT "the waters of Meribath-Kadesh": Aramaic *my mṣwt;* see Gen 14:7 (Ps.-J.), and Maher, *The Aramaic Bible* 1B, 56 n. 21; Num 20:13, 24 (Ps.-J.); 27:14; 34:11 (Ps.-J.); Deut 33:8 (Ps.-J.), and McNamara's note on this verse in *The Aramaic Bible* 5A, 161 n. 116.

Notes, Chapter 33

[1]Aramaic *dʾ* is feminine, whereas *sdr* is masculine; see Onq. and Nf *dʾ brkth;* see also v. 7 and Ginzberg, *Legends* 3.452–462.

[2]HT "man of God": the Tgs. describe Moses as a prophet as in Deut 34:10 (Ps.-J.) below; see Grossfeld, *The Aramaic Bible* 9, 102 n. 1 for a discussion of that idea in rabbinic sources.

[3]The Midrash is an explanation of why "Seir" and "Paran" are mentioned in addition to Sinai on the giving of the Law in the HT. The Lord offered the Law to the nations and this midrash deals with that rejection and the acceptance by Israel. Heinemann (1974) 156–157 considers the form of the midrash in Ps.-J. to be the earliest; see *Mekilta* on Exod 20:2 (II, 234–235), *Sifre Deut.* 351–356, Syrén (1986) 144–148, and McNamara's note on the midrash in this verse in *The Aramaic Bible* 5A, 162 n. 3.

[4]HT "the Lord came from Sinai": on the use of itp *gly* in the Tgs. see Chester (1986) 131–132, and ibid., 165–168 on the avoidance of direct action by God. Here the emphasis is on God's revelation and the giving of the Law to Israel; see *Sifre Deut.* 352 and *b.Zebaḥ.* 116a, which suggests that revelation is that of the Law.

[5]Aramaic here *zyw;* Onq. "splendor *(zyhwr)* of his Glory," and Nf only "Glory."

[6]HT and Onq. "Seir": normally "Gabla" is the word in the Pal. Tgs. to identify "Seir" of the HT; Nf as here; see Clarke (1984) 625 *(gbl / gblʾ / gblyʾ).* "Gabla" is an area in Edom that was known to Josephus (*Ant.* 2.6 and elsewhere). Also *1QGen.Apoc.* 21:29 "the mountain of Gebal *(gbl)*" identified Seir with Gabla; see McNamara (1972) 194, and Fitzmyer (1966) 132, 147.

[7]See *Sifre Deut.* 352, *Mekilta* on Exod 20:2 (II, 234), and *PRE* 319 on Esau's refusal.

[8]HT "shone" (RSV): here ap *ypʿ.*

[9]Aramaic *hdrt ʾyqr:* Onq. *gbwrt* "power" and Nf and Frg. Tg.(V) simply *yqr* "glory."

[10]Home of Ishmael; see Gen 21:21.

[11]Aramaic *qbl:* see *Sifre Deut.* 352, *Mekilta* on Exod 20:2 (II, 234), and *PRE* 319 for Ishmael's refusal.

[12]Aramaic *hdr wʾtgly,* literally "it returned and was revealed"; see also n. 3 above.

[13]HT *ʾth* "he came" is understood as being the preposition "with" *(ʾt)* as in Onq. and Nf; see McNamara's note on this word in *The Aramaic Bible* 5A, 162 n. 7.

[14]Aramaic *rbw rbwwn;* see Deut 34:5 (Ps.-J.) "two thousand myriads of angels."

[15]HT and Onq. "holy ones": here, Nf, and Frg. Tg.(V) specify "the holy ones" as "holy angels." *Sifre Deut.* 354 stresses that the HT "from" implies that not all the "holy ones" are to be understood; see Grossfeld, *The Aramaic Bible* 9, 103 n. 6 on "holy ones," and the preceding note 14.

midst of a flaming fire,[16] *he gave them the commandments.*[17] 3. *Also everything that was made known to the nations (he made known to them)* because he loved his people, *the house of Israel. He called them* holy *to keep the place where his Shekinah resides. When they were keeping the commandments of the Law, they were led*[18] *according to*[19] *the clouds*[20] *of your Glory,*[21] *resting and camping according to his words."*[22] 4. *The Israelites said: "Moses prescribed for us the Law that he gave* as an inheritance to the congregation of Jacob'*s tribes.* 5. *And it*[23] *(the Law) was* king in Israel,[24] when the chiefs of the people gathered together,[25] the tribes of Israel *obeyed it.* 6.[26] Let Reuben live *in this* world[27] and not die *by the death*[28] *that the wicked die in the world to come;*[29] and let his young men be numbered *with*[30] *the young men of his brothers of the house of Israel!"* 7. *And this is the blessing for the tribe of Judah: it united Simeon his brother in his portion (of territory)*[31] *and in his blessing;* and *so* he said: "Accept,[32] O Lord, Judah's *prayer*[33] *when he goes out to fight and from battle*[34] *make him return in peace*[35] *to his people.* Let his[36] hands *take revenge* for him from his enemies and be *a help* and a support[37]

Notes, Chapter 33

[16]HT *ʾšdt* "flaming fire" is interpreted as *ʾš* "fire" and *dt* "Law" and "flaming" *(šlḥwbyt);* see *Sifre Deut.* 355 on Deut 33:2: "This shows that the words of Torah are likened to fire."

[17]See Heinemann (1974) 156, who considers the Midrash here to be older than Nf; see Syrén (1986) 145–146.

[18]HT *tkw* "they followed" is interpreted as "led" *(dbr),* that is, out of Egypt.

[19]Aramaic *lrgyl* "according to" (Jastrow 1228; Le Déaut IV, 285 "au gré de") and not "to the foot (of the clouds)" as McNamara.

[20]HT "in your steps" is translated as "clouds" and HT "receiving direction from you" suggests action due to God's *Memra* as in Num 9:23; 33:2 (Ps.-J. and Nf); see Clarke, *The Aramaic Bible* 4, 213, 284.

[21]See Maher, *The Aramaic Bible* 1B, 22 n. 11 for the distribution of the phrase in the Tgs.

[22]Aramaic *kmn ps db(y)r* translated according to Jastrow (1191), as if based on *ps d byr:* the text of the MS seems corrupt; better to translate with Nf and Frg. Tgs.(PV) *ʿl pwm dbyrwy* "according to his words"; see n. 17 above.

[23]HT "Lord": Aramaic here *hwʾ;* Onq. as HT, but Nf "a king shall arise from those of the house of Jacob." *Sifre Deut.* 358–359 understands this as referring to God. Nf is apparently Messianic.

[24]HT "Jeshurun": see n. 65 on this word in Deut 32:15 (Ps.-J.).

[25]Aramaic *bʾ tknšwt;* also Onq. and Frg. Tgs.(PV), but Nf *knš* "he gathers." Syrén (1986) 118–119 suggests reading singular as in Nf, but McNamara suggests emending according to other Tgs.

[26]See Sysling (1991) 215–220, 228, 264 for a full discussion of this verse and its textual variants in the Tgs.; Syrén (1986) 123–124 for the eschatological emphasis and McNamara's note on this verse in *The Aramaic Bible* 5A, 164 n. 19.

[27]Also Onq. and Nf, and *b.Yoma* 88b considers the reference to be to "this world."

[28]Onq., Nf, and Frg. Tgs.(PV) "a second death" *(mwtʾ tnynʾ):* a phrase found only six times in the Tgs.; see Grossfeld, *The Aramaic Bible* 9, 104 n. 15; McNamara (1966) 118–125; Sysling as noted above in n. 26; Syrén (1986) 122–124, and *Sifre Deut.* 359–360 and Drazin (1982) 296 n. 22. "Second death" is an idea found in *PRE,* but that is later.

[29]Frg. Tgs.(PV) agree with Ps.-J.: Reuben is to live and not to die ever; hence *Sifre Deut.* 359–360 and *b. Sanh.* 92a, which interprets HT "not to die," that is, he will live in the world to come; see McNamara's note on this verse in *The Aramaic Bible* 5A, 165 n. 20.

[30]See McNamara's note in *The Aramaic Bible* 5A, 165 n. 21 on the Aramaic word *ʿm* in Ps.-J. being understood as the preposition rather than the noun *ʿm* "people"; see *Sifre Deut.* 361 "his people . . . meaning with him."

[31]See Josh 19:1, "Simeon . . . its inheritance was in the midst of the tribe of Judah."

[32]HT "hear": Onq. and here *qbl* but Nf *šmʿ;* see Maher, *The Aramaic Bible* 1B, 104 n. 7 for other passages where the same distribution of vocabulary is found.

[33]HT "voice," but Tgs. as here; see *Sifre Deut.* 360.

[34]The phrase "out to fight and from battle" is an idea found also in Onq. and Nf; see Gen 49:8 "your hand shall be on the neck of your enemies" and *Sifre Deut.* 360 "Hear, Lord . . . show that Moses prayed for the tribe of Judah, saying: 'Master of the Universe, whenever the tribe of Judah finds itself in trouble and prays unto you, deliver them from it.'"

[35]HT "in peace": also Onq. and Nf as here.

[36]HT "with thy hands contend for him" (RSV): all the Tgs. "his" to avoid expressing God's action.

[37]Aramaic *sʿd* and *smk,* as also Nf, but Onq. only *sʿd.*

for him against his adversaries." 8. *Then Moses, the prophet, blessed the tribe of Levi* and said: "With Thummim *and* Urim[38] you have clothed Aaron, the man *whom you found pious*[39] *before you, whom* you tested[40] *at the trial*[41] *and found perfect;*[42] *you examined*[43] *him at the Waters of Contention at Reqem*[44] *and found him faithful.*[45] 9. *The tribe of Levi came out for service at the Tent of Meeting and separated themselves from their dwellings, saying to their fathers and to their mothers:* 'I have never seen them.'[46] They were not made known[47] to their brothers *who were not yet thirty years of age* and their children they did not know *because they stood for twenty years in their service according to your Memra*[48] and kept the covenant *of your holy service.*[49] 10. *They are suited to*[50] teach your judicial ordinances to those of the house of Jacob and the Law[51] to those of the house of Israel. *Their brothers, the priests,* put the aromatic spices on the censers *in order to restrain the plague on the day of your anger,* and offered up the whole[52] offering[53] *for good will*[54] upon your altar. 11. Bless, Lord, the possessions[55] *of the house of Levi who give a tenth of a tithe* and accept *with good will the sacrifice*[56] *from* the hand *of Elijah, the priest,*[57] *who offered up at Mount Carmel.* Break the loins *of Ahab,*

Notes, Chapter 33

[38]See Exod 28:30; Lev 8:8; Ezra 2:63, and Neh 7:65 for these words; see Maher, *The Aramaic Bible* 2, 241 n. 27 for a midrash explaining the words as "light" and "fulfilled."

[39]HT *ʾyš ḥsyd* "godly one": Onq. *gbr ḥsyd* "a man pious before you"; here, Nf, and Frg. Tg.(V) *ʾḥrn gbrʾ ḥsydh,* but Frg. Tg.(P) *ʾḥrn ḥsydʾ;* see *Sifre Deut.* 363 and Grossfeld, *The Aramaic Bible* 9, 105 n. 22 for the same idiom.

[40]Aramaic *nsy* here, Onq., and Nfi, but Nf *npy* "to winnow" (Jastrow 923); see Exod 17:1-2; Num 20:2; Deut 6:16; 9:22; 32:51.

[41]HT "Massah": Onq. "Nisetha"; Nf as here *(nystʾ);* see *Sifre Deut.* 363 "you have proven him with many trials and he proved steadfast in all of them."

[42]Aramaic *šlym* here and Onq., but Nf and Frg. Tg.(V) "he remained steadfast" *(qwm).*

[43]HT "with whom you did strive": Tgs. avoid an anthropomorphism by "test/examine": here, Nf, and Frg. Tg.(V) *bdq,* but Onq. *bḥr* "chose"; a number of MSS of Onq. read *bḥn* "test."

[44]See Exod 17:7 ("Massah and Meribah") and n. 160 on Deut 32:51 (Ps.-J.) for other occurrences of the phrase.

[45]Aramaic *mhymn:* the Tgs. add this phrase for clarification as does *Sifre Deut.* 363 "and he proved steadfast in all of them."

[46]HT "I regard them not": Onq. "showed no mercy *(rḥm)* when they were condemned in judgment" and Nf "did not show favor *(nsb ʾp)* in the judgment." The Tgs. vary in their interpretations. Frg. Tg.(V) is the most specific and complete, citing the sins of Tamar, for the parents "did not show favor to his father and mother in the case of Tamar," the worship of the golden calf for his brothers "nor was he partial to his brothers in the incident of the (golden) calf," and the incident of Zimri for his sons, "nor did he have mercy upon his sons in the incident of Zimri." Onq. refers all the sins of all three groups to that of the golden calf where the Levites were told to kill all who had worshiped the golden calf (Exod 32:26-29). Nf is specific about the brothers and the sons as in the Frg. Tg., but Ps.-J. takes a very different line, not identifying the displeasure according to the Frg. Tgs. Rabbinic parallels are found in *Num. R.* 15.12 and *Ber. Rab.* 38.24.

[47]See Deut 1:17; here *ʾštmwdʿ,* but Onq. *nsb* "favor" and Nf *ḥkm* "know."

[48]HT "thy word": Onq. as here and HT, but Nf "the *Memra* of your mouth."

[49]HT "your covenant": Onq. as here and HT, but Nf "your decree *(gzr)* and your Law *(ʾwryyt)*"; echoes of the religious demands expressed here are found in Luke 14:26 and Matt 10:37.

[50]Here Aramaic *kšr* as in Onq. and Nf and Frg. Tg.(V).

[51]HT *twrtk* "thy law" (RSV): Nf *gzyrtk ʾwrytk* "your decree of your Law." The *editio princeps* as Onq. and Nf "(your)," but MS and Nfi "the (Law)." *Sifre Deut.* 363 considers that the HT refers to two Laws: oral and written.

[52]Aramaic *gmyr* in Tgs.

[53]*Sifre Deut.* 364 "parts of the burnt offering."

[54]Aramaic *rʿwʾ* describes the "burnt offering" in Lev 1:13 (Ps.-J.).

[55]HT *ḥyl* "substance": here *nykswy* "possessions/property" as in Palestinian Aramaic and *Sifre Deut.* 364 "(Bless him with) possessions. . . . Most priests are wealthy"; see Fitzmyer (1978) 329 "possessions" rather than "sacrifices" as suggested in Schürer-Vermes (1973) 215 n. 33.

[56]HT "works of his hands": Tgs. *qrbn.*

[57]See Syrén (1986) 171 for references where Elijah is described as a priest.

his enemy, *and the (neck-)joint*[58] *of the false prophets who arose against*[59] *him so that there will not be for the enemies of Johanan, the high priest,*[60] *a foot to stand on.*" 12. *Moses the prophet blessed the tribe of* Benjamin, *and* said: "The beloved[61] of the Lord shall live in safety with him. He will be a shield upon him all the days and it is *within his territory*[62] *the Shekinah*[63] dwells." 13. *And Moses the Lord's prophet blessed*[64] *the tribe of* Joseph, and said: "*Blessed shall be Joseph's land before* the Lord *with the abundance*[65] *of the heavens; it shall produce fine fruit, from the dew and the rain that come down from above,*[66] *and from the abundance of the springs of the deep that come up from below* and flow and irrigate the plants. 14. And from the abundance of fine fruits and produce *that his land ripens by the gift of the sun, and from the abundance of the first fruits of the trees that his land produces*[67] *at the beginning of each and every month;* 15. *and from the abundance* of the mountain *tops, the birthright*[68] *that the blessing of the fathers,*[69] *who resemble the mountains, caused him to inherit, and from the abundance of* the heights *whose produce never ceases that the blessing of the matriarchs from eternity, who resemble the hills,*[70] *caused him to possess,* 16. *and from the abundance of the praiseworthy fruits of* the land and its fullness. The good will *of the Lord that was revealed to Moses in the Bush*[71] *in the Glory of his Shekinah. Let all* these *blessings be gathered and be made a crown*[72] *of honor* for Joseph's head *and for* the head[73] of the man who was chief *and*

Notes, Chapter 33

[58]Aramaic here *pwrqt:* see Clarke (1984) 478 *pyrqt'*, but Gen 54:14 and Deut 33:29 (Ps.-J.) *pyrqt ṣwwry.*

[59]I.e., the Levites; see *Sifre Deut.* 364 "anyone who disputes the legitimacy of the (Levitical) priesthood."

[60]The various identifications of Johanan are discussed by Syrén (1986) 168–178. Since the Tgs. interpret the biblical text and not history the identification must be seen in its connection with the reference to Elijah and Ahab. Syrén argues that this passage may well refer to John Hyrcanus (135–104 B.C.E.), who effected the destruction of the Samaritan temple on Mount Gerizim in 128 B.C.E. None of the other Tgs. contains this addition. The preservation of this addition in Ps.-J. possibly represents an early tradition that has been censored in the other Tgs.

[61]HT *ydyd* "beloved": here *ḥbyb,* but Onq. and Nf *rḥym. Rḥym* is not common in the Tgs. of the Pentateuch, but see Gen 38:12, 20 (Onq., Ps.-J., and Nf) and Deut 13:7 (Nf). Outside the Pentateuch *rḥym* is more common. For *ḥbb* see Clarke (1984) 209 *(ḥbb).*

[62]HT "between his shoulders": see Grossfeld, *The Aramaic Bible* 9, 107 n. 36. *Sifre Deut.* 366 states that a strip of land in the shape of the head of an ox projected from Benjamin's territory into Judah's, and that the temple was built on the shoulders where the *Shekinah* dwelt.

[63]I.e., the temple was to be built in the territory of Benjamin; see Maher, *The Aramaic Bible* 1B, 162 n. 81 on Gen 49:27 (Ps.-J.) for rabbinic citations and Gordon (1994) 43 n. 12.

[64]See Gen 49:25 (Ps.-J.); see also vv. 22-24.

[65]HT "choicest gifts": Onq. *mgdnyn* "precious gifts" (Jastrow 726); here *ṭwb* (literally "good") and Nf *ṭwb 'wsry* ("best of the treasuries"), and frequently in the following verses.

[66]See Gen 49:25 (Ps.-J. and Nf). The whole phrase here is paralleled in Onq. of this verse. See Gen 27:28, 39 (Ps.-J.) "dew of heaven" and "the fatness of the earth."

[67]Aramaic *mbkr': bkr* "to produce" (Jastrow 170).

[68]See v. 17 (Ps.-J. and Nf) below.

[69]I.e., "Abraham, Isaac, and Jacob" as in Frg. Tgs.(PV) and Nf; see also Deut 28:15 (Ps.-J.) and Marmorstein (1968) 147 n. 4 and *Sifre Deut.* 369 "the patriarchs and matriarchs are called mountains and hills."

[70]See Gen 49:26 (Ps.-J.), Maher, *The Aramaic Bible* 1B, 162 nn. 79–80, and *Sifre Deut.* 369 (see previous note).

[71]See Exod 3:2-4 and Grossfeld, *The Aramaic Bible* 9, 107 n. 42 for rabbinic citations.

[72]HT "these" is understood here and Nf as "blessings" and *klyl* "crown"; see Grossfeld, *The Aramaic Bible* 9, 108 n. 43, who comments that the HT "these" is extensively expanded in Ps.-J., Nf, and Frg. Tg.(V); Maher, *The Aramaic Bible* 1B, 162 n. 79; Syrén (1986) 60–65.

[73]HT "crown *(qdqd)* of the head" (RSV): here Aramaic *qdqd;* similar phraseology is found in Gen 49:26 (Ps.-J.); Maher, *The Aramaic Bible* 1B, 162 n. 79 observes that the HT *nzyr* is understood as both "crown" and "leader." The whole midrash of v. 16 is found in its basic features in Gen 49:26 (Ps.-J.).

ruler[74] *in the land of Egypt and was custodian*[75] *for* his brother's *glory.*[76] 17. *The birthright belonged to Reuben, but it was taken*[77] *from him and was given formerly to Joseph. It is just that the splendor of the Glory and of the Praise*[78] *belong to him. For, just as it is impossible for a man to work with* the firstling of his oxen, *so is it impossible for Joseph's sons to become enslaved among the kingdoms.*[79] And just as the wild ox strikes *the wild animals* with its horns, *so shall Joseph's sons rule over the nations as one* in every corner of the earth. So these are the myriads *whom Joshua son of Nun*[80] *who was from the house*[81] *of Ephraim killed in Gilgal;* and they are the thousands *of the Midianites whom Gideon*[82] *son of Joash who was from the house*[83] *of Manasseh killed."* 18. *Then Moses, the Lord's prophet, blessed the tribe of* Zebulun and said: "Rejoice you *of the house of* Zebulun, when you go out *to your business*[84] and you *of the house of* Issachar in the tents *of your schools.*[85] 19. Many nations[86] will pray at the mountain *of the Temple;* there they will offer up their proper[87] offerings; for *they (Zebulun and Issachar) live on the coast of the Great Sea, and they will feast on its salted fish;*[88] *and they will take the (murex) shells and dye purple from its blood the threads (of the fringes) of their (prayer) cloaks,*[89] *and* from the sand *they shall make window glass*[90] *and vessels of glass,* for the treasures of their *depths*[91] *are revealed to them."* 20. *Then Moses, the Lord's prophet, blessed the tribe* of Gad and said: "Blessed is he who expands[92] *the borders of Gad! When he*

Notes, Chapter 33

[74]Aramaic *rb wšlyṭ:* see also Gen 27:29; 41:46; 49:26 (Ps.-J.).

[75]HT *nzyr* "prince": here, Nf, and Frg. Tgs.(PV) *zhyr* "custodian," but Onq. *gbr špyr* "a man distinguished"; see n. 73 above.

[76]See Gen 49:26 (Ps.-J. and Nf).

[77]See Gen 49:3 (Ps.-J. and Nf); 1 Chr 5:1 and Maher, *The Aramaic Bible* 1B, 157 n. 8; Syrén (1986) 129. Chiesa (1977) 417–440 has a full discussion of Gen 49:26 in targumic literature.

[78]Aramaic here *šybhwr'*, but Nf *hdr'* "majesty," which McNamara in his note in *The Aramaic Bible* 5A, 168 translates as "kingship and the glory and the majesty."

[79]Deut 15:19 (Ps.-J.) is interpreted as referring to the freedom of Joseph and his offspring from serving and being dominated; see *PRE* 131 ". . . his horns are taller than all kings and he will gore in the future towards the four corners of the Heavens."

[80]See *Sifre Deut.* 370 "this comes to a total of one hundred and thirty-five thousand."

[81]Nf and Frg. Tgs.(PV) "tribe of the children of" instead of "house of"; see n. 83 below.

[82]See Judg 6:35 and *Sifre Deut.* 379 "comes to a total of one hundred and thirty-five thousand."

[83]Aramaic *mbyt,* as also Onq., but Nf *mn šbṭh dbnwy* "from the tribe of the children of"; see n. 81 above.

[84]Aramaic here *prgmty* (Greek *pragmateia*); also Nf and Frg. Tgs.(PV); see n. 12 on Deut 24:7; 1 Chr 12:33 and *Sifre Deut.* 370 "Zebulun was an agent for his brothers. He would buy from his brothers and sell to the Gentiles," and Gen 49:13 (Onq.) and Grossfeld, *The Aramaic Bible* 6, 166 nn. 34–36.

[85]See Gen 49:14-15 (Ps.-J.); 1 Chr 12:22 and Maher, *The Aramaic Bible* 1B, 81 n. 34 for other references to "schools"; 159 n. 37 for the fact that Ps.-J. is the only Tg. that takes note of Issachar's knowledge of the Law; and see Syrén (1986) 132–133. Generally the same text is found in Nf and Frg. Tgs.(PV).

[86]Nf, on the other hand, specifies the HT "they" as referring to the house of Zebulun as mentioned in v. 18. Onq. agrees with Ps.-J. against Nf; see McNamara's note on this verse in *The Aramaic Bible* 5A, 169–170 n. 58.

[87]Aramaic *qšwṭ.*

[88]Aramaic *ṭryt'* (Greek *thrissa*) "salted or pickled fish" (Jastrow 554). In modern Hebrew the word means "sardines"; see *b.Meg.* 6a for reference to this midrash and *Sifre Deut.* 371, 511 n. 8. HT "hidden" refers to "a kind of fish used for pickling."

[89]Aramaic *gwlyyt:* see Clarke (1984) 138–139 (*gwlt'*) and Num 15:38 (Ps.-J.).

[90]Aramaic *'spqlry'* (Latin *specularia:* Jastrow 96); see *Sifre Deut.* 371 "sand refers to glassware."

[91]MS confuses *h* and *ḥ;* correctly *thwmy'* possibly because of *tḥwm* "border(s)" in the next verse.

[92]Aramaic ap *pty:* see *Sifre Deut.* 372 "the territory of Gad widens to the east . . .," and Gen 49:19 (Ps.-J.).

camps, he rests as a lion *in his resting place but when he goes out to fight against his enemies, he kills*[93] *kings*[94] *along with rulers:*[95] *his slain are known among all the slain,* for he cuts[96] off the arm[97] with the head." 21. And he saw the good land and accepted his portion *at the beginning;*[98] *for there a place was set with precious stones and pearls,*[99] *wherein Moses,*[100] *the scribe*[101] *of Israel, is deposited.*[102] *Just as he went in* and came out at the head of the people *in this world, so will he go in and come out in the world to come,*[103] because he did righteous deeds before the Lord and he taught the judicial ordinances *to the people of the house of* Israel. 22. *Then Moses, the Lord's prophet, blessed the tribe of* Dan and said: *"The tribe of* Dan is like a lion cub; *his land watered*[104] *from the rivers that flow from Mathnan*[105] *and his territory shall reach to Butnin."*[106] 23. *So Moses, the Lord's prophet, blessed the tribe of* Naphtali and said: 24.[107] "Blessed is Asher *among the sons of Jacob.* He will make reconciliation[108] with his brothers *and supply them with food in the years of release.*[109] *His territory will produce olives in quantity, making* oil, *sufficient* for dipping their feet in it. 25. *The tribe of Asher is as bright* as iron *and their feet*[110] *as hard* as bronze *to walk upon (the sharp) points of the rocks.*

Notes, Chapter 33

[93]HT "tears" *(trp),* but Tgs. as here *(qṭl).*

[94]HT "the arm": Onq. as here, but Nf and Frg. Tg.(V) have an entirely different text.

[95]HT "the crown of the head."

[96]MS *mgrr:* possibly incorrect for *gdd* "cut," which would be a pun on Gad; see Jastrow 279 and *Gen. R.* 30:11 (659); Nf and Frg. Tgs.(PV) "remove" *(prq).*

[97]NF and Frg. Tgs.(PV) "head with the arm."

[98]*Sifre Deut.* 372 "he was at the head, at first"; the subjugation of Gad's portion was the beginning of the conquest of the land.

[99]See Gen 50:1 (Ps.-J. and Nf) for the phrase "inlaid with precious stones" to describe the bier on which Joseph laid his father.

[100]HT *mḥqq* "commander" (RSV) is understood as referring to Moses ("the scribe who teaches the Law") in the Tgs. because of understanding the Hebrew from *ḥq* "statute/law"; see McNamara, *The Aramaic Bible* 1A, 220 n. 23 for rabbinic evidence.

[101]Moses is often described as "the scribe"; see preceding note and Maher, *The Aramaic Bible* 1B, 96 n. 20; Syrén (1986) 54–55, and Ginzberg, *Legends* 3.460.

[102]Aramaic here *gnz:* Onq., Nf, and Frg. Tgs.(PV) *qrb;* see McNamara's note on this word in *The Aramaic Bible* 5A, 171 n. 66, and *Sifre Deut.* 372 "this refers to the burial place of Moses which was in the portion of Gad," contrary to Deut 34:1-6 where it is said that Moses' tomb was in Reuben's territory. *B.Sukk.* 13b says Moses died in Reuben's territory but was buried in the territory of Gad; see *Sifre Deut.* 372 "Moses was carried on the wings of the *Shekinah* four miles from the portion of Reuben to the portion of Gad."

[103]The midrash is also in Nf and Frg. Tgs.(PV); see McNamara's note in *The Aramaic Bible* 5A, 171 n. 67 on "this world" and "the world to come" as an eschatological reference.

[104]HT *zqn* "leaps forth" (RSV) is understood, in the Tgs., to refer to water flowing with the Aramaic *šty.*

[105]See Num 21:33 (Ps.-J.) and Clarke, *The Aramaic Bible* 4, 250 n. 65 for a note on the consonantal shift and see Grossfeld, *The Aramaic Bible* 9, 111 n. 61 where Mathnan is Bashan in Onq.

[106]I.e., "Bashan," a play in Ps.-J.

[107]MS omits the balance of v. 23 and the beginning of v. 24 due to homoioteleuton on *wʾmr;* see *PRE* 141, which supplies some of what is missing in the MS: "and of them all he chose the Sea of Kinnereth only and gave it as an inheritance to the tribe of Naphtali."

[108]Aramaic ap of *rʿy* "reconcile/favor, welcome" (Jastrow 1486). All the Tgs. use the same verb; see *Sifre Deut.* 374 "when Reuben admitted the deed, however, they were reconciled with Asher."

[109]See *Sifre Deut.* 374–375.

[110]HT *nʿl* "door-locks": the texts of Onq. and Nf differ; LXX "his shoes shall be iron and brass."

Just as in their youth[111] so will they be strong *in their old age.*[112] 26. There is no god like the God of Israel[113] *whose Shekinah*[114] *and chariot dwell in the heavens; as for him, he will be your help. He will sit on his throne of Glory,*[115] *in majesty,* in the heavens *of clouds above.*[116] 27. God's dwelling[117] is from of old, and by his powerful arm[118] *the world is sustained.* He will scatter[119] your enemies[120] before you and shall give orders,[121] *by his Memra,* to destroy them. 28. Israel has dwelt safely from of old, *according to the blessing with which Jacob their father blessed them,*[122] *for by his merit he caused them to take possession of the good land that produces* wheat and wine. Also the heavens above provide[123] them with the dew *of blessing and the beneficent rains.* 29. Happy are you, Israel! Who is like you *among all the nations,* a people who has been redeemed *by the Name of the Memra*[124]*of* the Lord? And He is the shield[125] helping you and whose sword[126] is the strength of your majesty. So your enemies trembling *shall be proved false before* you and you shall walk *upon the neck-joint*[127] *of their kings.*"

Notes, Chapter 33

[111]HT *kymyk* "like your days": Tgs. "as in the days of your youth" (here *ṭlywt,* but Onq. and Nf *ʿlymwt;* see Grossfeld, *The Aramaic Bible* 9, 112 n. 67 for detailed rabbinic parallels.

[112]HT "your days" which the Tgs. expand as youth and old age. The expansion here in Ps.-J. *(sybwt)* depends on the obscure *dbʾ* in the HT which is translated as "old age." McNamara, *The Aramaic Bible* 5A, 172 n. 78 suggests reading *dbʾ* as *sbʾ*.

[113]HT "like God, O Jeshurun."

[114]Nf "Glory of his *Shekinah.*"

[115]See Maher, *The Aramaic Bible* 1B, 22 n. 12 for other instances in Ps.-J.

[116]HT "through the skies": the phrase "heavens on high" *(šmy mrwmʾ)* is found in the Tgs. and especially in Ps.-J. See Gen 3:22; 11:28; 18:16; 24:3, 7; 28:12; 38:25; Exod 2:23; 16:15; 24:10; Num 21:6; Deut 4:36; here and 34:5 (see Maher, *The Aramaic Bible* 1B, 51 n. 19, and Clarke [1984] 547). Genesis 3:22 is the only passage where the phrase is found in Nf and some Frg. Tgs. However, in this passage the phrase *šmy šḥqy mrwmʾ* is found as a variant on the more common phrase. The word *šḥqyn* "clouds" is also the name of one of the seven heavens (Jastrow 1551).

[117]Nf "the dwelling place of the Glory of the *Shekinah* of God."

[118]HT "underneath are the everlasting arms" (RSV): Onq. "by his *Memra* the world was made," whereas Ps.-J. and Nf retain the idea of "arm"; see Drazin (1982) 313 n. 104.

[119]HT *grš* "thrust out": here *bdr* (see Clarke [1984] 94), but Onq. *trk* "expel" and Nf *ṭrd* "drive out."

[120]A reference to Pharaoh and his forces destroyed at the Reed Sea (Exod 14:26).

[121]Aramaic *ʾmr.*

[122]See Gen 48:21 (Ps.-J.) and *Sifre Deut.* 377 "with the blessings with which their father Jacob blessed them."

[123]HT *ʿrp* "drop down": Onq. "serve them" *(šmš);* here *rss* "drop" (Jastrow 1484) and Nf ap *nḥt* "make descend."

[124]This phrase is only here among all the Tgs. of this verse. See also Deut 4:7; 5:11; 18:7 for the same phrase (Clarke [1984] 575–576 for the other passages in Ps.-J.). Syrén (1986) 99 suggests a special efficacy in pronouncing this phrase.

[125]HT *mgn* "shield" as also Nf: Onq. translates what is understood as a human instrument that applies to God. Ps.-J. and Frg. Tgs.(PV) translate literally as *trys.*

[126]HT *ḥrb* "sword": here and Frg. Tgs.(PV) *syypʾ* whereas normally Onq. and Nf use *ḥrb* as HT. In this text neither Onq. nor Nf translate the HT.

[127]HT "their backs" or "high places" (RSV), interpreted here as *pyrqt ṣwwry,* Nf "necks (of kings)" *(prqt ṣwʾry),* Frg. Tg.(P) "on the necks *(pyrqy)* of your enemy," and Frg. Tg.(V) "on the necks *(pwrqt)* of your kings"; see Gen 45:14 and Deut 33:11 for the similar phrase and see Grossfeld, *The Aramaic Bible* 9, 113 n. 75 and Clarke (1984) 478 *pyrqtʾ; Sifre Deut.* 378 "'put your feet on the necks of them' (Joshua 10:24)."

CHAPTER 34

1. Then[1] Moses went up from the plains of Moab to Mount Nebo, the summit *of the height*[2] that is opposite Jericho. And *the Memra of* the Lord showed him all *the strong ones of* the land,[3] *the mighty things that Jephthah of Gilead*[4] *would accomplish, and the victories of Samson, son of Manoah,*[5] *from the tribe of* Dan, 2. *and the thousand commanders from among those of the house of Naphtali who would associate with Barak*[6] *and the kings whom Joshua son of Nun, from the tribe of* Ephraim, *would kill, and the mighty acts of Gideon,*[7] *son of Joash, from the tribe of* Manasseh, *and all the kings of Israel and the kings of the house of* Judah *that ruled in the land until the last Temple*[8] *was destroyed;* 3. *and the king of* the south[9] *who associated with the king of the north*[10] *to destroy the inhabitants of the land, the Ammonites and the Moabites, inhabitants of* the plain, *who will oppress the Israelites;*[11] *and the exiles, students of Elijah who were exiled from* the valley of Jericho *and the exiles, disciples of Elisha who were exiled from* the city *of Galaad* of the palm trees[12] *because of their brothers of the house of Israel, two hundred thousand men; and the oppression of each successive generation, and the punishment of Armalgos,*[13] *the wicked, and the wars of Gog. But in the time of their great privation, Michael*[14] *will arise to redeem with his (strong) arm.* 4. *Then the Lord said to him: "This is the end of the discourse about the land:* And this is the land that I promised to Abraham, Isaac, and Jacob, saying: I shall give it to your children.[15] I have made you see it with your eyes but you shall not cross over there." 5. *On the seventh day of the month of Adar,* Moses *the Teacher*[16] *of Israel was born and on the seventh day of the month of Adar*[17] he was gathered *from the midst of the world. A celestial voice fell from the heavens and thus it said:*

Notes, Chapter 34

[1]I.e., "on the seventh day of Adar"; see v. 5 below and Deut 32:48 (Ps.-J.) for the specific time.

[2]HT "Pisgah": see Grossfeld, *The Aramaic Bible* 8, 127 n. 15.

[3]Aramaic *tqypy ʾrʿʾ,* not in the other Tgs.

[4]See Gen 31:21 (Ps.-J.) and Maher, *The Aramaic Bible* 1B, 109 n. 15. Jephthah would be a future liberator of Israel (Judges 11).

[5]See *Sifre Deut.* 378: "who was the man? Samson, son of Manoah," Gen 49:18 (Ps.-J.); Maher, *The Aramaic Bible* 1B, 160 n. 43, and Syrén (1986) 113–115.

[6]MS and *editio princeps* incorrectly "Balak"; see *Sifre Deut.* 379: "he showed him Barak, son of Abinoam who waged war against Sisera."

[7]See Gen 49:18 (Ps.-J.): Gideon and Samson are considered future redeemers; see Maher, *The Aramaic Bible* 1B, 160 n. 45.

[8]A reference found only in Ps.-J.

[9]HT "Negeb."

[10]Aramaic *ṣypwnʾ.*

[11]Literally "them, Israel."

[12]HT "city of palm trees," as also Onq.: Nf "city that produces (date) palm trees"; Frg. Tg.(P) "the city that produces dates, that is Zeir."

[13]Aramaic *ʾrmlgws:* also Ginsburger; Jastrow (123) suggests a corruption of Romulus. The MS mg reads "*ʾrmylws* the wicked whom the nations of the world call *ʾntqrystw*" (Antichrist). Gordon (1994) 145 n. 28 notes other arguments for *ʾrmylws* deriving from *armillae,* "armbands," and hence a reference to the Caesars.

[14]See Dan 12:1 and Clarke (1984) 663 *mykʾl* for the seven instances in Ps.-J.

[15]HT "your seed."

[16]Aramaic *rb dysrʾl:* see Num 3:3 and Clarke, *The Aramaic Bible* 4, 195 n. 2 for other occurrences of the phrase in Ps.-J.

[17]See Deut 32:48 (Ps.-J.).

"Come all who enter the world and see the grief of Moses, the Teacher of Israel, who toiled but did not gain fulfilment. But he has been honored with four good crowns:[18] *the crown of the law is his, that he carried off*[19] *from the high heaven*[20] *and the Glory of the Lord's Shekinah was revealed to him with two thousand myriads of angels and with forty-two thousand chariots of fire; the crown of the priesthood that was his during the seven days of the ordination*[21] *(of the priests); the crown of the kingdom was to him as a possession from the heavens; he did not draw a sword or harness a horse or trouble the soldiers; the crown of a good name he acquired by good deeds and by humility." Therefore was Moses, the servant of the Lord,* gathered[22] there in the land of Moab *by the kiss*[23] *of the Memra of the Lord.* 6.[24] *Blessed be the Name of the Master of the World who taught*[25] *us his established way. He taught us to clothe the naked because of his having clothed Adam and Eve; he taught us to join*[26] *grooms and brides because of his having united Eve with Adam; he taught us to visit the sick because he was revealed in a vision to Abraham when he was ill from the incision of circumcision; he taught us to console the bereaved because he was revealed to Jacob again, when he returned from Padan in the place where his mother died; he taught us to feed the poor because of his having sent down bread from the heavens to the Israelites; he taught us to bury the dead from (the time of the burial of) Moses because he revealed himself to him by his Memra and with him was a company of ministering angels: Michael*[27] *and Gabriel*[28] *arranged the golden couch, set with diamonds,*[29] *sardonynx, and beryl, arranged with silk cushions and purple cloth and white robes; Meṭaṭron*[30] *and Jophiël and Uriël and Jephephia, the four masters of wisdom, brought him upon it. Then by his Memra, the Lord led him four miles* and buried[31] him in the valley[32] opposite Beth Peor,[33] *that whenever all raised (their eyes) at Peor, it would be a reminder to Israel of their sin; (whenever all) examined carefully the place of Moses' burial place then they*

Notes, Chapter 34

[18]See *Num. R.* 4, 5 (112), *Sifre Num.* 18, 20, and *m.Abot* 4.13.

[19]Aramaic *šbʾ* (*šby,* Jastrow 1513).

[20]See Maher, *The Aramaic Bible* 1B, 51 n. 19 for other instances of the phrase in Ps.-J.

[21]Aramaic *ʾšlmwwtʾ:* see Lev 8:33-34; 9:1 (Ps.-J.) and Maher, *The Aramaic Bible* 3, 142 n. 34, 38, and 143 n. 1.

[22]Aramaic itp *knš:* HT, Onq., Nf, and Frg. Tg.(V) "die"; CG MS Heb.e 43, fol 65r (Klein [1986] 361) as here; but see v. 7 below for a different vocabulary distribution among the Tgs.

[23]HT *ʿl py* "according to the Word of the Lord": Onq. "by the *Memra* of the Lord"; Nf "by the decree of the *Memra* of the Lord." Hence the HT *py* (literally "mouth") is understood in Ps.-J. as "kiss." *Tanhuma* says that Moses died by the kiss of God. Ps.-J. combines that idea with the interpretation of the other Tgs.; see also *Deut. R.* 31.4.

[24]See Gen 35:9 (Nf) for a parallel midrash of this verse; see McNamara, *The Aramaic Bible* 1A, 166–167 and notes.

[25]See *b.Sot.* 14a and *Eccl. R.* 7.2.

[26]Aramaic *zwg:* see Deut 32:4 (Ps.-J.) and Gen 35:9 (Nf).

[27]See n. 14 on v. 3 above.

[28]See *Deut. R.* 31.14 (186).

[29]MS *wwrdyn* and *editio princeps ywrkyn* but read with Ginsburger *ywhryn* "diamonds" (Jastrow 568); see Gen 6:16 for the only other instance in Ps.-J. of the same vocabulary and Gen 50:1 for a description of Joseph's preparation for his father to lie on "a bed of ivory, overlaid with pure gold, inlaid with precious stones. . . ."

[30]The only references to *Meṭaṭron* in Ps.-J. are here and Gen 5:24 (Ps.-J.); see Maher, *The Aramaic Bible* 1B, 37 n. 10. In Gen 5:24 Ps.-J. calls *Meṭaṭron* "the great scribe." On the other hand, in Exod 24:1 (Ps.-J.) it is Michael who spoke to Moses and who is called "*srkn* (prince) of Wisdom," but in *b.Sanh.* 38b it is *Meṭaṭron.*

[31]Aramaic *qbr* (singular) as HT, Onq., and Frg. Tg.(V), but Nf, CG, and Frg. Tg.(P) *qbrw* (plural); see *m.Sot.* 1.4: God himself buried Moses.

[32]HT adds "in the land of Moab."

[33]According to Num 32:38 (Ps.-J.), but also in Gad (Deut 33:20-23 [Ps.-J.]); see Sysling (1991) 206 n. 109.

would grieve.[34] But no man knows to this very day[35] his grave. 7. So Moses was one hundred and twenty when he lay[36] (with his fathers). The *pupils of* his eyes were not dimmed, *nor were his molar teeth decayed.*[37] 8. And the Israelites cried for thirty days for Moses on the plain of Moab. The days of weeping for Moses' mourning were completed *on the eighth of Nisan and on the ninth of Nisan the people of the house of Israel prepared their affairs and harnessed their animals and crossed the Jordan on the tenth of Nisan. However, the manna ceased for them on the sixteenth of Nisan. They found manna to eat because of Moses' merit for thirty-seven days after he died.*[38] 9. Then Joshua son of Nun was filled with the spirit of wisdom, because Moses had placed his hands upon him. The Israelites received[39] instruction from him and they did just as the Lord had commanded for Moses. 10. No more did a prophet such as Moses[40] arise again in Israel; because *the Memra of* the Lord knew him, *speaking to him literally,*[41] 11. *at the occasion of* all the signs and miraculous wonders[42] that *the Memra of* the Lord sent him to do in the land of Egypt, against[43] Pharaoh, and against all his servants and against all the people of his land, 12.[44] *and on the occasion of* all the strength[45] of his mighty *hand, as he carried the rod that weighed forty seah*[46] *and split the sea and struck the rock,* and on the occasion of all the great fear[47] that Moses worked, *at the time he received the two tablets of sapphire stone, whose weight is forty seah, and he carried them in his two hands,* in the sight of all of Israel.

Notes, Chapter 34

[34]See *b.Sot.* 14a.

[35]Aramaic *ʿd zmn ywmʾ hdyn;* HT "to this day": Onq. as HT, but Nf as here.

[36]Aramaic here *škb:* Nf and Frg. Tg.(V) itp *knš* "was gathered," but Onq. "died" as HT; see also v. 5 above where there is a different vocabulary distribution *(knš).*

[37]HT "natural force not abated": here *ntr* "decay" (Jastrow 946); Onq. "the radiance of the Glory of his face remained unchanged"; Nf "the splendor of his face had not changed"; see Drazin (1982) 316 n. 7 and 317 n. 8.

[38]See Exod 16:35 (Ps.-J.) for a different tradition: "ate manna for forty years, during the life of Moses" and "ate manna for forty days after his death"; see Maher, *The Aramaic Bible* 2, 209 n. 31 for the rabbinic evidence. Malina (1968) 62 considers this a very ancient tradition.

[39]HT *šmʿ* "obeyed," also Nf, but Onq. and here *qbl.*

[40]See Deut 33:1 (Ps.-J.).

[41]HT "face to face": here, Nf, and Frg. Tg.(V) *mmll klw qbl mmll:* see Exod 33:11; Num 12:8; Deut 5:4 (Ps.-J. and Nf); Etheridge (1968) 685 "word by word"; see Grossfeld, *The Aramaic Bible* 9, 114 n. 6 for other comments.

[42]HT *hʾ twt whmwptym* "signs and wonders": here *ʾtyʾ wtymhy pryštʾ* and Nf *ʾtyyh wnysy pryšth.*

[43]Literally "*lprʿh,* etc."

[44]MS records the whole verse in Hebrew before presenting the Tg.

[45]HT "mighty power" (RSV): *hyd hḥzgh;* Onq., Nf, and Frg. Tg.(V) as HT, but here and CG MS Heb.e 43 fol 65r (Klein [1986] 361) *gbwrt ydh tqyph.*

[46]See Exod 4:20 (Ps.-J.) and Maher, *The Aramaic Bible* 2, 172 n. 20.

[47]HT *mwrʾ* "terror": here *dḥyl;* Onq. *ḥzwwnʾ rbʾ* "great manifestations"; Nf *ḥzwwyh rbrbyyh. Sifre Deut.* 383 speaks of "the terror" as the division of the Reed Sea or the revelation at Sinai. Ps.-J. opts for the second part of *Sifre Deut.* Jethro (*b.Zebaḥ.* 116) heard of the division of the Reed Sea and the victory over the Amalekites and so joined the Israelites.

SELECTED BIBLIOGRAPHY

Manuscript

Pseudo-Jonathan: London, British Museum Add. 27031

Editions of Targum Pseudo-Jonathan

Clarke, Ernest G., with W. E. Aufrecht, J. C. Hurd, and F. Spitzer. *Targum Pseudo-Jonathan of the Pentateuch: Text and Concordance*. Hoboken, N.J.: Ktav, 1984.

Díez Macho, A. *Biblia Polyglotta Matritensia.* Series IV. *Targum Palaestinense in Pentateuchum.* Additur Targum Pseudojonathan ejusque hispanica versio. Editio critica curante A. Díez Macho, adjuvantibus L. Díez Merino, E. Martínez Borobio, T. Martínez Saiz. Pseudojonathan hispanica versio: T. Martínez Saiz. Targum Palaestinensis testimonia ex variis fontibus: R. Griño. Madrid: Consejo Superior de Investigaciones Científicas, 5, *Deuteronium,* 1980.

Ginsburger, M. *Pseudo-Jonathan.* (Thargum-Jonathan ben Usiël zum Pentateuch). Nach der Londoner Handschrift (Brit. Mus. Add. 27031). Berlin: Calvary, 1903; reprint Hildesheim: Olms, 1971.

Rieder, D. *Pseudo-Jonathan:* Thargum Jonathan ben Uziel on the Pentateuch copied from the London MS. (Brit. Mus. Add. 27031). Jerusalem: Salomon's, 1974. Reprinted with Hebrew translation and notes; 2 vols. Jerusalem, 1984–1985.

Translations

Etheridge, J. W. *The Targums of Onkelos and Jonathan Ben Uzziel on the Pentateuch, with Fragments of the Jerusalem Targum from the Chaldee.* 2 vols. London: Longman, Green, Longman, 1862, 1865. Reprint in one volume, New York: Ktav, 1968.

Déaut, R. Le, with J. Robert. *Targum du Pentateuque. Traduction des deux Recensions Palestiniennes complètes.* 4 vols. Sources Chrétiennes 245, 256, 261, 271. Paris: Cerf, 1978–1980.

Martínez Saiz, T. Spanish translation in the Díez Macho edition in *Biblia Polyglotta Matritensia* Series IV. *Targum Palaestinense in Pentateuchum.* Madrid: Consejo Superior de Investigaciones Cientificas, 1980.

Rabbinic Sources

Midrash Rabbah Deuteronomy, edited by H. Freedman and M. Simon, translated by J. Rabbinowitz. London: Soncino Press, 1939.

Mekilta de Rabbi Ishmael. 3 vols.; edited and translated by J. Z. Lauterbach. Philadelphia: JPS, 1933–1935; reprinted 1949.

Sifre. A Tannaitic Commentary of the Book of Deuteronomy, translated by R. Hammer. Yale Judaica Series 24. New Haven: Yale University Press, 1986.

Sifre to Deuteronomy. An Analytical Translation, edited by Jacob Neusner. 2 vols. Brown Judaic Studies 98, 101. Atlanta, Ga.: Scholars Press, 1987.

General

Alexander, P. S.: 1974. *The Toponomy of the Targumim with Special Reference to the Table of Nations and the Boundaries of the Land of Israel.* Diss. Oxford.

idem: 1976. "The Rabbinic Lists of Forbidden Targumim," *JJS* 27, 178–191.

idem: 1985. "The Targumim and the Rabbinic Rules for the Delivery of the Targum," *VTSupp* 36, 14–28.

Allony, N.: 1975. "The Jerusalem Targum Pseudo-Jonathan. Rieder's Edition" (in Hebrew), *Beth Miqra* 62, 423–425.

Bacher, W.: 1906. "Targum," *JE* 12, 57–63.

Barnstein, H.: 1899. "A Noteworthy Targum MS in the British Museum," *JQR* 11, 167–171.

Beer, B.: 1857. "Eldad und Medad im Pseudjonathan," *MGWJ* 6, 346–350.

Bienaimé, G.: 1984. *Moïse et le Don de l'Eau dans la Tradition juive ancienne: Targum et Midrash.* Analecta Biblica 98. Rome: Biblical Institute Press.

Bloch, R.: 1955, 1978. "Note méthodologique pour l'étude de la littérature rabbinique," *RSR* 43, 194–227. Also published in English as "Methodological Note for the Study of Rabbinic Literature," trans. W. S. Green and W. J. Sullivan, in *Approaches to Ancient Judaism: Theory and Practice.* Edited by W. S. Green. Brown Judaic Studies 1. Missoula, Mont.: Scholars Press, 1978, 51–75.

Chester, A.: 1986. *Divine Revelation and Divine Titles in the Pentateuchal Targumim.* Texte und Studien zum Antiken Judentum 14. Tübingen: Mohr (Siebeck).

Chiesa, B.: 1977. "Contrasti ideologici de tempo degli Asmonei nella Aggádáh e nelle versioni di Genesi 49,3," *Annali del Istituto Orientale di Napoli* 37, 417–440.

Cook, E. M.: 1986. *Rewriting the Bible: The Text and Language of the Pseudo-Jonathan Targum.* Diss. University of California, Los Angeles. Ann Arbor, Mich.: University Microfilms International.

Cook, J.: 1983. "Anti-Heretical Traditions in Targum Pseudo-Jonathan," *JNSL* 11, 47–57.

Dalman, G. H.: 1897. "Die Handschrift zum Jonathantargum des Pentateuch, Add. 27031 des Britischen Museum," *MGWJ* 41, 454–456.

idem: 1938, 1967. *Aramämaisch-Neuhebräisches Handwörterbuch zu Targum, Talmud und Midrasch.* Göttingen, 1938; reprint Hildesheim: G. Olms, 1967.

idem: 1905, 1927, 1960. *Grammatik des Jüdisch-Palästinischen Aramäisch. Aramäische Dialektproben.* Leipzig: J. C. Hinrichs, 1905, 2nd ed., 1927; reprint Darmstadt: Wissenschaftliche Buchgesellschaft, 1960.

Danby, Herbert: 1933. *The Mishnah.* Oxford: Oxford University Press.

Davies, G. J.: 1972. "Additional Note: *Reqem*," *VT* 22, 152–163.

Déaut, R. Le.: 1970. "Aspects de l'intercession dans le Judaïsme ancien," *JStJ* 1, 35–57.

idem: 1974. "The Current State of Targumic Studies," *BTB* 4, 3–32.

Drazin, I.: 1982. *Targum Onqelos to Deuteronomy.* Hoboken, N.J.: Ktav.

Emerton, J. A.: 1962. "Unclean Birds and the Origin of the Peshitta," *JSSt* 7, 204–211.

Esterlich, P.: 1967. "El Targum Pseudojonathán o Jerosolimitano," *Studi sull' Oriente e la Bibbia offerti a P. Giovanni Rinaldi.* Genoa: Studio e Vita, 191–195.

Fitzmyer, J. A.: 1966, 1971. *The Genesis Apocryphon of Qumran Cave 1. A Commentary.* Biblica et Orientalia 18; 2nd, rev. ed. 18a. Rome: Pontifical Biblical Institute.

Ginzberg, L.: 1909–1946. *The Legends of the Jews.* 7 vols. Philadelphia: JPS.

Ginsburger, M.: 1900. "Verbotene Thargumim," *MGWJ* 44, 1–7.

idem: 1903. *Pseudo-Jonathan.* (See above under "Editions.")

Gordon, R. P.: 1978. "The Targumist as Eschatologist," *VTSupp* 29, 113–130.

idem: 1994. *Studies in the Targum to the Twelve Prophets from Nahum to Malachi.* Leiden: E. J. Brill.

Grabbe, L. L.: 1979. "The Jannes/Jambres Tradition in Targum Pseudo-Jonathan and its Date," *JBL* 98, 393–401.

Greenshield, J. C.: 1970. "*HAMARAKARA > ʿAMARKAL," in *W. B. Henning Memorial Volume*, edited by M. Boyce and I. Gershevitch. London: Lund Humphries, 180–186.

Gronemann, S.: 1879. *Die Jonathan'sche Pentateuch-Uebersetzung in ihren Verhältnisse zur Halacha.* Leipzig: Friese.

Grossfeld, B.: 1972. "Targum Neofiti I to Deuteronomy 31:7," *JBL* 91, 533–534.

idem: 1976. "Neofiti I to Deut 31:7—the Problem Re-analyzed," *Abr Nahrain* 24, 30–34.

idem: 1979. The Relationship between Biblical Hebrew ברח and נוס and their Corresponding Aramaic Equivalents in the Targums—ערק, אפך, אזל: A Preliminary Study in Hebrew-Aramaic Lexicography," *ZAW* 91, 107–123.

idem: 1984. The Translation of the Biblical פקד in the Targum, Peshitta, Vulgate and Septuagint," *ZAW* 96, 83–101.

Hayward, Robert: 1978. "Phinehas—the same is Elijah: The Origin of a Rabbinic Tradition," *JJS* 29, 22–34.

idem: 1978. "The Holy Name of the God of Moses and the Prologue of St John's Gospel," *NTS* 25, 16–32.

idem: 1980. "Memra and Shekinah: A Short Note," *JJS* 31, 210–213.

idem: 1981. *Divine Name and Presence: The Memra.* Totowa, N.J.: Allanheld, Osmun.

idem: 1989A. "The Date of Targum Pseudo-Jonathan. Some comments," *JJS* 40, 7–30.

idem: 1989B. "Targum Pseudo-Jonathan and Anti-Islamic Polemic," *JSSt* 34, 77–93.

idem: 1991. "Pirqe de Rabbi Eliezer and Targum Pseudo-Jonathan," *JJS* 42, 215–246.

idem: 1992. "Red Heifer and Golden Calf: Dating Targum Pseudo-Jonathan," in *Targum Studies* 1, edited by P. V. M. Flesher. Southern Florida Studies in the History of Judaism 55. Atlanta, Ga.: Scholars Press.

Heineman, J.: 1974. *Aggadah and its Development* (in Hebrew). Jerusalem: Keter.

Jastrow, M.: 1950 (etc.; reprints; preface 1903). *A Dictionary of the Targumim, the Talmud Babli and Yerushalmi, and the Midrashic Literature.* 2 vols. New York: Pardes.

Jaubert, A.: 1963. "La Symbolique du puits de Jacob et Jean 4.12," in *L'homme devant Dieu. Mélanges offerts au Père Henri de Lubac.* Theologie: Etudes publiées sous la direction de la Faculté de Théologie 56/1, 63–73.

Kaufman, S. A.: 1973, review of J. P. M. van der Ploeg et al., *The Targum of Job from Qumran, JAOS* 93, 317–327.

idem: 1974. *The Akkadian Influence on Aramaic.* Assyriological Studies 19. Chicago: University of Chicago Press.

Kaufman, S. A., and Y. Maori: 1991. "The Targumim to Exodus 20: Reconstructing the Palestinian Targum," *Textus* 16, 13–78.

Kaufman, S. A., and M. Sokoloff: 1993. *A Key-Word-In-Context Concordance to Targum Neofiti. A Guide to the Complete Aramaic Text of the Torah.* Baltimore: The Johns Hopkins University Press.

Klein, M. L.: 1975. "A New Edition of Pseudo-Jonathan," *JBL* 94, 277–279.

idem: 1976. "Converse Translation: A Targumic Technique," *Biblica* 57, 515–537.

idem: 1979. "The Preposition *qdm* ('before'), a Pseudo-Anti-Anthropomorphism in the Targum," *JTS* n.s. 30, 502–507.

idem: 1980. *The Fragment-Targums of the Pentateuch.* Analecta Biblica 76. Rome: Biblical Institute Press.

idem: 1981. "The Translation of Anthropmorphisms and Anthropopathisms in the Targumim," *VTSupp* 32, 162–177.

idem: 1982A. *Anthropomorphisms and Anthropopathisms in the Targumim of the Pentateuch*, with parallel citations from the Septuagint (in Hebrew). Jerusalem: Makor.

idem: 1982B. "Associative and Complementary Translation in the Targumim," *Eretz Israel* 16 (H. M. Orlinsky volume), 134*–140*.

idem: 1986. *Genizah Manuscripts of Palestinian Targum to the Pentateuch.* Cincinnati: Hebrew Union College Press.

idem: 1988. "Not to be translated in Public"—*l' mtrgm bṣybwr*," *JJS* 39, 80–91.

idem: 1992. *Targumic Manuscripts in the Cambridge Genizah Collection.* Cambridge University Library Genizah Series 8. Cambridge: Cambridge University Press.

Koehler, Ludwig, Walter Baumgartner, et al., eds.: 1958, 1974. *Lexicon in Veteris Testamenti Libros.* 2 vols. 2nd ed. 1974. Leiden: E. J. Brill.

Kuiper, G. J.: 1972. *The Pseudo-Jonathan Targum and its Relationship to Targum Onkelos.* Studia Ephemeridis "Augustinianum" 9. Rome: Institutum Patristicum "Augustinianum."

Kutscher, E. J.: 1976. *Studies in Galilean Aramaic.* Bar Ilan Studies in Near Eastern Languages and Culture. Translated from Hebrew with annotation by M. Sokoloff. Jerusalem: Ahva.

Lange, N. A. M. de: 1976. *Origen and the Jews. Studies in Jewish Christian Relations in the Third Century.* Cambridge: Cambridge University Press.

Levey, S. H.: 1974. *The Messiah: An Aramaic Interpretation.* The Messianic Exegesis of the Targum. Monographs of the Hebrew Union College 2. Cincinnati and New York: Hebrew Union College–Jewish Institute of Religion.

Levine, E. 1971A. "Some Characteristics of Pseudo-Jonathan Targum to Genesis," *Augustinianum* 11, 85–103.

idem: 1971B. "A Study of Targum Pseudo-Jonathan to Exodus," *Sefarad* 31, 27–48.

idem: 1972. "British Museum Additional MS 27031," *Manuscripta* 16, 3–13.

Levy, B. Barry: 1986, 1987. *Targum Neophyti I. A Textual Study.* 2 vols. Lanham, New York, and London: University Press of America.

Levy, J.: 1966. *Chaldäisches Wörterbuch über die Targumim und einen grossen Theil des rabbinischen Schriftthums.* Leipzig 1867–1868; reprint Cologne: Melzer.

Lieberman, S.: 1962. *Hellenism in Jewish Palestine* 2. 2nd ed. New York: Jewish Theological Seminary.

Lund, S., and J. Foster: 1977. *Variant Versions of Targumic Traditions Within Codex Neofiti I.* SBL Aramaic Studies 2. Missoula, Mont.: Scholars Press.

Luzarraga, J.: 1973. *Las tradiciones de la nube en la Biblia y en el judaísmo primitivo.* Analecta Biblica 54. Rome: Pontifical Biblical Institute.

McNamara, M. J.: 1966A, 1978. *The New Testament and the Palestinian Targum to the Pentateuch.* Analecta Biblica 27. Rome: Pontifical Biblical Institute 1966; reprint 1978.

idem: 1966B. "Some Early Rabbinic Citations and the Palestinian Targum to the Pentateuch," *Rivista degli studi orientali* 41, 1–15.

idem: 1972. *Targum and Testament. Aramaic Paraphrases of the Hebrew Bible; A Light on the New Testament.* Shannon: Irish University Press.

idem: 1991. "Early Exegesis in the Palestinian Targum (Neofiti) Numbers Chapter 21," *SNTU* 16, 127–149.

Maher, M.: 1971. "Some Aspects of Torah in Judaism," *IThQ* 38, 310–325.

idem: 1990. "The Meturgemanim in Prayer," *JJS* 41, 226–246.

idem: 1993. "The Meturgemanim in Prayer (2)," *JJS* 44, 220–235.

idem: 1994. "Targum Pseudo-Jonathan of Deuteronomy 1:1-8," *The Aramaic Bible: Targums in their Historical Context,* edited by D. R. G. Beattie and M. J. McNamara. JSOT.S 166. Sheffield: JSOT Press, 264–290.

Malina, Bruce: 1968. *The Palestinian Memra Tradition. The Memra Tradition in the Palestinian Targums and its Relationship to the New Testament Writings.* AGSU 7. Leiden: E. J. Brill.

Maori, Y.: 1983. "The Relationship of Targum Pseudo-Jonathan to Halakhic Sources" (in Hebrew), *Te'uda* 3, 235–250.

Marmorstein, A.: 1905. *Studien zum Pseudo-Jonathan Targum.* Pozsony: Alkalay.

idem: 1920, 1927, 1937, 1968. *The Doctrine of Merits in Old Rabbinic Literature.* 3 vols. (1920, 1927, 1937) reprinted in 1 (1968). New York: Ktav.

Martin, D. J.: 1973. "New Directions in Biblical Scholarship. Targum Yerushalmi to the Pentateuch Tradition," *Journal of Orthodox Thought* 13/14, 201–208.

Martin, E. G.: 1983–1985. "Eldad and Medad," *The Old Testament Pseudepigrapha,* edited by James H. Charlesworth, 2.463–465. New York: Doubleday.

Muñoz León, D.: 1971. "Apéndice sobre el Memra de Yahweh en el MS Neophyti I," in *MS Neophyti I. III: Levitico* (Madrid 1971), *70–*83.

idem: 1974. "Dibbura y Memra," in *Dios Palabra. Memrá en los Targumim del Pentateuco.* Granada: Santa Rita-Monachil, 668–679.

idem: 1977. *La Gloria de la Shekina en los Targumim del Pentateuco.* Madrid: Consejo Superior de Investigaciones Científicas. Instituto "Francisco Suarez."

idem: 1986. *Salvación en la Palabra. Targum. Derash. Berith.* En memoria del profesor Alejando Díez Macho. Madrid: Ediciones Cristiandad.

Ohana, M.: 1975. "La polémique judéo-islamique et l'image de Ismaël dans Targum Pseudo-Jonathan et dans Pirke de Rabbi Eliezer," *Augustinianum* 15, 367–387.

Pérez Fernández, M.: 1981. *Tradiciones Mesiánicas en el Targum Palestinense.* Estudios exegéticos. Institución San Jerónimo 12. Valencia and Jerusalem: Institución San Jerónimo and Casa de Santiago.

Philo. *Philo with an English Translation.* Edited and translated by F. H. Colson and G. H. Whitaker. 10 vols. and 2 supplementary vols. Loeb Classical Library. London: Heinemann; Cambridge, Mass.: Harvard University Press, 1929–1941. Reprint 1956–1962.

Press, I.: 1951. *Historical-Topographical Encyclopedia of Palestine* (in Hebrew). 4 vols. 2nd ed. Jerusalem 1951.

Pseudo-Philo. *Pseudo-Philo's Liber Antiqitatum Biblicarum.* Edited by G. Kish. Publications in Mediaeval Studies. Notre Dame, Ind.: University of Notre Dame Press.

Rabin, C.: 1969. "The Nature of the Origin of the Saf'el in Hebrew and Aramaic," *Eretz Israel* 9, 148–158.

Rappaport, S.: 1930. *Aggada und Exegese bei Flavius Josephus.* Vienna: Alexander Kohut Memorial Foundation.

Revel, D.: 1924–1925. "Targum Jonathan to the Torah" (in Hebrew). *Ner Ma'aravi* 2, 17–122.

Ribera, J.: 1983. "La expresión aramaica *mn qdm* y su traducción," *Aula Orientalis* 1, 114–115.

Rieder, D.: 1968. "On the Ginsburger Edition of the 'Pseudo-Jonathan' Targum of the Torah" (in Hebrew). *Leshônenu* 32, 298–303.

Schürer, Emil.: 1973, 1979, 1987. *The History of the Jewish People in the Age of Jesus Christ (175 B.C.–A.D. 135).* A new English version revised and edited by Geza Vermes, Fergus Millar, and Matthew Black. Literary editor P. Vermes. 3 vols. Edinburgh: T & T Clark.

Shinan, A.: 1975. "'Their Prayer and Petitions.' The Prayers of the Ancients in the Light of the Pentateuchal Targums" (in Hebrew). *Sinay* 78, 89–92.

idem: 1975–1976. "*lyšn byt qwdš'* in the Aramaic Targums of the Torah" (in Hebrew). *Beth Miqra* 21, 472–474.

idem: 1979. *The Aggadah in the Aramaic Targums to the Pentateuch* (in Hebrew). 2 vols. Jerusalem: Makor.

idem: 1982–1983. "On the Theoretical Principles of the Meturgemanim" (in Hebrew). *Jerusalem Studies in Jewish Thought* 2, 7–32.

idem: 1983A. "Folk Elements in the Aramaic Targum Pseudo-Jonathan" (in Hebrew), in *Studies in Aggadah and Jewish Folklore.* Presented to Dov Noy on his 60th Birthday. Edited by I. Ben-Ami and J. Dan. Jerusalem: Magnes, 139–155.

idem: 1983B. "Miracles, Wonders and Magic in the Aramaic Targums of the Pentateuch" (in Hebrew), in *Essays on the Bible and the Ancient Near East.* Festschrift I. L. Seeligman. 2 vols. Edited by A. Rofé and Y. Zakovitch. Jerusalem: Rubinstein, 2.419–426.

idem: 1983C. "The Angelology of the 'Palestinian' Targums on the Pentateuch," *Sefarad* 43, 181–198.

idem: 1985. "The 'Palestinian' Targums—Repetitions, Internal Unity, Contradictions," *JJS* 36, 72–87.

idem: 1986. "On the Characteristics of Targum Pseudo-Jonathan to the Torah" (in Hebrew), in *Proceedings of the Ninth World Congress of Jewish Studies.* Jerusalem: World Union of Jewish Studies, A.109–116.

idem: 1990. "Dating Targum Pseudo-Jonathan: Some More Comments," *JJS* 41, 57–61.

idem: 1994. "The Aggadah of the Palestinian Targums," in *The Aramaic Bible: Targums in their Historical Context.* Edited by D. R. G. Beattie and M. J. McNamara. JSOT.S 166. Sheffield: JSOT Press, 203–217.

Singer, I., et al.: 1901–1907. *The Jewish Encyclopedia.* New York: Funk and Wagnalls.

Sokoloff, M.: 1990. *A Dictionary of Jewish Palestinian Aramaic of the Byzantine Period.* Ramat-Gan, Israel: Bar-Ilan University Press.

Splansky, D. M.: 1981. *Targum Pseudo-Jonathan: Its Relationship to Other Targumim, Use of Midrashim and Date.* Diss. Hebrew Union College, Cincinnati.

Syrén, R.: 1986. *The Blessings in the Targums. A Study on the Targumic Interpretations of Genesis 49 and Deuteronomy 33.* Acta Academiae Åbonensis, ser. A, vol 64, no.1. Åbo: Åbo Akademi.

Sysling, H.: 1991. *Techiyyat Ha-Metim. De opstanding van de Doden in de Palestijnse Targumim op de Pentateuch en overeenkomstige Tradities in de Klassieke Rabbijnse Bronnen.* Zutphen: Terra.

Urbach, E. E.: 1975. *The Sages. Their Concepts and Beliefs.* 2 vols. English translation. Jerusalem: Magnes Press.

Vermes, Geza: 1961, 1973. *Scripture and Tradition in Judaism.* Studia Post Biblica 4. Leiden: E. J. Brill; 2nd rev. ed. 1973.

idem: 1987. *The Dead Sea Scrolls in English.* New York: Penguin (3d revision).

York, A. D.: 1974. "The Dating of Targumic Literature," *JStJ* 5, 49–62.

idem: 1979. "The Targum in the Synagogue and in the School," *JStJ* 10, 74–86.

Wainright, A.: 1956. "Caphtor—Cappadocia," *VT* 6, 199–210.

INDEXES TO TARGUM PSEUDO-JONATHAN: DEUTERONOMY

HEBREW BIBLE

5:11 103
5:16-21 22
5:16-33 22
5:22 18
5:22-29 22
5:31-33 22
6:8 36
6:9 37, 56
6:12 35
6:14 36
6:16 99
7:4 36
8:4 29
8:11 25
8:14 25
8:19 25, 36
9:1 19
9:2 12
9:9 18
9:19 7
9:22 99
11:1 37
11:18 25
11:20 25
11:26 25
11:26-29 37
11:28 35
11:29-30 37
12:17 48, 59
13:7 41, 79, 100
13:18 72
14:28 45
15:2 57
15:23 92
16:2 47
16:15 59
16:19 57
16:22 86
17:1 28
17:5 50
17:7 41
17:8 58, 66, 84
17:12 41, 66
17:15 59
17:18 57
18:7 103
18:14 52
18:12 28
19:21 41
20:5 25
21:2 57
21:3 57
21:19 50
21:21 41
22:5 28
22:15 50
22:22 62, 66
22:24 50
23:19 28
24:7 74, 101
24:15 67
25:5 67
25:7 50
26:12 45
26:13-18 72
27:1 57
27:12ff. 37
27:6 52
27:15-26 73
28:12 25
28:14 82, 85, 87
28:15 6, 7, 30, 70, 100
28:17 70
28:28 25
28:35 25
28:54 41
28:56 41, 79
29:9 25, 57
30:1ff. 37
32:1 19, 88, 89
32:1-3 89
32:3 25
32:4 25
32:14 25
32:34 65
32:50 57
32:51 99
33:2 98
33:11 103
33:15 7
33:20 87, 105
33:28 7
34:1 16
34:1ff. 102
34:3 90
34:6 90

Joshua
3:7 14
10:24 103
12:4 12
12:5 16
13:11 16
13:12 12
13:13 16
15:8 12
19:1 98
23:5 26

2 Samuel
23:34 16

1 Kings
4:13 15

2 Kings
25:23 16

Ezra
2:63 99

Nehemiah
7:65 99

1 Chron
5:1 101
11:15 12
12:22 101
12:33 101
14:9 12
17:22 72
20:4 12
20:6 12

Isaiah
1:2 88, 89
5:6 89
13:22 91
34:13 91
35:7 91
42:13 95
44:2 92
51:6 89
59:17 95
65:17 89

Jeremiah
2:27 58
6:13 64

Micah
2:6 89

NEW TESTAMENT

Matthew
10:37 99

Luke
3 15
3:1 15

TARGUMIM

Targum Neofiti

Genesis
7:4 36
7:23 36
30:22 75
35:9 105
36:20 12
36:21 12

Leviticus
1:16 16

Numbers
7:89 18
34:11 16

Deuteronomy
5:4 106
5:10 27
6:9 56
10:16 83
11:17 76
11:20 56
13:7 100
14:23 71
24:16 22
27:8 90
32:1 19

Neofiti Margin

Targum Onqelos

Targum Pseudo-Jonathan

Fragment Targum V

RABBINIC LITERATURE

Midrash

INDEX OF SUBJECTS

Bold type indicates entries found in the text.
Non-bold indicates entries found in the notes.

INDEX OF AUTHORS